"Miscegenation"

"*Miscegenation*"

Making Race in America

ELISE LEMIRE

PENN

UNIVERSITY OF PENNSYLVANIA PRESS

Philadelphia

Copyright © 2002 University of Pennsylvania Press
All rights reserved
Printed in the United States of America on acid-free paper

10 9 8 7 6 5 4 3 2 1

Published by
University of Pennsylvania Press
Philadelphia, Pennsylvania 19104-4011

Library of Congress Cataloging-in-Publication Data

Lemire, Elise Virginia.
  "Miscegenation" : making race in America / Elise Lemire.
      p. cm.
  Includes bibliographical references (p.) and index.
  ISBN 0-8122-3664-5 (cloth : alk. paper)
      1. American literature—19th century—History and criticism. 2. Miscegenation in literature.
3. Literature and society—United States—History—19th century. 4. Jefferson, Thomas,
1743–1826—In literature. 5. Racially mixed people in literature. 6. Race relations in literature.
7. Racism in literature. 8. Race in literature. I. Title.

PS217.M57 L46 2002
810.9'355—dc21   2002018048

For Jim

Contents

Illustrations

Introduction: The Rhetorical Wedge Between Preference and Prejudice

Between the Revolution and the Civil War, descriptions and pictorial representations of whites coupling with blacks proliferated in the North. Novelists, short-story writers, poets, journalists, and political cartoonists, among others, devoted a vast amount of energy to depicting blacks and whites dancing, flirting, kissing, and marrying one another. Invariably, the blacks are portrayed as ugly, animal-like, and foul-smelling. This makes them easily distinguishable from the whites, who are usually portrayed as physically attractive. In most cases, the whites portrayed coupling inter-racially are abolitionists. In all cases, the depictions appear when and where the question of black political rights was debated most vociferously. In this book, I read depictions of inter-racial couplings created in New York, Pennsylvania, and Massachusetts during three distinct waves of hysteria about inter-racial sex and marriage between 1776 and 1865. I focus on what these depictions can tell us about both the racialization of sexual desire in the wake of attempts to expand the purview of liberal democracy and the concomitant invention of "race" as a set of traits that are more or less sexually desirable.[1]

The first widespread discussion in American history about inter-racial sex was sparked by a report published in Richmond, Virginia, in 1802, that the author of the Declaration of Independence was having sex with one of his slave women. Thomas Jefferson's political opponents, the Federalists, responded with numerous poems in Philadelphia about the affair that linked it to Jefferson's embrace of liberal democracy. The Federalists argued that Jefferson's personal behavior was a corollary to his political beliefs and that those like Jefferson who viewed all men as equal would foolishly find black women attractive sexual partners.

In the 1830s, after the immediate abolitionists began to organize widely and effectively, there was a much bigger explosion of anxiety about black political rights, expressed in the form of far more graphic images and descriptions of inter-racial sex. Detailed rumors abounded in the anti-abolitionist press about all of the imagined ways that white abolitionists intent on eradicating prejudice were flirting with blacks at their integrated meetings. Lithographed images of abolitionists in various forms of inter-racial embraces, as well as maritally coupling inter-racially, were everywhere. The power of these images to express and further goad white anxiety is evidenced by the widespread mob action they galvanized against the abolitionists across the span of the decade. Two of the biggest riots occurred in Philadelphia and New York City.

A third wave of concern in the North about inter-racial sex and marriage was in direct response to the urgent question raised by Lincoln's Emancipation Proclamation: "What will you do with the negro when he is free?"[2] Slavery had clearly defined blacks as politically and socially unequal to whites. Lincoln's opponents reasoned that, if blacks were now free to earn wages and to thereby rise to the highest economic and social positions, whites might want to marry them. Political pamphlets in New York City aimed to convince readers that inter-racial marriage would begin to happen not just in the South but across the nation if Lincoln was reelected. Like the anti-abolitionists, the Democrats were not pro-slavery. But, like most Northern whites, they wanted clearly demarcated limits to black freedom.

Since the seventeenth century, all of the Southern states had been ensuring that social and economic equality would not occur between whites and blacks and that slavery would be perpetuated as a race-based system by making inter-racial marriage illegal.[3] The laws prohibiting inter-racial marriage promoted and legally substantiated the idea that blacks are not fit for whites to marry because they are socially and physically inferior to whites. They also made the children of inter-racial couples bastards and thereby concentrated frreedom and wealth in white families by not allowing these illegitimate children to inherit. Such laws outlived slavery, were eventually enacted in 44 states at one time or another, and were finally declared unconstitutional in 1967.[4]

But even as the depictions of inter-racial sex from New York, Pennsylvania, and Massasschusetts indicate that many whites there clearly feared social and economic equality would follow political equality, New York never had laws prohibiting inter-racial marriage, Pennsylvania overturned theirs in 1780, and Massachusetts would overturn theirs in 1843. I show in this book that the numerous depictions of inter-racial couplings that dotted the Northern cultural landscape did the work of prohibiting inter-marriage by teaching whites that blacks are physically and socially inferior and to thereby treat them accordingly.[5] The power of these depictions, literary, pictorial, and otherwise, cannot be overstated, particularly because, in doing the work of prohibiting what we now call "inter-racial" sex and marriage, and of thereby limiting "black" economic and social mobility, the depictions did so much more as well. In particular, I argue, they helped make the racial categories they aimed to police.

In order for an imagined group of people to be deemed universally ugly, they had to be identifiable as a group with shared traits meant to ellicit disgust. In all of the depictions of inter-racial couplings, "blacks" are depicted as having certain traits that easily distinguish them from "whites." They are shown with unrealistically dark skin. Hair is imagined as so coarse that it can stand up in shapes that defy gravity. Noses and lips are portrayed as inordinately wide. Jaws jut out beyond all proportion. And the imagined foul smell of "blacks" is noted obsessively. Conversely, whites are protrayed with pale skin, flowing hair, thin noses and lips, and vertical profiles. "Race" thus referred to an imagined composite of skin color, hair color and texture, nose and lip thickness, what was called "facial angle," and smell. It was these physical traits that readers were trained to isolate and read until they believed a "black" person looked as different from a "white" person as, say, a dog from a flower. And insofar as a person's imagined race thus makes them ugly or beautiful in these depictions of inter-racial coupling, race was imagined even more specifically as a set of traits that are more or less sexually desirable. Of course, concomitantly, desire, then termed "preference," thus became racialized. When Thomas Jefferson insisted in his *Notes on the State of Virginia* (1785), for example, that blacks "prefer" whites the same way that orangutans "prefer" blacks, what makes a person sexually desirable in his formulation is specifically their imagined race traits.[6]

I show how soon after "preference," or desire, was racialized, it was biologized. Normal preference was construed as the desire to sexually couple and reproduce with someone who has not only the same supposedly racial features as oneself but also the same source of these features: namely, what was imagined as race blood. *Intra*-racial desire was imagined, in other words, as an instinct to perpetuate what were imagined as distinct biological entities. Blacks were depicted as the near relatives of primates and thus as a separate species from whites so that *inter*-racial sex, on the other hand, could be declared against the biological laws of Nature. In the wake of abolitionism, this rhetoric of blood and species allowed the demonization of inter-racial sex and marriage and the concomitant invention of intra-racial desire to seem completely unrelated to the prejudicial ideas on which the demonization was founded.

The vocabulary developed in the North for referring to what we now term "inter-racial" sex and marriage grew out of the desire to substantiate this view that intra-racial desire is an instinct and that race is a biological category. Beginning in the second decade of the nineteenth century, the term "amalgamation" was borrowed from metallurgy to refer to, as one Boston-based newspaper explained in 1834, the "physical commixture of the white and colored races."[7] "Amalgamation" meant that different race bloods were blending in the way that molten metals do. To be sure, some of the earliest uses of "amalgamation" to describe race mixing can be found in Jefferson's writings. But the term was most widely used in the North in the 1830s where the concept became a great concern for those opposed to the immediate abolitionists or, as they were so often called, the "amalgamationists." In 1864, the word "miscegenation" was coined in New York City from the Latin *miscere* (to mix) and *genus* (race), seeming then, like "amalgamation," to refer to reproduction across race lines.[8] To use these terms and to thereby demonize certain desires and couplings as outside of a biological norm was also implicitly to make the claim that whiteness is a biological category made and maintained through instinctual intra-racial reproduction. I show, however, that when we look at the Northern depictions of inter-racial sex and marriage that led to the coining of the these terms, we see that whiteness is an identity people can only claim if they have certain sexual race preferences. For the concern voiced about liberal democracy, abolitionism, and emancipation in these depictions was not that a large "mulatto" class would arise in the wake of black political rights. Rather, the concern was about the loss of the racial preferences or desires that comprised "whites" as a group with certain tastes, including, in particular, a distaste for blacks that ensured white social and economic superiority. "Amalgamation" and "miscegenation" were terms that did the work of enforcing the prohibition against certain marriages, such that social and economic equality would not follow the granting of any black political rights, and of thereby making whiteness a category of people with certain sexual race preferences, all without seeming prejudicial due to the insistence implicit in the terms on the biological real. Again, what subsequently became a nationwide rhetoric for ensuring white supremacy without seeming racist was born in the North.

It should be clear, then, that this is not a book about actual biological acts or states of being. While I began this introduction with references to "whites" and "blacks" as if there are such people, I show in this book that these were categories coming into existence through the discourses of what came to be called "miscegenation," itself a cultural fiction, as is the term that has replaced it: "inter-racial." Thus, even though I don't always use scare quotes in this book in my references to "blacks," "whites," and "inter-racial" sex to indicate their socially constructed nature, they should always be assumed.[9]

My book is organized around the waves of anxiety about inter-racial sex and marriage in the North, the last one of which culminated in the coining of the term "miscegenation" in 1864. It is thus a genealogy of this term, the usage of which does much of the work of prohibiting inter-racial sex and marriage, of thereby ensuring white supremacy, and of biologizing race so as to mystify the constructed nature of whiteness. Each chapter marshals evidence from a range of texts that contributed to the various waves, with each chapter focused in particular on a work of belles lettres (or several in the case of the poetry I examine in Chapter 1) that was both a result of and an attempt to shape the particular historical context I am delineating.

In the first part of The book, I focus on the first national discussion about what we now term inter-racial sex and the subsequent borrowing from metallurgy of "amalgamation" as a means of referring to sexual reproduction as a mixture of race blood. In Chapter 1, "Race and the Idea of Preference in the New Republic: The *Port Folio* Poems about Thomas Jefferson and Sally Hemings," I examine the poems published in the Philadelphia *Port Folio* about Jefferson and the woman we know now to be Sally Hemings as well as a political cartoon that depicts them as a sexual couple. According to the Federalists, what attracted Jefferson to his slave were the black race traits they repeatedly enumerated and declared disgusting. I show that they were thus responding directly to Jefferson's own contribution to the topic of race relations in his *Notes on the State of Virginia*. There, Jefferson had developed the idea of an aesthetic hierarchy of the races. He imagined what we would now term sexual desire as "preference" specifically and solely for the race traits above one on the Great Chain of Being. The Federalists never disagreed with Jefferson on this point, finding him perverse precisely because he had violated the terms of the aesthetic hierarchy they shared with him. I argue that the Jefferson and Hemings rumors illustrate why liberal democracy failed to result in a society without race hierarchies. It is not that the discourses of "preference" ensured that there would be no so-called mixed-race or "mulatto" people, a purely metaphorical means of imagining people anyway, but that the established link between preference and the aesthetics of the chain helped consolidate a group of people who would find those they imagined to be "black" as undesirable and therefore as unequal.

Within ten years, the term "amalgamation" would make "preference" seem a fully biological impulse to mix one's supposed race blood with another person's of the same race. In that way, the inter-racial preferences imagined in the likes of the Federalists' poems about Jefferson and "Monticellian Sally" seemed all the more unlinked to prejudice and therefore not in contradiction to the philosophical underpinnings of liberal democracy. While James Fenimore Cooper does not have his characters use the term "amalgamation" in his 1826 novel *The Last of the Mohicans*, the characters' use of the blood rhetoric implicit in the term demonstrates that blood rhetoric disguises the labor required of the culture to train people in what was being newly imagined as same-race desire. As I discuss in my second chapter, "The Rhetoric of Blood and Mixture: Cooper's 'Man Without a Cross,' " when Cooper has Hawk-eye claim that "young women of white blood give the preference to their own colour," he is claiming that same-race desire is solely a natural physical urge.[10] While Cooper's novel is ostensibly about the relations between Anglo-Americans and Indians during the French and Indian War, Cora's black lineage reveals that the concept of "amalgamation" was meant to police, not white relations with Indians, the latter of whom were vanishing from the East anyway, but the perceived biological boundary between "whites" and "blacks." That Cora nevertheless functions as a "white" woman in so much of the narrative also reveals that her own sexual race preferences trump her imagined lineage in determining her race. Cooper thus created a blueprint for whiteness in his novel.

In the middle section of the book, I consider the particular anxieties that resulted from immediate abolitionism and the resulting shifts in how race and sex were imagined in the North. Each of the two chapters in this part is focused on the debates that accompanied and spurred one of the many riots that erupted across the North as a result of the threat of "amalgamation." In Chapter 3, "The Barrier of Good Taste: Avoiding *A Sojourn in the City of Amalgamation* in the Wake of Abolitionism," I consider the July riots in New York City in 1834, focusing in particular on the anti-abolitionist novel Jerome B. Holgate penned after witnessing them. Holgate made the by-then standard argument that whites would be forced by the abolitionists to inter-marry as part of their plan to eradicate prejudice. He then insisted that thereafter the inter-married whites would vomit continuously when in proximity to their black spouses. The lesson taught by *A Sojourn in the City of Amalgamation* (1835) was thus based on the long-standing stereotype about how blacks smell. Holgate argued that if whites naturally prefer members of their own race it is because blacks are so bad smelling that whites ruin their health when forced to socialize with them. He thus aimed to carefully distinguish preference from prejudice. If whites simply "prefer" to couple with other whites this is to be expected, is indeed required by Nature, and therefore is completely unlinked to prejudice of any kind. That he can assert as much in the wake of equating blacks with the smell of excrement is a testimony to the power of the rhetoric of preference.

The narrator of Holgate's novel concludes it with the question that defined the anxiety of the period. His narrator declared of slavery that "The point to be settled . . . is not what concerns the abusing or maltreating of a fellow creature, but what disinclines one to the companionship or presence of a particular individual."[11] Presumably everyone could easily agree that the abuse and maltreatment of blacks must stop. But social equality must not follow, Holgate insists, insofar as whites cannot help preferring their own. During the New York City riots, the media labeled this preference "good taste" and thereby tapped one of the most important principles of the middle class. I show that later, in 1843, the abolitionists were able to overturn one of the remaining laws in the North against inter-marriage because they were in agreement with their opponents that good taste would serve as the social and therefore marital barrier between "whites" and "blacks."

In Chapter 4, "Combating Abolitionism with the Species Argument: Race and Economic Anxieties in Poe's Philadelphia," I show of the debates swirling around the Philadelphia riots of 1838 that the anti-abolitionists feared not only that social equality might arise in the wake of abolitionism, but that economic equality or even economic reversals might result as well. Reprinted here in their entirety for the first time, an 1839 series of anti-abolitionist lithographs by Philadelphian E. W. Clay depicts blacks rising socially and economically by inter-marrying with white abolitionist women and thereby forcing white men to replace them as the servant class. Clay depicts the black men as winning these white abolitionist women with what he insists is their phallic potency and hypersexuality, evidenced in the prints by the jutting jaws, or "facial angles," that he uses to link them to nonhuman primates and thus to the animal noted for desiring those above it on the Great Chain of Being. I argue that Edgar Allan Poe's 1841 tale "The Murders in the Rue Morgue," published in Philadelphia's *Graham Magazine*, uses many of Clay's terms to respond to the Philadelphia riots. In it, a marauding orangutan assaults and kills two white women in their bedroom where they are undressing for the night. The murder weapon is a barber's razor at a time, I show, when the barbers of Philadelphia were some of the wealthier blacks of the city. Poe thus strengthens the perceived link between black economic mobility and "amalga-mation" that had set the anti-abolitionists rioting.

In the last part of Chapter 4, I argue that Clay and Poe made presenting blacks as the relatives of orangutans a powerful weapon in the battle against social and economic equality for blacks. If blacks were viewed as related to simians then they could be imagined as belonging to a wholly separate species. Sexual contact between whites and blacks thus could be declared utterly unnatural. I show that, in the 1840s, scientists were following the likes of Poe and Clay when they increasingly argued in favor of separate species origins for blacks and whites as a means of arguing that same-race preference is a species instinct. What had once been viewed as good taste was now more fully natu-ralized with the result that preference had never seemed so far from prejudice.

In my last chapter, "Making 'Miscegenation': Alcott's Paul Frere and the Limits of Brotherhood After Emancipation," I focus on the wave of concern about inter-racial sex and marriage during the Civil War. By then, it was widely believed that race was a biological difference in the blood and that inter-racial sex was therefore a violation not only of "the faculty of taste"[12] but also of what one scientist termed "the natural repugnance between individuals of different kinds."[13] This is evidenced by the fact that these beliefs were mobi-lized for political effect in the 1864 presidential election. I provide a detailed reading of the seventy-two-page pamphlet authored by two Democrats aim-ing to foil Abraham Lincoln's bid for reelection by accusing him of advocating what they termed "miscegenation." The authors meant the neologism to encompass all of the beliefs about race and sex that had been developed since the Jefferson rumors. For while "miscegenation" translated from the Latin meant the "mixing" of "races," its use in the pamphlet and immediately there-after proved that "miscegenation" was used to mark a violation both of Nature, because of the presumed blood or species differences between blacks and whites, and of good taste, insofar as blacks were deemed unattractive and foul-smelling. On both of these fronts, the invented concept of "miscegena-tion" prohibited certain sexual couplings as a means of constructing and pre-serving whiteness as a category of people with a certain sexual race preference.

Chapter 5 also explores the power of the taste argument to co-opt even the most liberal abolitionist positions. In 1863, Louisa May Alcott was well aware that the taste argument made blacks appear socially unequal by eliciting disgust at the idea of inter-mixing. In an attempt to counter antiblack preju-dice, she thus published a short story, "M. L.," that celebrates an inter-racial marriage by depicting it as the crowning achievement of two genteel characters, a white woman named Claudia and Paul Frere, born to a "Quadroon" slave mother. At the end of the story, Claudia will only accept the friends who had turned against her when hearing of her nuptials if they will "come up here with me."[14] She seems to be instructing her old friends to either inter-marry themselves or to embrace the inter-racial romantic love of others. Alcott understood precisely the point I am making in this book, namely that the only way that Paul, or any other "black" person for that matter, can claim the political and social status of "brother"—the stated goal of the abolitionists who had long rallied around this term, not coincidentally Paul's last name—would be through his full acceptance by "whites" as a lover and husband as well. She thus works hard in her story to portray Paul as attractive and sweet-smelling.

But even in this attempt to argue against the naturalness of race prejudice, Alcott perpetuates the last barrier to brotherhood by ultimately fearing that inter-racial desire is in bad taste. Paul Frere's body is wholly absent from the opening scene when Claudia hears him singing and promptly falls in love. Then, when Paul does appear, he is so light skinned that Claudia does not recognize his slave ancestry. Alcott thus avoids depicting racial blackness as attractive. On the other hand, to have presented readers with depictions of more obviously "inter-racial" kisses would have been to risk providing what had become a popular form of pornographic writing. For as much as the Federalists, Clay, Poe, and Holgate meant to demonize inter-racial sex, they were also providing a form of pornography with their descriptions and pictorial representations of lascivious embraces and sexualized violence. While these often pornographic texts might have served as the safety valves that allowed people to claim whiteness through the publicly performed intra-racial desires the culture was demanding of them in the name of good taste and later, species instinct, they nevertheless made inter-racial coupling erotic and erotically perverse in ways that Alcott could not afford to do.

A year after Alcott published her short story, the word "miscegenation" would do the work of placing limits on the brotherhood that emancipation might otherwise have ushered in. The authors of the pamphlet in which the term was coined provided a means of summoning with one word all of the scientific and aesthetic justifications against social and economic equality between "blacks" and "whites." The debates of the previous seventy-five years were now crystallized in one term, the perceived usefulness of which is indicated by the fact that it caught on right away and has been used ever since. In my epilogue, " 'Miscegenation' Today," I consider two recent texts which use the term "miscegenation" or the concept: the entry for "miscegenation" in

Africana (2000), the encyclopedia of African and African-American experience edited by Henry Louis Gates, Jr., and Kwame Anthony Appiah, and a 1994 article in *Discover* magazine by Pulitzer Prize–winner Jared Diamond. I show that the ideas embedded in the word "miscegenation" live on today in the word "inter-racial." These terms still make certain sexual couplings seem against the laws of Nature and thereby still disguise prejudice with biology.

1 Race and the Idea of Preference in the New Republic

The *Port Folio* Poems About Thomas Jefferson and Sally Hemings

On a tour of North and South Carolina in 1773, Bostonian Josiah Quincy, Jr., took note of what he perceived to be the prevailing attitudes there about inter-racial sex. He recorded his findings in his private journal:

The enjoyment of a negro or mulatto woman is spoken of as quite a common thing: no reluctance, delicacy or shame is made about the matter. It is far from being uncommon to see a gentleman at dinner, and his reputed offspring a slave to the master of the table. . . . The fathers neither of them blushed or seem[ed] disconcerted. They were called men of worth, politeness and humanity. Strange perversion of terms and language![1]

A Revolutionary patriot who despised the slave system, Quincy is not only appalled because men were enslaving their own children. He is also and seemingly more appalled that sexual desire was traversing race boundaries. Note that he stresses not only the existence of the enslaved children but the implied act, the "enjoyment," that resulted in their birth. It is about this "enjoyment" of a negro or mulatto woman" that society, he believes, should feel some "delicacy or shame." But while the lack of embarrassment about desired sex between a "gentleman" and a "negro or mulatto woman" is shocking to Quincy, himself from a state where inter-racial marriage and "fornication" had been illegal since 1705, he seems to have limited his comments, themselves brief, to his journal.[2]

By the turn of the century, however, the political colleagues of Quincy, Jr.'s Federalist son were commenting extensively and publicly on a particular Southern gentleman and the slave woman he supposedly "enjoyed," following rumors published about that gentleman in the Richmond *Recorder*.[3] On September 1, 1802, Republican malcontent James T. Callender had written that "the man, *whom it delighteth the people to honour,* keeps, and for many years past has kept, as his concubine, one of his own slaves. Her name is SALLY." [4] This was the first printed report about President Thomas Jefferson and the woman now known to be Sally Hemings.[5] For Callender, the crime is not only the fact that Jefferson, a widower since 1782, is presumably having sex with a woman to whom he is not married, nor even that Jefferson is enslaving his own children. He goes on to note in this first of many articles he wrote on the matter, not that the "several" children he claims "the African Venus" has born Jefferson are bastards or slaves themselves, both of which they would have been, but that they have, he insists, what he terms "sable"-colored skin. The eldest child is said to be a son named Tom whose features "bear a striking although sable resemblance to those of the president himself."[6] Callender deems the fact that Jefferson has chosen "an African stock whereupon . . . to engraft his own descendants" "an act which tends to subvert the policy, the happiness, and even the existence of this country." While there would not be a term for another decade with which to name Jefferson's crime (even my use of the term "inter-racial" is ahistorical), it is spelled out here as the crime of wanting to sexually and reproductively bridge a perceived racial divide. Jefferson fathered "sable" children of "African stock," thereby creating a frightening hybrid of the presidential and the primitive, and he did so because he imagined a slave woman his "African Venus, " his "concubine." For Callender, as for Josiah Quincy, Jr., it is inter-racial desire that makes these Southern gentlemen unworthy of their society's and, in Jefferson's case, the nation's honor.

While propertied Virginians found Callender a "sad fellow" for violating what Joshua D. Rothman terms "a cultural code of public silence" about sex between masters and slaves and themselves remained silent in the face of Callender's weekly harangues over the course of four months in the *Recorder,* Federalists in the North filled their newspapers and magazines with poems and editorials about the president and Sally Hemings in the fall of 1802 and spring of 1803, thereby hoping to hurt Jefferson's chances for reelection.[7] Much of the commentary issued from Philadelphia, a center of the publishing industry at the time and a hotbed of debate between the Federalists and the Republicans. Joseph Dennie's weekly *Port Folio* carried an item about Jefferson and Hemings in almost every issue during that period, including ten poems devoted exclusively to attacking Jefferson for his relationship with Hemings.[8] Political caricaturist James Akin read and heard enough in Philadelphia to prompt him to issue an engraving depicting the author of the

Declaration of Independence and his slave as sexual partners (Figure 1).[9] The story also spread along the eastern seaboard. Dennie had large numbers of subscribers, as many as two thousand per week, from Georgia to Canada.[10] The commentary on Jefferson and Hemings in his and other Federalist papers also found large audiences through reprinting practices and oral transmission. "A Song Supposed to Have Been Written by the Sage of Monticello," for example, reprinted in the *Port Folio* from the *Boston Gazette*, was comprised of verses about the president and "Monticellian Sally" set to the melody of "Yankee Doodle." As well known as "Yankee Doodle" was and as popular as parodies of it were at the time, it is probable that this particular parody was spread beyond the parameters of print culture.[11] By 1808, the story of the pres-

1. [James Akin], *A Philosophic Cock*, 1804. Courtesy American Antiquarian Society.

ident and his slave had been so widely reprinted and repeated that the thir-teen-year-old son of a Federalist on the western Massachusetts frontier would know to include it in a poem on Jefferson's Embargo Act of 1807 as part of a longer list of presidential sins.[12]

Jefferson's national prominence does not explain why the charge of sex with a slave should have been a Federalist means of attacking him. Rather, something had changed in the Northeast between 1773 and 1802 such that sex between a master and slave came to be regarded as requiring lengthy discussion and as shocking enough that the charge of its occurrence could serve as a political weapon. The *Port Folio* poems and Akin's engraving of *A Philosophic Cock* reveal that, for the Federalists, it was in large part the recent founding of the new nation on the principle of liberal democracy that seemed to increase the, for them, frightening possibility of sex between whites and blacks. Liberal democracy was based on two concepts: natural rights and political equality. If every person was deemed politically equal, the Federalists reasoned, wouldn't blacks claim the right to white spouses? And, because they viewed blacks as their equals, wouldn't whites want to marry them?

The *Port Folio* had already linked liberal democracy to what was depicted as the monstrosity of inter-racial sex in a poem published prior to Callender's comments in the Richmond *Recorder*. Indeed, one can imagine his tale of presidential misconduct otherwise falling on deaf ears. Published in July 1802, two months before Callender's first comments about "Sally," the poem pre-tends to be by a fictional slave of Jefferson's named Quashee who demands for himself a white wife on the premise that Jefferson had declared all men equal.

Our massa Jeffeson [sic] he say,
  Dat all mans free alike are born;
Den tell me, why should Quashee stay,
  To tend de cow and hoe de corn?
  Huzza for massa Jeffeson!

And if all mans alike be free,
  Why should de one, more dan his broder,
Hab house and corn? for poor Quashee
  No hab de one, no hab de oder.
  Huzza, &c.

And why should one hab de white wife,
  And me hab only Quangeroo?
Me no see reason for me life!
  No! Quashee hab de white wife too.
  Huzza, &c.

For make all like, let blackee nab
  De white womans . . . dat be de track!
Den Quashee de white wife will hab,
  And massa Jef. shall hab de black.
  Huzza, &c.

Why should a judge (him always white)
  'Pon pickaninny put his paw,
Cause he steal little? dat no rite!
  No! Quashee say he'll hab no law.
  Huzza, &c.

Who care, me wonder, for de judge?
  Quashee no care. . . . no not a feder;
Our party soon we make him trudge,
  We all be democrat togeder.
  Huzza, &c.

For where de harm to cut de troat
  Of him no like? or rob a little?
To take him hat, or shoe, or coat,
  Or wife, or horse, or drink, or vittle?
  Huzza, &c.

Huzza for us den! we de boys
  To rob and steal, and burn and kill;
Huzza! me say, and make de noise!
  Huzza for Quashee! Quashee will
  Huzza for massa Jeffeson![13]

If, as Jefferson asserted, "all mans free alike are born," then why should Jefferson "hab de white wife" and the slave "only Quangeroo"? The slave asserts that he too will "take" a white wife while "massa Jef. shall hab de black" so as to "make all [a]like," to make "all be democrat togeder." It's never imagined here, however, that black and white women become equally desirable. Quashee wants "de white wife" because he finds her superior to a black one. His wife is "*only* Quangeroo" (emphasis added). The reader experiences Quashee's desire as a nightmare precisely because the poem's depiction of democracy still includes this hierarchy of race. Quashee's white wife will find herself married to a man who plans "To rob and steal, and burn and kill." The Federalists often argued that, in a democracy, which they understood in its classical sense as rule by the *demos,* or mob, those at the bottom of the American hierarchy would claim privileges for which they were unworthy and unprepared.[14] Prior to the public revelations about Jefferson and Hemings, this Federalist poet was already imagining that one of the privileges that would be claimed were spouses of different races and that such a claim was horrifying. For the Federalists, then, Callender's accusation only proved this concern to be a valid one.

Akin's print depicts a caricature of Jefferson proclaiming,"Tis not a set of features or complexion Or tincture of a Skin that I admire." The "Philosophic Cock" views all skin colors as equally admirable presumably because he believes in the philosophy of human equality, on which Jefferson had famously based the Declaration of Independence. Behind Jefferson is a caricature of a woman whose turban and dark complexion are used to signify her status as a slave. Viewers of the print would have thus read her as the "Sally" of the, by then, repeated commentary in the Federalist press. Jefferson is depicted in the print as prepared to act on his admiration for "Sally." He is graphically portrayed as the male bird to which the title's "cock" refers. Since "cock" has been slang for penis since the seventeenth century (*OED*), the sexual allusion resulting from the depiction of Jefferson as a rooster, coupled with the slave woman's adoring gaze, makes clear that their relationship is a sexual one. The print thus asks how the nation can trust a man whose philosophy serves to provide the justification for this sexual behavior. If all men are perceived as equal, thanks to Jefferson's political efforts, who is to say that a slave owner can't prefer to couple with a slave woman? And since Hemings is defined here by her skin color, her "tincture of skin," the question becomes a question of race. Who is to say that, if all men are perceived as equal, a white man won't prefer to have sex with a black woman? Since the rooster was also a symbol of the French Revolution, the print makes the point not only that Jefferson is a Jacobin, or misguided supporter of the French, a frequent Federalist accusation, but that to democratically have no preferences for certain complexions, and thus perhaps to prefer a black person, is a kind of disastrous end on the same scale as France's. In other words, the print makes the point that liberal democratic rule is dangerous because the philosophy of equality that underwrites it leads to the traversal of a revered race boundary. As the Quashee poem also indicates, it was thus the inception of liberal democracy in a race-based society that, for the Federalists, led to the specter of inter-racial sex. It seems the Federalists did not want so much equality that what they regarded as important race boundaries would be sexually traversed. For while Northern Federalists may have considered enslavement unjust, there is no sympathy in Akin's print for Hemings.[15] Hemings is simply a means to attack Jefferson because sex with her is viewed as deviant. The Federalists were arguing that the nation should be wary of liberal democracy because the natural rights philosophy underpinning it was creating a forum for inter-racial sex. And even if this argument was merely a political tactic, it demonstrates the Federalist confidence that there were now enough people like Josiah Quincy, Jr., who were disgusted or frightened at the prospect of desired inter-racial sex that they could use that prospect as an argument against liberal democracy.

By not only depicting Jefferson as a rooster, and thus as a reminder of what democracy had led to in France, but by also depicting Hemings as a chicken, Akin is making another important point about how liberal democracy will lead to inter-racial sex. An early draft of the Declaration of Independence makes clear that the assumption behind the idea "all men are created equal" is the fact of a shared and thereby equal creation as one species. Jefferson wrote that "We hold these truths to be sacred & undeniable; that all men are created equal & independent, that from that equal creation they derive rights inherent & inalienable."[16] One of Jefferson's sources here was John Locke, the principal architect of natural rights philosophy, who wrote in his *Second Treatise of Government* (1689) that there is "nothing more evident, than that Creatures of the same species and rank promiscuously born to all the same advantages of Nature, and the use of the same faculties, should also be equal one amongst another without Subordination or Subjection."[17] Jefferson was drawing, too, on the findings of Swedish scientist Carolus Linnaeus, who in 1740 had reimagined the relationship between people in the second edition of his immensely popular and influential *Systema Naturae*, dividing them into four basic varieties dictated by geography: *Americanus, Europaeus, Asiaticus, and Afer.* Linnaeus's understanding was a radical departure from the older way of understanding all living things in a minutely stepped, hierarchical order, the so-called Great Chain of Being, from the lowest insects and animals up to humans and, finally, God himself.[18] Before Linnaeus, humans were ranked within the Chain of Being according to kind: Europeans were ranked right below God and above the Africans, who were themselves situated right above the apes, the most humanlike of all the brutes, and to whom it was thus implied the Africans were related. Conversely, Linnaeus's ordering was not vertical and hierarchical but cartographic and therefore horizontal.[19] He based it on the ancient test of inter-fertility. Georges-Louis Leclerc, comte de Buffon, formulated this test in scientific terms in the second volume of his *Histoire Naturelle* (1749): "We should regard two animals as belonging to the same species if, by means of copulation, they can perpetuate themselves and preserve the likeness of the species; and we should regard them as belonging to different species if they are incapable of producing progeny by the same means."[20] Liberal democracy is based on the idea that all men were deserving of equal rights because all men, able as they were thought to be to reproduce with one another, thus must have shared an "equal creation." Akin is arguing that the sexual liaison between Sally and the author of the Declaration of Independence demonstrates Jefferson's belief that Sally is the same species as himself, a chicken to his rooster, and thereby sexually and reproductively compatible with him.

That the Federalists were not just motivated by their anti-Jefferson feelings but by their concerns about liberal democracy is indicated by the fact that Thomas Paine is also a target in the poems about Jefferson and Hemings. Like Jefferson, Paine was a philosopher of and for democracy. In an untitled poem reprinted in the April 9, 1803, *Port Folio* from the *Boston Gazette*, Jefferson says to Sally, "I fear that *Tom Paine*, with his air and his art, / Has made, or will make, an attack on your heart." When Paine shows up in the president's absence, he quickly succeeds in seducing the slave woman, "For he argued so sharp, saying *Sally* you know, / That *his* name is *Thomas* and *mine* is *so too*, / And therefore you can't be to *Thomas untrue*."[21] Inter-racial sex is here again the dangerous outcome of liberal democracy, according to the Federalists. Since Paine was in favor of liberal democracy, his desire for Sally is, according to the poet, a logical corollary of his views. Anyone who believes in liberal democracy must also want to have sex with Sally. Paine will achieve his desire through the ridiculous argument that, because he shares Jefferson's first name, Sally cannot be untrue to Thomas Jefferson by having sex with Thomas Paine. For the Federalists, Paine was a talented dissembler for democracy who could lead the country into dangerous waters.

In another poem, one of two imitations of Horace's "Ode to Xánthias"

(Book 2, Ode 4) published anonymously on October 30, 1802, in the *Port Folio*, Paine is again made to reveal his own attraction to Hemings.[22] "Ode to Xánthias" (Book 2, Ode 4) was deemed applicable to Jefferson for, like Xánthias, he also loved a slave woman and, as was the case for Xánthias, another man, specifically the speaker of the poem, also loved that slave woman. In the original, Horace seems to provide a seemingly generous compliment as a means of chastising Xánthias for what may be the lowly origins of the slave woman he loves: "your golden-haired Phyllis' parents / May prove rich and famous and do you honor; / She is doubtless grieving for royal forebears / Woefully fallen." But Horace thus also disfavorably compares Xánthias's beloved slave woman, Phyllis, to the slave woman loved by the ancient heroes such as Agamemnon, who "For a kidnapped girl . . . languished." By implication, Xánthias falls short of the ancient heroes for having selected poorly. Of course, while Horace means to satirize Xánthias for loving a woman with no stature, he also aims to convince himself not to love the slave woman whose "features, . . . arms . . . [and] shapely / Ankles" he praises and whose golden hair and faithfulness he takes note of carefully. The ode concludes with the poet's insistence that he is uninterested in Phyllis and that his age proves the impossibility of any attraction:

Oh, I praise her features, her arms, her shapely
Ankles,—quite objectively! Stop suspecting
One whose years have hurried along to bring their
   Total to forty.[23]

But the focus on Phyllis's loveliness and the fact that Xánthias suspects the poet raises the possibility for the reader that the poet is indeed quite smitten. In other words, two Federalists chose to imitate a poem in which the speaker, not just the subject of the poem, expresses attraction to a slave woman.

John Quincy Adams, the anonymous author of one of these Horatian imitations, takes advantage of this dynamic by couching his poem as an address to Thomas Jefferson from his friend Thomas Paine.[24]

Dear Thomas, deem it no disgrace
   With slaves to mend thy breed,
Nor let the wench's smutty face
   Deter thee from the deed.
At Troy's fam'd siege the bullying blade

Who swore no laws for *him* were made,
　Robs, kills, sets all in flame—
A SLAVE in petticoats appears,
And souse! in love! head over ears
　The Lion's heart is tame!

Lord of the world, when *Nero* reign'd,
　When fires were his delight
A SLAVE the Tyger's bosom chain'd,
　That slave indeed was white.
Lo! at his feet the fawning train,
His Smith, Blake, Cheetham and Duane,
　Howling his praise are seen!
Vice turns to virtue at this nod;
Imperial Nero, grows a GOD
　And ACTE grows a Queen.

Speak but the word! alike for thee
　Thy venal tribe shall swear,
PUREST OF MORTALS thou shalt be
　And SALLY shall be fair.
No blasted brood of Afric's earth
Shall boast the glory of her birth
　And shame thy daughter's brother,
To prove thy panders shall conspire
Some king of Congo was her sire -
　Some Ethiop Queen her mother.

Yet, from a princess and a king
　Whatever be their hue,
Since none but drivelling idiots spring,
　And GODS must spring from you.
We'll make thy Tommy's lineage lend;
Black and white genius both shall blend
　In him their rays divine.
From Phillis Wheatley we'll contrive
Or brighter Sancho to derive
　Thy son's maternal line.

Though nature o'er thy Sally's frame
  Has spread her sable veil,
Yet shall the loudest trump of fame
  Resound your tender tale.
Her charms of person, charms of mind
To you and motley scores confin'd
  Shall scent each future age;
And still her jetty fleece and eyes
Pug nose, thick lips and ebon. . . . [*sic*]
  Shall blacken Clio's page.

Nay, Thomas, fumble not thy head,
  Though Sally's worth I sing,
In me, no rival canst thou dread,
  I cause no horns to spring.
Besides my three score years and ten
I was not form'd like other men
  To burn for beauteous faces—
One pint of brandy from the still
My soul with fiercer joys can fill
  Than Venus and her graces.[25]

The speaker begins by noting that Jefferson is just like the Ancients who themselves fell in love with slaves. Jefferson suffers by way of comparison, however, because his slave has a "smutty face," a "sable veil," "jetty fleece and eyes / Pug nose, thick lips and ebon," all of which are described in terms meant to sound particularly unattractive, whereas the Ancients' were simply "white" and presumably beautiful as such, at least by comparison. Jefferson is further reviled for heading a political party that will invent a lineage comprised of Phillis Wheatley or Ignatius Sancho for his son "Tommy." Readers would know that Jefferson had discussed Wheatley and Sancho in his *Notes on the State of Virginia* as less accomplished than their white counterparts. Five new editions of *Notes* had been published in 1801, the first year of Jefferson's administration, making his comments there more widely read than any other "scientific" discussions about blacks until the mid-nineteenth century.[26] So *Port Folio* readers knew that Wheatley and Sancho were hardly considered by Jefferson black "geniuses" to celebrate. His coupling with Hemings and his party's spin on it thus would have been taken as completely hypocritical. As in the original, the speaker, in this case Paine, finishes by assuring Jefferson that he is not interested in the slave woman: "Though Sally's worth I sing, / In me, no rival canst thou dread." Paine insists he does not "burn for beauteous faces" because "One pint of brandy from the still" fills his "soul with fiercer joys . . . Than Venus and her graces." But, of course, the act of Paine calling Sally "beauteous" and comparing her to Venus is meant to show that he is indeed interested in Sally even though this is only because he suffers from drunken delusions. And his drunkenness and inter-racial lust prove his championing of natural rights philosophy is dangerous insofar as some people, himself included, don't have the requisite virtue and reason to participate in a republic.

In their assertion that inter-racial desire was what made Jefferson monstrous, the *Port Folio* poets were taking a different tack from the one Callender had taken in the *Recorder*. Callender had hoped to turn the public against Jefferson by raising the specter of hundreds of thousands of mulattoes. On September 22, 1802, Callender followed his initial assertion that "By the wench Sally our president has had several children," with an ominous warning, also in the *Recorder*: "if eighty thousand white men in Virginia followed Jefferson's example, you would have FOUR HUNDRED THOUSAND MULATTOES in addition to the present swarm. The country would no longer be habitable, till after a civil war, and a series of massacres."[27] Callender implicitly invokes the census of 1800 which had just counted 100,000 white men between sixteen and forty-five in Virginia and over 260,000 white men of all ages. He argues that eighty percent of the men in their reproductive prime might follow Jefferson and thus also produce five "mulatto" children each, for that is the number that he claimed Jefferson fathered. For him, a "swarm" of "mulattoes" would be a nightmare, perhaps because he is imagining a slave revolt, "another St. Domingo," as one of the Federalists expressed it.[28] Peace, he argues, would thus only come once the mulattoes were "massacred."

Akin's print and the poems in the *Port Folio* on Jefferson and Hemings make few references, however, to their reported offspring. Rather, Akin and the *Port Folio* poets comment extensively and in some cases almost exclusively on what is described as Jefferson's and Paine's shocking preference not for a person named "Sally" but specifically for what are deemed "Sally's" race traits, namely her skin's color and texture, her hair texture, her nose and lip width, her facial angle, as it was called then, and her smell.[29] In other words, the *Port Folio* poets' specific fear of liberal democracy was that it would result in desire for blackness. Adams's Horatian ode, for example, details Sally's skin color, smell, "Pug nose," and "thick lips." That Thomas Paine desires these black traits and these traits in particular is precisely what is perverse and horrifying about natural rights philosophy. Akin also argues in his print that Jefferson's preference for Sally is a preference solely for her dark skin and that it is this sexualization by Jefferson of blackness that will lead to national chaos on the order of France's. Similarly, "A Song Supposed to Have Been Written by the Sage of Monticello" devotes an entire stanza to "Sally's" "black" skin color and another to what is imagined as her bad smell. Jefferson is the imagined speaker or singer here for whom "Black is love's proper hue" and for whom black sweat is a "perfume" when it is in bed with him:

OF all the damsels on the green,
  On mountain, or in valley,
A lass so luscious ne'er was seen,
  As Monticellian Sally.
Yankee doodle, who's the noodle?
  What wife were half so handy?
To breed a flock, of slaves for stock,
  A blackamoor's the dandy.

Search every town and city through,
  Search market, street and alley;
No dame at dusk shall meet your view,
  So yielding as my Sally.
  Yankee doodle, &c.

When press'd by loads of state affairs
  I seek to sport and dally,
The sweetest solace of my cares
  Is in the lap of Sally.
  Yankee doodle, &c.

Yet Yankee parsons preach their worst—
  Let Tory Whittling's rally!
You men of morals! and be curst,
  You would snap like sharks for Sally.
  Yankee doodle, &c.

She's *black* you tell me—grant she be—
  Must colour always tally?

Black is love's proper hue for me -
  And white's the hue for Sally.
      Yankee doodle, &c.

What though she by the glands secretes;
  Must I stand shil-I shall-I?
Tuck'd up between a pair of sheets
  There's no perfume like Sally.
    Yankee doodle, &c.

You call her slave - and pray were slaves
  Made only for the galley?
Try for yourselves, ye witless knaves—
  Take each to bed your Sally.

Yankee doodle, whose the noodle?
  Wine's vapid, tope me brandy—
For still I find to breed my kind,
  A negro-wench the dandy![30]

One problem for the Federalists with Jefferson having sex with Hemings was that he would thus produce more slaves for himself and thereby more political representation as a result of the three-fifths rule. "What wife were half so handy?" the poem has Jefferson ask, "To breed a flock, of slaves for stock." Thomas Green Fessenden would complain similarly in *Democracy Unveiled* (1806) that "Great men can never lack supporters, / who manufacture their own supporters."[31] But these concerns comprise only two stanzas of the nine-stanza "Song," the second and the last. Most of the song is devoted to what are deemed Sally's race traits. Jefferson is portrayed as trying to convince readers who would have clearly believed otherwise that black skin and the smell of Sally's sweat are sexually preferable. He urges readers to "Take each to bed your Sally," meaning that each man should find a black woman because they are best for "sport and dally." So while the song is another example of the standard Federalist argument that Jefferson's case proves liberal democracy will lead to inter-racial liaisons and that liberal democracy should thus be opposed on those terms, the stated problem with liberal democracy is that it makes the likes of Jefferson sexually attracted to blackness. "Yankee Doodle," to which the song is set, was a British song co-opted by the Revolutionaries in such a way as to swell patriotic fervor. That Jefferson, the "Sage of Monticello," could set his song of inter-racial desires to "Yankee Doodle" boded ill for democracy. It is not merely that Jefferson is using patriotic sentiment to sing about sexual "sport," which is bad enough, but the more damaging implication of this poem is that patriotic sentiment might somehow be responsible for sending Jefferson across a boundary described here as a race boundary. The constant refrain of "Yankee Doodle" makes the point that liberal democracy necessarily leads to the belief that a woman with black skin and who smells bad will be considered the most "luscious" "of all the damsels" and thus lead those "press'd by loads of state affairs" into bed and away from their civic duties.

The focus on race traits is also obsessive in "A Philosophic Love-Song. *To Sally.*" This poem examines in detail Sally's supposed race traits and Jefferson's imagined attraction to them. He is made to sing the following:

Let poets sing, and striplings sigh,
  For damsels bright and fair,
The ruby lip, the sapphire eye,
  The silken, auburn hair:

My philosophic taste disdains
  Such paltry charms as those—
Scorns the smooth skin's transparent veins,
  And cheeks that shame the rose.

In glaring red, and chalky white,
  Let others beauty see;
Me no such tawdry tints delight—
  No! *black's* the hue for me!

What though my Sally's nose be flat,
  'Tis harder, then, to break it—
Her skin is sable — what of that?
  'Tis smooth as oil can make it.

If down her neck no ringlets flow,
  A fleece adorns her head—
If on her lips no rubies glow,
  Their thickness serves instead.

Thick pouting lips! how sweet their grace!
  When passion fires to kiss them!
Wide spreading over half the face,
  Impossible to miss them.

Thou, Sally, thou, my house shalt keep,
  My widow'd tears shall dry!
My virgin daughters—see! they weep—
  Their mother's place supply.

Oh! Sally! hearken to my vows!
  Yield up thy swarthy charms—
My best belov'd! my more than spouse,
  Oh! take me to thy arms![32]

What makes Jefferson's behavior particularly scandalous, according to this Federalist poem, is that he insists that the traits of black women are more sexually desirable, even as he realizes they are less than aesthetically pleasing. A flat nose might not be pretty but it can't be broken during what can thus only be imagined as the most passionate of lovemaking. Black skin is well oiled, which, presumably, is a sensuous quality. A black woman's lips might be an unfortunate color and out of what readers would consider good proportion, but, during sex, they thus provide a big target. On the other hand, despite ostensibly serving Jefferson here as a sexually undesirable point of contrast to black women, white women are lovingly described in these poems as having the "ruby lip, the sapphire eye, / The silken, auburn hair," not to mention their "smooth skin's transparent veins, / And cheeks that shame the rose." In this, in "A Song Supposed to Have Been Written by the Sage of Monticello," and in other Federalist texts, racial difference is a difference in aesthetic value and thus a difference that governs sexual desire, drawing desire toward the most attractive race such that "Quashee" understandably wants a white wife. Jefferson's attraction to those traits at the bottom of the imagined aesthetic hierarchy is supposedly a result of liberal democracy and is what makes him sexually perverse. The poems and Akin's print thereby remind readers of what, by implication, is the *right* response to the aesthetic hierarchy of race traits imagined here, namely that they should desire other whites and other whites only and that the danger of endorsing liberal democracy is that it will teach them the *wrong* response.

The rationalization of race as an aesthetic hierarchy of traits with supposedly built in dynamics of sexual desire had been popularized by Jefferson himself in his *Notes on the State of Virginia*. In Query XIV of *Notes*, on "the administration of justice and description of laws," Jefferson lays out his views on racial difference and desire in the process of recounting the work of the committee appointed by Virginia's House of Delegates to make the former colony's statutes and common law commensurate with Virginia as a sovereign commonwealth. The committee, on which Jefferson served in 1776, drafted an amendment proposing gradual emancipation with colonization. Colonization was a new idea and one regarded warily by a nation that pinned its hopes for success on population growth.[33] So although the amendment was never presented, but because Jefferson continued to advocate colonization, he felt compelled to address the fact that his readers will wonder "Why not retain and incorporate the blacks into the state, and thus save the expense of supplying, by importation of white settlers, the vacancies they will leave?"[34] That deported blacks left "vacancies" that must be filled was a foregone conclusion. It was the expense of deportation that deserved justification. Jefferson's rationale was that blacks must be "removed beyond the reach of mixture" so as not to "stain the blood of . . . [their] master[s]" (270). Removal, he explains, would ensure that blacks and whites remain "as distinct as nature has formed them" (270). Those "physical distinctions [that] prove . . . a difference of race" and that Jefferson thus wanted to remain distinct were, for him, those of skin color, "the first difference," he argues, "which strikes us" (264), as well as those of hair, smell, memory, and reason, among others. And he wants these traits to remain distinct only because black traits are, in his view, so much less attractive than white traits. He insists, for example, that blacks "secrete less by the kidnies [sic], and more by the glands of the skin, which gives them a very strong and disagreeable odour" (265). And he argues of skin that

Whether the black of the negro resides in the reticular membrane between the skin and scarf-skin, or in the scarf-skin itself; whether it proceeds from the colour of the blood, the colour of the bile, or from that of some other secretion, the difference is fixed in nature, and is as real as if its seat and cause were better known to us. And is this difference of no importance? Is it not the foundation of a greater or less share of beauty in the two races? Are not the fine mixtures of red and white, the expressions of every passion by greater or less suffusions of colour in the one, preferable to that eternal monotony, which reigns in the countenances, that immoveable veil of black which covers all the emotions of the other race? (264–65)

For Jefferson, whiteness is a superior color and one which he wants to remain "distinct" because it is more expressive of "every passion," whereas "black" skin "covers all the emotions." The white "race" thus also has, in his view, inner beauty whereas he envisions blacks as both unintelligent because expressionless and as tricksters, veiled characters who use their skin color for the purposes of duplicity. The imagined aesthetics of color are thus also indicators of moral value. To argue for removal in the face of emancipation is, in Jefferson's view, a moral imperative based on what Jefferson wants to argue is a science of aesthetics. "The circumstance of superior beauty, is thought worthy attention in the propagation of our horses, dogs, and other domestic animals; why not in that of man?" (265). Jefferson further argues that even those who are "advocates" of the slaves, "while they wish to vindicate the liberty of human nature, are anxious also to preserve its dignity and beauty" (270). Seemingly fearful of the same racial implications of natural rights philosophy that worried the Federalists, Jefferson argues that liberal democracy must be coupled with disdain for inter-racial sex and reproduction because he assumes that blacks are ugly and therefore a threat to white beauty should the two mix.

In arguing for white isolation based on white beauty, Jefferson insists that the beauty of white race traits and thus the place of whites on the top of a hierarchy of race is proved by the black "preference of them, as uniformly as is the preference of the Oranootan for the black women over those of his own species" (265).[35] The perception that orangutans desire African women goes back to the late sixteenth/early seventeenth centuries and was widely credited by the scientists of Jefferson's day.[36] Jefferson would have been familiar with the frontispiece of an English translation of Linnaeus entitled *A Genuine and Universal System of Natural History*, which showed an orangutan snatching an African woman from her human mate. And Jefferson's friend Benjamin Rush had recently asserted similarly in his "Observations Intended to Favour a Supposition That the Black Color (As It Is Called) of the Negroes Is Derived from the Leprosy" (1797) that African women are "debauched" by orangutans.[37] Jefferson's assertion that blacks prefer whites was also a white commonplace by the eighteenth century. In his *New Voyage to Guinea* (1744), William Smith asserted, for example, of the reputedly "hot constitution'd Ladies" there that they possess a "temper hot and lascivious, making no scruple to prostitute themselves to the *Europeans* for a very slender profit, so great is their inclination to white men."[38] By insisting that orangutans desire blacks and that blacks desire whites, Jefferson is laying out the old Chain of Being organized by kind where blacks and primates are together on the bottom of the hierarchy. Jefferson is putting a new spin on the chain, however. He imagines that the chain is organized into biological kinds who are knowable as distinct through their relative beauty. And he envisions each race or species desiring to couple with that race or species above it on the chain out of "preference" for its greater beauty. In *Notes*, "preference" or desire thus becomes, by definition, thoroughly racialized. Preference for a person is imagined as desire for the race traits that supposedly distinguish them.

Given the position of whites on the chain and the upward direction of desire, it should be the case that whites desire other whites and other whites only. That Jefferson advocates black deportation indicates, however, that he was not completely confident in this premise. A sign of his wariness is that he poses his questions about the relative beauty of black and white skin as a series of rhetorical questions. He thus means to assert with them that he believes he can count on readers to agree that those with "the fine mixtures of red and white" *are* more beautiful. But rhetorical questions are often posed not only when the answer is obvious, but when the answer must be elicited. Pressed with these questions, a reader would feel compelled to agree that those people without the imagined "immoveable veil of black" are aesthetically preferable even as, importantly, he might not have thought these issues through in the same way before. That Jefferson attempts to make his ultimate point in a series of rhetorical questions reveals, in other words, that he is attempting to school or train readers in the right kind of preferences. The reward for compliant readers is that white intra-racial desire, within the terms that Jefferson describes it, proves the reader's aesthetic competency, the reader's superior judgment. To "prefer" a person had come to be experienced as desire for their race traits and thus a means to demonstrate one's knowledge and appreciation of beauty. In *Notes*, Jefferson was helping create an identity based on aesthetic competencies demonstrated through one's sexual desires.

The *Port Folio* poets use precisely this logic to argue in their poems that to desire "Sally" must be to desire her black race traits and thus to be a perverse man, whereas to desire white traits, by implication, proves one's good taste. Both Jefferson and the Federalists responded to liberal democracy and the question it raised of emancipation with the dissemination of thoroughly racialized rules of desire.[39] Jefferson thus helped create the rhetoric with which he was attacked.

Both *Notes* and the Federalist poems about Jefferson and "Sally" thus demonstrate that desire for another person imagined to be of one's own race is not a fact of nature, as is commonly believed, but, rather, at this moment, was being produced as a kind of race "preference" in response to liberal democracy and its ideologies of equality and freedom. And while whiteness was coming to be imagined by both Jefferson and the Federalists as a set of physical traits that still needed to be enumerated and described ("the fine mixtures of red and white," "the ruby lip," "the silken . . . hair," etc.), it was an emergent category, the inclusion of which was based squarely on a supposedly innate but really learned aesthetic appreciation for these imagined features and distaste for others ("sable" skin, a flat nose, thick lips, and so on) in which their texts schooled readers. One of the Federalist poems about Jefferson and Hemings reveals this point that what makes a person able to claim membership in the white race is their supposedly inborn taste for the supposedly more attractive "race" traits. In "The Metamorphosis," Jefferson becomes black himself, presumably as a means of attracting Hemings, but also because his supposed attraction to her means he is no longer really white.

In days of yore, as poets tell,
When Jove in love with mortals fell,
He stripp'd off dignity and pride,
Laid all his thunder-bolts aside;
From high Olympus made escape
To beastly deeds, in beastly shape. . . . [*sic*]
By turns, as lewdness spurr'd him on,
A bull, a serpent or a swan. . . . [*sic*]
Yet, when the lustful fit was o'er,
He rose, resplendent, as before:
Ascended heav'n's bright throne again,
Majestic king of gods and men!
Again the blasting thunder hurl'd,
And snuff'd the incense of a world.
Say, then, ye scoundrel tory crew,
Who make of morals such ado:
Since Jove could make himself a beast,
On Grecian beauty's charms to feast;
If he, whom jacobins adore,
Should lust to kennel with a wh. . . .e[*sic*],
If, scorning all his country's dames,
No tint, but jet, his blood inflames,
Why should our demi-god forbear
A transient veil of soot to wear,
Why not his godship put away,

Invest himself in Afric's clay
Smear with lamp-black his pallid wax,
And look and smell like other blacks,
To charm the lovely Sally's eye,
And wallow in a negro-sty:
Then take his proper form again,
The pride of virtue. . . .[*sic*] first of men.
In vain you prate of moral rules,
The net of priests. . . . [*sic*] the bait of fools;
He shall not lose beneath your rod,
The ancient birth-right of a god. . . . [*sic*]
Lo, while his wonted form I seek,
The rosy hue forsakes his cheek,
And straight, by transformation strange,
From white to black his features change!
His tresses fall, and in their stead,
A fleece shoots curling from his head,
Flat sinks the bridge, that prop'd his nose,
Which round his nostril plumper grows:
His jaw protrudes, his lip expands,
Pah! he secretes by all the glands:
His legs inflect: his stature shrinks,
And from his skin all Congo stinks:
Behold him now, by Cupid sped,
In darkness sneak to Sally's bed:
With philosophic nose inquire,
How rank the sable race perspire.
In foul pollution steep his life,
Insult the ashes of his wife:
All the paternal duties smother,
Give his white girls a yellow brother:
Mid loud hosannas of his knaves,
From his own loins raise herds of slaves,
With numbers to outvote the free,
With smoke the yankies, five for three.
Yet shall he not be long confin'd
To the base mould of Afric's kind:
But with the morrow's dawning light
Resume his native red and white. . . . [*sic*]

Then pure to jacobinic eyes,
Claim the full tribute of their lies.
Still under Smith's and Jones's pen,
Appear the first of mortal men.
Still in the prime of Dallas shine,
Still seem to Lincoln all divine.
Still worshipp'd as a god remain,
By Cheetham, Grainger and Duane:
And, spite of all you tories can,
Still wield the state. . . . [*sic*] THE PEOPLE'S MAN.[40]

Once again, a Federalist poet reiterates those traits that were repeatedly desig-
nated by Jefferson and others as race traits at the time: skin color, hair texture,
nose and lip width, facial angle, and smell. But in this poem, the stress is not
on Hemings's black traits but rather on Jefferson's "fleece," "flat" nose, pro-
truding jaw, wide lips, and foul smell. Jefferson is said to be attracted to these
traits of the "sable race"—"No tint, but jet, his blood inflames"—and to act
on that attraction in secret by transforming himself into a black man in order
to win Sally. He is thus politically attacked in the poem for his hypocrisy. He
only "appear[s]" "the first of mortal men" when in fact he is "lust[ing] to kennel with a wh. . . . e." But by linking Jefferson's lust for Sally with his own
blackness, the poem makes the point that the objects of people's sexual attraction are not only what make people honorable or not but also comprise their
racial membership. Jefferson literally loses the whiteness that made him "THE
PEOPLE'S MAN" because of his inter-racial lust.

Finally, even as the *Port Folio* poems ostensibly were meant solely to
politically critique the Republicans, and implicitly served to train readers in
the proper desires, the inter-racial desire they portrayed also must have titillated readers. Readers are treated, for example, to the exposure of sexual
secrets in voyeuristic fashion. Consider again "The Metamorphosis." Even as
the poem propounds the hypocrisy of Jefferson, the reader is asked to imagine
watching Jefferson and Hemings in bed: "Behold him now, by Cupid sped, /
In darkness sneak to Sally's bed." Also, when Jefferson declares his attraction
to Sally in the many first-person Federalist poems in which Jefferson is the
speaker, the reader must also enunciate that attraction in the first person. In
using the first person in the form of "Yankee Doodle," a popular song that
might easily be repeated with these lyrics on the street, in a pub, or elsewhere
long after the issue of the *Port Folio* it was in had been discarded, the Federalist author of "A Song Supposed to Have Been Written by the Sage of Monti-

cello" makes his readers and their repeaters enunciate such lines as "The sweetest solace of my cares / Is in the lap of Sally." So spoken, the "my" is both Jefferson's and the reader's who thus become one and the same. The reader, in other words, by virtue of the poem's first-person construction, is forced to assert that *his* "sweetest solace" "Is in the lap of Sally." In other words, the reader has to ventriloquize Jefferson's own lust, thereby speaking inter-racial desires himself. In a poem in which a black woman is noted in typical fashion for being sexually "yielding" and good for "sport and dally," the reader might have to admit that, as the speaker asserts, "You men of morals! and be curst, / You would snap like sharks for Sally."

"A Philosophic Love-Song. *To Sally*" works similarly. Even while, as we've seen, the poem argues that black traits are inferior to white traits, its linkage of black traits with heightened sexual passion makes those traits appealing, particularly when the reader has to ventriloquize Jefferson's attraction to them. "Oh! Sally! hearken to my vows! / Yield up thy swarthy charms — / My best belov'd my more than spouse, / Oh! take me to thy arms!" The mythology that black women were more sexually satisfying not only reveals its appeal here to white men, but shows that, even as they meant to discredit one man for succumbing to it, they do so themselves.

But perhaps the guilt and shame that resulted from desiring that which was deemed revolting served to heighten the impression that inter-racial sex is degrading and generally repulsive. And because the poems lure readers into imagining touching, smelling, and looking at sexualized black race traits, both desire and revulsion would have been experienced on the most physical level. In short, the Federalist poems were thus naturalizing the sexual responses that comprised racial identity as fast as they could culturally construct them.

Since Callender first broached it publicly, the story of Thomas Jefferson and Sally Hemings has cropped up repeatedly in American history and always to serve some political ends.[41] Most recently, now that DNA evidence has proven that Thomas Jefferson did indeed father at least some of the children of Sally Hemings, the story of their relationship has been invoked to make the point, among others, that academic historians were racist in long ignoring African-American oral history.[42] In 1802–3, the story was deployed first to heighten hysteria about liberal democracy but also finally to further Jefferson's idea that there is an aesthetic hierarchy of so-called "race" traits that must be honored by those who want to be praised as what Josiah Quincy, Jr., termed "men of worth, politeness, and humanity." A person proved his worthiness as a "white" man through the manifestations of his sexual desire, desire that, in the United States, was thoroughly racialized. The lasting legacy of the Thomas Jefferson and Sally Hemings affair may well be that liberal democracy would not result in a society without race, or at least without race hierarchies, because what we might now term intra-racial desire was invented. In the wake of a state-sanctioned philosophy of equality, intra-racial desire was an important means of maintaining a race-based culture, not because mixed-race people would otherwise result—although this was raised as a concern at times—but because it proved one's affiliation to the idea of white superiority and thus to whiteness itself.[43]

2 The Rhetoric of Blood and Mixture

Cooper's "Man Without a Cross"

In *The Last of the Mohicans* (1826), a historical novel about the New York frontier during the French and Indian War and the most popular novel of the 1820s, James Fenimore Cooper has the main protagonist refer repeatedly to race in terms of blood and fractions of blood.[1] Hawk-eye states that he is "the whole blood of the whites" and, on another occasion, that he is "a man of white blood." On still another occasion, he claims to be "a white man who has no taint of Indian blood."[2] Hawk-eye uses the rhetoric of blood in these statements to make the point that he has not one Indian ancestor and that this is precisely what makes him "white" to the core of his being. He makes these repeated assertions about his "whole" blood because, as he notes, he "may have lived with the red skins long enough to be suspected!" (35). In other words, to claim that he has only "white blood" is to invoke a biological white identity supposedly inherited from his ancestors that negates any cultural practices that might seem to indicate otherwise. Only rarely does Hawk-eye say simply that "I am genuine white" (31) or that he is "a white man" (121), although this clearly meant the same thing to him as having "the whole blood of the whites." "White man" was—and still remains—the shorthand version of these ideas about inheritance and blood. Because he is a simple woodsman who lives with Indians, readers are meant to understand that, in constantly referring to blood, Hawk-eye is using the most basic and even perhaps pre-cultural terms to describe the essence of being a "white man." If someone like him who lives in Nature asserts that race is a quality of the blood and that it thus has nothing to do with one's cultural practices or behaviors, then it must be true. So at the same time that whiteness was becoming an identity demonstrated through social behavior, namely the demonstrations of sexual race "preference" indicated by the *Port Folio* poems, it was imagined by Cooper and his readers to be, on the contrary, a purported biological identity one inherited from one's ancestors and that manifests itself in one's blood. Indeed, it was by understanding sexual relations across an imagined race barrier as blood mixture that the role of the culture in creating the rules of preference that governed inclusion in "whiteness" could be ignored in the face of what seemed to be a purely biological category.

The perception that blood carries family history and thus physically embodies kinship comes from the ancient belief that sperm is comprised of blood. Aristotle wrote that "men and women are tired after ejaculation, not because the quantity of material emitted is so great but because of its quality: it is made from the purest part of the blood, from the essence of life."[3] In the fourteenth century, Dante similarly envisioned the sex act as two bloods sprayed on each other.[4] Without an understanding of the capillaries and other bodily systems only visible in the seventeenth century with the invention of the microscope, there was, in the words of historian Thomas Laqueur, "a physiology of fungible fluids."[5] In other words, the body was not envisioned as a composite of separate systems, as it is today. A child was thus imagined as made from and comprised of her parents' blood. And this is precisely why, as explained in a seventh-century encyclopedia,

Consanguinity is so called by that which from one blood, that is from the same semen of the father, is begotten. For the semen of the male is the foam of blood according to the manner of water which, when beaten against rocks, makes white foam, or just as dark wine, which poured into a cup, renders the foam white.[6]

That kinship ties were imagined as ties of shared blood infused those ties with powerful sentiments. The Ancients knew that losing large amounts of blood was fatal and thus hypothesized the role of this precious fluid in sustaining life. Claudius Galen argued that the basic principle of life, "spirit" (*pneuma*), is drawn into the lungs by breathing where it charges the blood before it is sent out through all of the arteries. In medieval Europe, blood was also viewed as powerful. It was deemed the "father" of the four humors that regulated one's health and personality: blood, phlegm, yellow bile, and black bile.[7] All of these ideas about blood's life-sustaining role were so powerful that the Christian faith was built on the idea that a savior redeemed the world by shedding his blood for all. For believers, partaking of the transubstantiated wine of the Eucharist was an ecstatic experience that healed both body and soul.[8] To invoke the seventeenth-century aphorism about family ties "blood is thicker than water" is to refer to a substance thickened with all of these meanings.[9]

The stress on lineal kinship that blood marks in modern genealogical thinking originated in the medieval period, according to R. Howard Bloch, when lineal kinship became the central means of imagining one's identity over the earlier privileging of horizontal kin. Bloch notes that, in ninth- and tenth-century France, there were dynastic houses but no patronyms. People knew others and themselves by a single Christian name. It seems the noble family imagined itself more in relation to living relatives than ancestors. In his terms, "Descent was a less potent force of family cohesion than affiliation with living relatives."[10] Due to various changes that occurred in the eleventh century—principally the transformation of provisional benefices into heritable fiefs—nobility came to represent a quality of birth. Bloch states: "The kin group as a spatial extension was displaced from within by the notion of the blood group as a diachronic progression." In other words, what Bloch calls the "horizontal clan" took on "through increased emphasis upon time and blood, a necessarily tighter and more 'vertical' slant."[11] The history of relationships became, for the nobility and increasingly for all Westerners, its genealogical records of the "blood" ties of lineal kinship.

The discovery of DNA and the fact that many cultures do not celebrate or even recognize biogenetic ties make clear, however, that the rhetoric of blood is a purely metaphorical means developed in Western history to refer to modern family formations. Indeed, anthropologist David Schneider has found that when Americans perceive a person as a "blood relative," they mean not a person who shares biogenetic material, but one who follows voluntarily what he terms a kinship "code of conduct," whether that be expressing affection or helping with financial or other responsibilities.[12] The rhetoric of blood is the means used to naturalize the role of reproduction and procreation in creating these family formations. In other words, the invocation of blood is a means of insisting that family ties are grounded in the biological real rather than in what Pierre Bourdieu terms the "strategies" for interacting with other people in order to maximize "material and symbolic interests."[13]

Before race became linked to lineal kinship and thus defined by the rhetoric of blood, it was imagined by the English and the earliest English colonialists to be a product of the climate. Blackness was often described as a "universal freckle," while light skin was believed to be the result of *not* living in a torrid climate.[14] Thus, in *The Merchant of Venice* (1596–97), Shakespeare had the Prince of Morocco describe his "complexion" as "The Shadow'd livery of the burnish'd sun, / To Whom I am a neighbor and near bred" (II, I, 2–3). The climatological argument held that people who moved from one climate to another changed into a different race. But after the large migrations that resulted from the slave trade proved otherwise and after the egg and sperm were discovered in the seventeenth century, it came to be assumed widely that reproduction was the means by which race was made.[15] By 1816, Dr. Samuel Latham Mitchill was arguing that "If by the act of modeling the constitution in the embryo and foetus a predisposition to gout, madness, scrofula and consumption, may be engendered, we may rationally conclude . . . that the procreative power may also shape the features, tinge the skin, and give other peculiarities."[16] Interestingly, Mitchill can insist that his is a "rational" conclusion only on the strength of an analogy. Reproduction was only thought to result in race traits through some largely mysterious "procreative power." But race and reproduction became linked nonetheless and blood was the means by which they were joined. Each parent contributed his or her race blood through the act of procreation. While many continued to believe in the importance of the environment in initially shaping what was thought of as race, most believed that racial categories were perpetuated over time as inherited identities carried in the blood. Just as Sir William Blackstone wrote in his *Commentaries on the Laws of England* (1768) that "So many different bloods is a man said to contain in his veins, as he hath lineal ancestors," so too was race believed to be in the blood and also devisable in relation to a person's family history.[17] Those interested in creating a science of race generated complex equations based on this idea that race is an amount of blood inherited through lineal kinship and thus linked directly to reproduction. One such interested person wrote in 1815, for example:

Let us express the pure blood of the white in the capital letters of the printed alphabet, the pure blood of the negro in the small letters of the printed alphabet, and any given mixture of either, by way of abridgment in MS. letters.

Let the first crossing be of a, a pure negro, with A, pure white. The unit of blood of the issue being composed of the half of that of each parent, will be $a/2 + A/2$. Call it, for abbreviation, h (half blood).

Let the second crossing be that of h and B, the blood of the issue will be $h/2 + B/2$, or substituting for $h/2$ its equivalent, it will be $a/4 + A/4 + B/2$, call it q (quarteroon) being 1/4 negro blood.

Let the third crossing be of q and C, their offspring will be $q/2 + C/2 = a/8 + A/8 + B/4 + C/2$, call this e (eighth), who having less than 1/4 of a, or of pure negro blood, to wit 1/8 only, is no longer a mulatto, so that a third cross clears the blood.[18]

Race blood is a finite "unit" here that is neatly devisable. Each parent contributes exactly one half of his or her blood to the offspring. While the alge-

braic component of the equations seems excessive, they are entirely represen-
tative of the rhetoric employed by Hawk-eye when he terms himself of "whole
blood." Degrees of whiteness and blackness were imagined by this author and
Cooper as so much blood of one race or another. Only the assumption voiced
in 1815 that black blood can be "cleared" in three "crosses" is not typical for
the period. For others, "one drop" of "negro blood," as it was termed, was
enough to make a person black.[19]

Hawk-eye not only describes his blood as "whole," however, but asserts
obsessively for a total of nineteen times in the course of the novel that, as he
variously phrases it, he is "a man without a cross" or "no cross in his blood"
(70, 35). This repeated use of the term "cross" is often interpreted by scholars
as a reference to Hawk-eye's Christianity or lack thereof. Richard Slotkin
argues that the phrase "is ambiguous, since . . . [Hawk-eye] is not a Christian
and has no conception of being a member of a fallen race. Hence he neither
identifies with the cross nor bears the cross of guilt, punishment or expia-
tion."[20] Forrest G. Robinson follows suit, seeing the phrase as Hawk-eye's
"assertion of moral and spiritual preeminence. But . . . he is protesting too
much. For all his advocacy of Christian principles, he is at least as predatory
and quite as vengeful as the Indians he so habitually condemns."[21] But, in
Cooper's day, after one hundred years of fairly sophisticated animal and plant
breeding in British North America, the term "cross" littered the pages of nineteenth-century guides to horticulture and to animal husbandry and thus
would have been easily understood by contemporary readers as a mixture
between two separate species or, in regard to people, two different races, the
latter a concept often synonymous with the idea of species. In *The American
Gardener* (first edition, 1819), for example, a book reprinted often, William
Cobbett defined "degenerate" seed as that which has "become *mixed*, or
crossed, in generating."[22] At least by 1815, the term "cross" had been appropriated to refer to race mixing. Cooper thus knew readers would understand
that, with his denial of any "crossing," Hawk-eye is summoning an all-white
genealogical past. No one in his bloodline has coupled or "crossed" with an
Indian, meaning that the blood flowing in his veins, which gives him all of his
inherited familial traits, including his race traits, is "pure" white. Again, for
Hawk-eye, race is not a set of behaviors—otherwise he could be deemed an
Indian—but a genealogical and biological condition.

By drawing on the rhetoric of blood and referring to race mixture as
"crossing," Hawk-eye makes clear his view that the races comprise different
kinds or species that do not normally and should not mix or "cross." For as
set forth by Buffon, a species is comprised of those animals who will and can

perpetuate themselves. According to this definition, animals from separate species are not meant nor are even able to procreate. Cooper's title for the novel and the plot of *The Last of the Mohicans* to which the title refers is driven by this view that the races comprise separate species that would not naturally mix. Both depend on an understanding of race as both species and a biological inheritance. In his introduction to the first edition of the novel, Cooper writes of the Lenni Lenape, of which the Mohicans are one branch, that their name translates into "unmixed people." They are "a people who sprang from the same stock" (2). This is a means of proving the Mohicans the "good" Indians—like Hawk-eye, they are not "crossed"—whose demise white readers should thus mourn. And Chingachgook and his son, Uncas, can be the "last" of these "unmixed people," which Cooper describes as an "inevitable fate" (6–7), only because Uncas will produce no "unmixed" offspring. His race will die out because he cannot reproduce with another Mohican, the women of whom are presumably already gone and who are thus noticeably absent from the novel. Even if he sexually coupled with a non-Indian woman, he should still be considered the last Mohican, according to Cooper's logic. In his introduction to the 1831 edition of the novel, Cooper elaborates on this link between species and race, dismissing the "Mosaic account of the creation" (6), which held that all humans are descended from one couple, when he argues that climate cannot have produced the "substantial difference" in the Indian's color (5). Rather than view all people as related through their common descent from Adam and Eve, Cooper believes the Indians are a separate species who were born in Asia and then migrated hither (5).[23] Cooper's story of the "last" of the Mohicans gets its purchase, therefore, not only from the fact of Indian removal and death, but from this definition of racial difference as species difference that is transmitted through familial inheritance. That the Indians can be imagined as completely removed or all dead depends on the assumption that they are a separate race, no fraction of which has been or could be incorporated into "white" America.

If, as Philip Fisher has argued, Cooper's novel helps readers mourn the passing of these Indians so that they can benefit from that removal and genocide without experiencing the guilt of their own implication in it, then Cooper's narrative must enable *intra*-racial marriages and defuse and disable the *inter*-racial desires that swirl around the novel's two heroines and that might otherwise undermine the species premise behind the removal fantasy.[24] If one of the two heroines coupled with the last Mohican, it would be harder for Cooper to declare him the last. To this end, *The Last of the Mohicans* is structured as much by the marriage plot as by the removal plot. What was once the first volume of the novel traces the attempt of two half sisters, Alice and Cora Munro, to get to their father, a Scottish commander, at his besieged British fort near what is now called Lake George in New York during the French and Indian War. They are accompanied by Hawk-eye; Uncas's father Chingachgook; Major Duncan Heyward of the Royal Americans; David Gamut, a singing master; and Magua, an outcast Iroquois or, more generically, a Huron, the latter the name for those Indians of Canada who were allied, albeit precariously, with the French. After the party has arrived at the fort toward the end of the first part of the novel, Colonel Munro erroneously thinks Heyward desires Cora and feels compelled to reveal to him that Cora has black ancestry. But all is not happily-ever-after when this confusion is cleared up. For, at the end of the volume, Cora and Alice are lost to their father again when kidnapped by Magua and the Hurons. The second part is divided into two quests, in one of which Uncas attempts to rescue Cora from Magua, who wishes to take her to his wigwam as his wife, and in the other of which Heyward attempts to rescue Alice, who Magua has also kidnapped as a means of making Cora follow him into the wilderness. Structured as it is by the marriage plot, the novel aims to create satisfying matches for its various protagonists with which to bring the narrative to resolution.

What defines a satisfying match in the novel is the right kind of blood mixture. This is first made clear when Colonel Munro stops in the middle of delicate political negotiations to discuss giving the hand of one of his two daughters to Heyward. Munro begins by acknowledging, "I did not think it becoming an old soldier to be talking of nuptial blessings, and wedding jokes, when the enemies of his king were likely to be unbidden guests at the feast! But I was wrong, Duncan, boy, I was wrong there; and I am now ready to hear what you have to say" (157). When Duncan warns that they had better attend instead to the message he has just brought from the French, Munro exclaims that he feels "too much pressed to discharge the little domestic duties of . . . [my] own family!" He then explains why he should be so eager to converse about these matters with this particular young man: "Your mother was the only child of my bosom friend, Duncan; and I'll just give you a hearing, though all the knights of St. Louis were in a body at the sally-port, with the French saint at their head, craving to speak a word, under favour" (157). Munro wants Duncan for a son-in-law, he claims, "for the sake of him whose blood is in your veins" (158). For Munro, one's lineage is a set of historical facts about the past preserved in a biological essence in the present: blood. Sex and procreation thus become loaded with significance, for each coupling has an outcome presumably written in blood. But if Munro is anxious to engage his daughter to Duncan at the peril of their lives and of the security of the fort, this is because blood is also the carrier of race. With Indians ready to invade with the French and his daughter's black ancestry to conceal, Munro's concern is specifically with race blood.

After Duncan clarifies that it is Alice and not Cora he loves, the Colonel reveals to Duncan that Cora's mother "was the daughter of a gentleman of those [West Indian] isles, whose misfortune it was, if you will, . . . to be descended, remotely, from that unfortunate class, who are so basely enslaved" (159). Recalling that Duncan was born in the South and assuming that blood is as important to Duncan as it is to himself, Munro feels compelled to ask him, "You scorn to mingle the blood of the Heywards, with one so degraded —lovely and virtuous though she be?" (159). Munro assumes that for Duncan, as for himself, race is an essence in the blood. Because of Cora's ancestry, she has what is imagined as black blood and is thus perhaps undesirable to Heyward, no matter how beautiful she is nor even, for that matter, how "white" she might look. Even as Duncan denies what he terms a "prejudice" against Cora's lineage, he is, the narrator explains, "at the same time conscious of such a feeling, and that as deeply rooted as if it had been engrafted in his nature" (159). To be sure, Southern planters, like West Indian colonialists, frequently had sexual relationships with black women, but they usually avoided marriage where blood becomes particularly important because it is legitimated. The language of horticulture ("deeply rooted" and "engrafted") is used to describe this prejudice in a way that helps naturalizes it. If Duncan would consider blood a factor in a marriage decision, this is because such a consideration is an inherent part of his biological makeup. Cooper makes it clear that Duncan is invested in good blood in the exact same way Munro is when Munro considers him a good prospect as a son-in-law because of his blood.

Duncan's own preoccupation with blood status is further revealed when he declares his love to Alice. As in his earlier discussion with Munro, Duncan broaches the subject with Alice in the midst of great danger. In *The Last of the Mohicans*, men stop to discuss their hearts when, one might argue, they should be plotting to save lives. In both instances, this has nothing to do with Cooper's ineptitude as a writer and everything to do with the fact that, because he envisions the real danger as inter-racial sex, plans to divert it through *intra*-racial unions are imperative. In this second case, there is the danger that Alice might have to live out her life with the Indians and thus presumably accept one as her husband. Duncan's ambiguous reply to Alice's request that he not forget Cora reveals that white blood is precisely what is at stake in his preference for the younger sister. "Your venerable father knew of no difference between his children; but I—Alice you will not be offended, when I say, that to me her worth was in a degree obscured " (260). Here Alice cuts him off. But having informed us of Duncan's secret prejudice, we might be meant to wonder if Duncan was going to confess that Cora's worth was obscured by her black blood, rather than by her sister's own worth. The former is likely, given Duncan's admitted prejudice. In the midst of the threat of Indians and particularly of Indian men in proximity to white women, it seems Cooper must have Duncan secure what is imagined as an intra-racial blood bond.

If any of Cooper's characters can claim responsibility for securing the coupling between Alice and Duncan, it is Hawk-eye, a man who clearly understands that race dynamics are a key aspect of their coupling because of his own concern about "white blood." It is Hawk-eye who persuades Duncan to wash off the Indian paint that has allowed him to infiltrate the camp where Alice is being held so that he can approach his beloved and declare his love: " 'your streaked countenances are not ill judged of by the squaws, but young women of white blood give the preference to their own colour. See,' he added, pointing to a place where the water trickled from a rock . . . , 'you may easily get rid of the Sagamore's daub' " (258). That women who have "white blood" "give the preference to their own colour" is made understandable here by the fact that that color is associated with cleanliness. But whereas Jefferson realized the need to teach aesthetic "preference" in his *Notes*, here it is firmly believed to be located in one's biological makeup. Preferences are said here to spring directly from the blood. It seems that, in the wake of whiteness becoming a category of "preference," as the writings of Jefferson and the Federalists make clear, certainly one of the reasons the rhetoric of blood was used more frequently and, in Cooper's case, obsessively, was because blood could help naturalize preference. If "preference" is driven by one's blood, then intra-racial desire is natural and to be expected, and "whiteness" can be imagined as simply the inherited biological result of those desires. Similarly, the case can be made that Heyward is naturally disgusted at the prospect of race blood mixing. And at the end of the novel, after Hawk-eye has rescued Alice and Duncan, we learn that Duncan's and Munro's concern for the right kind of blood has prevailed: Duncan and Alice will be married (348).

Cora's marriage plot, which takes center stage once Alice and Duncan are united, is structured by the same concerns but only because, for the rest of the narrative, she functions mainly as, and is even called, a "white maiden" (348). When Magua proposes and later when Tamenund, the Delaware leader, orders that she live in Magua's wigwam as his wife, the level of her disgust is thoroughly indicative of her status as and indeed of the supposed "nature" of a white woman. When Tamenund argues that her "race will not end," her reply precisely echoes her sister's own reaction to the prospect. Where Alice had asserted in response to Magua's proposal to Cora, "Name not the horrid alternative again; the thought itself is worse than a thousand deaths" (109), Cora similarly asserts to Tamenund, "Better, a thousand times [my race should end] . . . than meet with such a degradation" (313). Tamenund, assuming Cora is white, insists that one woman's inter-racial marriage will not result in the end of the entire white race. Cora can disagree only because she views her race as a so-called "pure" one. One person, in other words, can dilute and thus spell its downfall. Finally, when taken by Magua, or "le Subtil," as the French call him, Cora does in fact choose death over a coupling with him. Stopping on a ledge of rocks, she cries, "Kill me if thou wilt, detestable Huron, I will go no farther!" Magua responds, "Woman . . . choose: the wigwam or the knife of le Subtil!" (337). Both of them use language here that makes clear that the choice is perceived and repudiated in racial terms. She does not call him by name but rather by his race. He does not ask her to choose him but rather the life of an Indian. He attaches his personal importance in the equation only to the knife that will otherwise kill her. In choosing death over Magua, Cora makes the classic sacrifice of the white virgin. What makes this descendent of slaves in this portion of the book "white" is her "preference" for other "whites" and her distaste for nonwhites, just as Jefferson's "preference" for Hemings made him, in the eyes of the Federalists, "black."

Because she functions in this part of the narrative as white, Cora is not even permitted by Cooper to marry a "good" Indian. As literary critic Nina Baym notes, the parallel nature of the two quests seems to require that Uncas rescue Cora and live with her ever after, just as Duncan rescues Alice and wins her hand.[25] But Uncas's attempt to rescue Cora is, uncharacteristically for the strong young warrior, an impotent one. After a leap that leaves him "prostrate" on the outcropping of rock where the struggle between Cora and her assailant is taking place, Magua is easily able to stab Uncas in the back (337).

Cora is eventually joined with Uncas in a marriage of sorts but one that the "Indian maidens" imagine taking place in the "world of the spirits" (342). And yet even as this coupling in death is described as a "path [that] should be pleasant," the narrator and Hawk-eye, the character obsessed with blood, undercut some of the satisfaction with the union by reminding readers of the inappropriateness of its inter-racial nature, indicating that, here again, Cora functions as a white woman. When the Indian maidens "spoke of the future prospects of Cora and Uncas, . . . [Hawk-eye] shook his head, like one who knew the error of their simple creed. . . . Happily for the self-command of both Heyward and Munro, they knew not the meaning of the wild sounds they heard" (344). Contrary, then, to Hawk-eye's stated role to serve as "a link between ... [the Delaware's] and civilized life," his actual role in the narrative is to register disapproval of inter-racial sexual unions and to otherwise disallow them while instead enabling the intra-racial ones (348).

Perhaps because they have themselves been schooled in the "one-drop" rule, scholars have been unwilling to see Cora's shifting identity and instead read her as defined throughout the narrative by her slave ancestry. Forrest G. Robinson, for example, fails to recognize Cora as defined by anything but "black blood," which he invokes as obsessively as Hawk-eye invokes his own "white blood":

Cora's *black blood* 'explains' her sexuality; for Cooper and his audience, it makes her sexually attractive to Indians. . . . Her *black blood* may be said to liberate the lover in Uncas; it frees Cooper to step outside his comforting assumption that 'the native warrior of North America' is 'commonly chaste'. . . in his address to white women. . . . Take away the trace of *Negro blood,* and all this would have been inconceivable for a large American audience. . . . Cora's *mixed blood* also enflames Magua's revengeful passion, thereby raising the specter of miscegenation that calls out and 'justifies' white fear and violence, and that leads ineluctably to her death, and to the death of Uncas, the last hope of the Mohicans. (emphasis added)[26]

It is true that Cooper uses blood to essentialize race, although Robinson reinscribes rather than examines such rhetoric. But as a "bad" Indian, Magua does not need the excuse of mixed blood to act in a lascivious and violent manner. And Uncas never voices his love, much less "liberate[s] the lover" within. Rather, that Cora functions in the narrative as white sometimes and black other times explains, on the one hand, how she justifies the destruction of the Indians who want to mix with her—and, on the other, how she clears the way for Duncan to marry not this most attractive and outspoken woman but Munro's younger daughter whose passivity and pure white blood better suit her for the role of exchange object between the two men.

That Alice is the more passive sister as well as the one throughout *The Last of the Mohicans* with pure "white blood" reveals that the novel's investment in intra-racial marriage stems in part from the perceived importance of forming intra-racial bonds between men. When Munro stops in the middle of political negotiations to discuss the marriage of his daughter with Heyward, he castigates the French for having an aristocracy that can be purchased "with sugar-hogsheads" to which he contrasts Heyward's ancestry: "The Thistle is the order for dignity and antiquity; the veritable 'nemo me impune lacessit' of chivalry! Ye had ancestors in that degree, Duncan, and they were an ornament to the nobles of Scotland" (157). It seems that at precisely the moment his military and colonial endeavors are failing, Munro must ensure that the political bonds between himself and other men with status back in Europe are secure. As Claude Lévi-Strauss has theorized, "The total relationship of exchange which constitutes marriage is not established between a man and a woman, but between two groups of men, and the woman figures only as one of the objects of exchange, not as one of the partners."[27] When Heyward opens his bid by asking Munro for "the honour of being your son," this is certainly meant to show his respect for the older man but it also proves that, for Duncan as well, the bond under consideration is one that will ensure patriarchal succession of aristocratic title. Magua operates similarly. When he asks Cora to come to his wigwam, he proposes that "the daughter of the English chief follow and live in his wigwam for ever" (104). His aim, he reveals, is that "The daughter of Munro would draw his water, hoe his corn, and cook his venison. The body of the gray-head would sleep among his cannon, but his heart would lie within reach of the knife of le subtil" (105). Magua's proposal reveals that he aims not only to extract revenge for the travesties committed by Munro and his people against the Indian, but to build a political alliance or at least a seemingly good measure of political respect via the exchange of women. For if the English accept Magua's proposal and replace the wife Magua lost with Cora, they would be acknowledging a debt and, by putting one of their own in his hands, would therefore be operating as political equals. Cora explains that the inter-racial aspect of the proposed bond is precisely what makes it unacceptable when she asks of Magua, "what pleasure would Magua find in sharing his cabin with a wife he did not love; one who would be of a nation and colour different from his own? It would be better to take the gold of Munro, and buy the heart of some Huron maid with his gifts" (104). For Cora, it is because of a difference in "colour" that there can be no love nor any marriage. Better to have a purchased marriage with a woman of the same race, which presumably can work despite its unromantic origins precisely because of those shared race traits, than embark on one that involves partners of different colors. Of course, the suggested "gift" of gold from Munro is meant to remove Magua from the picture, not to form an alliance of the kind marriage would necessarily entail. Cooper is clear that those marriages that are shunned in the novel are shunned for racial reasons and in large part out of fear for the inter-racial alliances that would result.

It wasn't always the case that inter-marriage with Indians was demonized in this way. In the eighteenth and early nineteenth centuries, a good number of Anglo-Americans advocated inter-marriage with Indians as a means of speeding up efforts to "civilize" the Indians or as a means of acquiring Indian land. In 1803, for example, the same year Jefferson was refusing to comment on the Federalist accusation that he was having a sexual liaison with his "negro" slave, he wrote a letter to Creek agent Benjamin Hawkins, in which he argued that inter-marriage would solve the problem of what to do with the Indians: "In truth, the ultimate point of rest & happiness for them is to let our settlements and theirs meet and blend together, to intermix, and become one people."[28] In some instances where Indians were still in the vicinity, state governments considered rewarding those citizens who would intermarry with them. In 1797, Virginia contemplated "offering bounties to such men and women as would intermarry with the Indians."[29] In Georgia, for another example, Secretary of War William Harris Crawford recommended in 1816 that those Indians who did not choose to migrate beyond the Mississippi should inter-marry with the whites.[30] In contrast, no such suggestions were ever made by the government regarding blacks. While many of the colonies and then states in the United States legislated against fornication and marriage between whites and blacks, there was far less legislation concerning mixture between whites and Indians. By the 1820s, out of the twenty-three states in existence, only New Jersey, New York, Connecticut, New Hampshire, Vermont, and Pennsylvania did not prohibit black/white marriage. In the same period, only seven states prohibited marriage between Indians and whites: Virginia, North Carolina, South Carolina, Georgia, Massachusetts, Rhode Island, and Maine. And importantly, these latter three states, all in the Northeast, legislated against Indian/white marriage solely out of the belief that the remaining Indians had inter-married with blacks.[31] As Winthrop Jordan asserts of the period from 1550 to 1812, "the entire inter-racial complex did not pertain to Indians."[32]

The greater tolerance in the colonial and early national periods for the idea of Indian inter-marriage with whites, especially compared to the intolerance for black inter-marriage with whites, had much to do with the fact that Anglo-Americans were not compelled to view Indians as significantly different physically from themselves. Colonists such as John Smith, William Wood, Thomas Morton, and Roger Williams believed that Indians were born with "white" skin and only later became "tawny" from the sun and from the paint many of them were known to put on their bodies.[33] Later, in *Notes on the State of Virginia*, Jefferson concluded of the Indians that "we shall probably find that they are formed in mind as well in body, on the same module with the 'Homo sapiens Europæus' " (187). Indeed, the physical differences were thought slight enough that it was commonly believed any offspring of an Anglo-American coupling with an Indian would become "white" within two or three generations.[34] All that separated the Indians from the Anglo-Americans, it was widely thought, were cultural differences, and many believed those could be overcome.[35] Thus, when Englishman John Rolfe married Pocahontas in 1614, his only concern was that it might not be appropriate to marry a woman of "rude education, [with] manners barbarous."[36]

However, by the end of the eighteenth century, whites were beginning to view the Indian as less compatible with them than they had previously.[37] Some whites were beginning to counter the Linnaean view of humans, insisting instead that the Indians comprised a separate species. North Carolinian Dr. Charles Caldwell argued, for example, in his *Thoughts on the Original Unity of the Human Race* (1830) that God created not one but four original species: Caucasians (a term introduced by Johann Friedrich Blumenbach in 1795), Mongolians, Indians, and Africans. Nor, in his mind, were the different races equal. "Caucasians," he asserted, were "superior ... in native intellectual faculties," whereas the "African" and "Indian" were "inferiorly organized and endowed."[38] In short, Indians were no longer viewed as darkened by the sun, but as innately different and as biologically inferior to "Caucasians." They were thus less frequently referred to in national or tribal terms and more in racial terms such as "redskins."[39] This shift was, in part, a result of Indians rejecting efforts to move and/or civilize them. Shawnee chief Tecumseh made a lasting impression in the first decade of the nineteenth century, for example, when he organized massive Indian resistance in the Ohio River basin before going to the Northwest, where in 1812 he played a major role in driving Anglo-Americans out. The shift was also a result of the effort to define blacks as a separate species. Once race and species became commensurate, it was easier to view the Indians as equally inappropriate partners. By 1840, the theory of polygenesis, namely that there were multiple creations, different ones for each race, was fast gaining ground in the United States on a stage set by Caldwell and men such as Samuel George Morton (1799–1851), the latter of whom argued in his *Crania Americana* (1839) that measurements of the skulls in his immense collection proved that the "intellectual faculties" of the American Indians "appear to be of a decidedly inferior cast when compared with those of the Caucasian or Mongolian races."[40] "The Indian," asserts historian Alden T. Vaughan, "was no longer considered a member of the same race."[41]

Not surprisingly, this shift affected the dominant attitudes toward Indian/white marriages. William Harris Crawford's proposal in favor of such marriages, for example, dogged his presidential campaign in 1824. Also in 1824, a bill introduced in the U.S. Congress to reward whites for marrying Indians never made it out of committee.[42] And when Lydia Maria Child published a radical novel in that year in which a white woman marries an Indian, a book reviewer complained in the *North American Review* of *Hobomok* that "this is a train of events not only unnatural, but revolting, we conceive, to every feeling of delicacy in man or woman."[43] A year later, in 1825, the American Board of Commissioners for Foreign Missions was forced to repudiate its earlier encouragement that its missionaries marry Indian women in order to promote Christianity when there was an uproar over two missionary intermarriages in Connecticut.[44] And one year after that, Timothy Flint reported of the Indians that "There seems to be as natural an affinity of . . . [the French] for them, as there is repulsion between the Anglo-Americans and them."[45] After traveling throughout the United States in the early 1830s, Alexis de Tocqueville concluded similarly in *Democracy in America* (1835) that the English refused to follow the French in inter-marrying with the Indians because they despised them.[46] That there was no rash of new laws outlawing white/Indian marriages was because, by then, Indian removal east of the Mississippi had become government policy, as evidenced by the treaties forced on the Indians in the Old Southwest between 1815 and 1820 by Andrew Jackson. There was thus little perceived cause to worry that widespread white/Indian marriages would occur anyway. What was important was that "whites" fully understand and express their disgust at the *idea* of inter-marriage with "Indians."

In *The Last of the Mohicans*, published after the shift toward viewing the Indians as a distinct racial group, the concern about Indian/white mixture is not a symptom of any real concern that Indian/white mixing will take place in New York, but is rather, in part, a means of justifying, in retrospect, a violent removal that had already taken place. Readers could extrapolate that just as Magua must die for desiring Cora, so did all of the Indians in the eighteenth century, when the novel was set, also have to die. Any current and future removal in other parts of the United States was also justified. But the disappearing story line of Cora's black ancestry indicates that the voiced concern in the novel about Indian/white mixing, like the legislation against Indian/white marriages in the Northeast, was also a symptom of a more pressing concern in the 1820s, the concern about black/white mixing. The project of Cooper's novel was to naturalize white intra-racial preference with a rhetoric of blood, not so as to solely help prevent Indian/white mixing—after all, most of those people imagined as "the Indians" had already vanished from the Northeast— but *any* "crossing" with whites.

And yet, despite Cooper's obvious investment in intra-racial marriage in *The Last of the Mohicans*, he also reveals in this novel, perhaps unwittingly, his own inter-racial desires. Consider that Cooper devotes considerable narrative space to describing the beauty and erotic appeal of Cora and of Uncas. He devotes few adjectives and little energy, in contrast, to the insipid Alice and Duncan. In his introductory descriptions of them, Alice is compared simply to the light and air of the "opening day," whereas Cora's darker visage is described in detail without the use of such a conventional metaphor. Furthermore, Alice is immediately revealed to readers while Cooper teases us with Cora. Her face is initially veiled but curiosity is piqued when her figure is described as "rather fuller and more mature than that of her companion." Finally, like a stage curtain, her veil is parted, revealing the already desired face behind it. Cooper closes this initial description of Cora by again drawing the curtain on her "surpassingly beautiful" face, further associating Cora with the tantalizing exotic and further whetting the reader's interest (18–19). Indeed, Cora is so much more beautiful than Alice that Munro can only assume Heyward must prefer her. Add to this that Alice spends most of the novel in nervous prostration, whereas Cora speechifies and wonderfully stands her ground, and it is clear that Cooper finds the older sister, to whom he gives a slave ancestry, to be by far the more interesting, compelling, and desirable character. Similarly, Uncas's leadership skills and Adonis-like physique warrant much narrative attention from Cooper, whose narrator notes that

The ingenious Alice gazed at his free air and proud carriage, as she would have looked upon some precious relic of the Grecian chisel, to which life had been imparted, by the intervention of a miracle; while Heyward, though accustomed to see the perfection of form which abounds among the uncorrupted natives, openly expressed his admiration at such an unblemished specimen of the noblest proportions of man. (53)

Readers would most certainly have found themselves riveted by and attracted to both Cora and Uncas. And that Cooper couples them at the end, although in a compromised fashion, reveals the presumed satisfaction he imagined his readers deriving from it. As Donald Davie notes of this coupling, "Cooper's imagination continually plays with the possibility [of inter-marriage] and invites it in order to repress it hysterically."[47] In short, like the Federalist poetry about Jefferson and Hemings, *The Last of the Mohicans* reveals that racializing desire can have the effect of eroticizing forbidden inter-racial desires.

In the midst of such temptations and at the same time that whiteness was coming to be a category of sexual race "preference," there was a need for a rhetoric such as "blood" that could help naturalize intra-racial preference. A special term was needed to describe in shorthand what Jefferson termed the "mixture" and Cooper the "crossing" of this race blood, the use of which would disguise the role of acculturated preferences in making the category of whiteness. The word "amalgamation" was thus appropriated from the field of metallurgy where, since the early seventeenth century, it has indicated a substance composed of two or more metals mixed together when molten. A term from metallurgy was particularly appropriate insofar as race had come to be imagined as a biological trait in the blood and race blood was perceived, in the words of the 1815 author of race equations quoted earlier, as a "mathematical problem of the same class with those mixtures of different liquors or different metals." Whereas Jefferson had not used "amalgamation" in *Notes*, nor had the Federalists used it in their attacks prior to the finish of Jefferson's term as president in 1809, in an 1813 letter to Alexander von Humboldt, Jefferson used it to express his regret that war had prevented whites and Indians from becoming one people: "They would have mixed their blood with ours, and been amalgamated and identified with us within no distant period of time."[48] That Indians could have come to "identify" with whites would have only come about, Jefferson argues, through the "mixture of blood," through Indians becoming, he argues, biologically part white. Jefferson cannot imagine that a person with both white and Indian ancestry might remain politically aligned with Indians because, for him, the biology of blood and presumably of white blood in particular is a stronger force than politics or culture. One cannot be completely Indian-identified, in his mind, if one is biologically part white. In 1814, he again used the term "amalgamation" when he wrote to Edward Coles of white liaisons with blacks that "amalgamation with the other color produces a degradation to which no lover of his country, no lover of excellence in the human character can innocently consent."[49] Jefferson argues implicitly here with his use of the term "amalgamation" that reproduction between "whites" and "blacks" is a mixture of race blood. The term is his way of insisting that something biological is happening in the supposedly physical field of race. The results, a "degradation" of the "human character," are thus not debatable and are certainly not questionable even by a "lover of his country" or a "lover of excellence," both of whom would presumably be the most intelligent people on such topics. Writing before the shift on the other side of which Cooper penned *The Last of the Mohicans,* Jefferson's views on white "mixture" with nonwhites, or "amalgamation," are completely different depending on whether mixture with Indians or blacks is at stake. What is important for our purposes is that he is using the term "amalgamation" to describe both by the second decade of the nineteenth century in order to insist that something biological and thus quantifiable is happening when two people "mix" and that that biological act is of more substance than behavior. While Cooper does not use the term "amalgamation" in *The Last of the Mohicans,* his understanding of blood and genealogical race reveals the kind of thinking that gave rise to the term's appropriation from metallurgy. In 1826, Hawk-eye's use of the term "cross" betrays not only his personal preference for a white family tree but makes the same point made by the term "amalgamation," namely that inter-racial reproduction is biological because it is a mixture of blood and that it is outside of the natural order of things. Hawk-eye's location on the frontier would have precluded Cooper from putting such a scientific sounding word as "amalgamation" in his mouth. And, of course, doing so would have been ahistorical. So instead, Cooper has Hawk-eye use the definition of "amalgamation," the blood rhetoric behind the term. The result of having his character sound slightly old fashioned or naive is that *The Last of the Mohicans* strengthens the authority of "amalgamation" by making it seem an old concept.

Only when a new term was coined to refer to inter-racial sex and marriage in 1864 did the popularity of the word "amalgamation" dwindle. Until then, as we will see in the next two chapters, the debates about race relations and politics, particularly the abolitionist debates, were defined in large part by a term that meant the mixture of race blood through sex and reproduction, but the use of which would reveal that the sexual race preference naturalized by blood rhetoric was always what was at stake. While Cooper's Indian tale contributed to these developments in the rhetoric of race, it is the seemingly awkward and certainly inconsistent inclusion in it of Cora's black ancestry that best exemplifies why "blood mixture" and "amalgamation" were becoming the most prevalent means of describing the level at which inter-racial sex occurred. The boundary between "black" and "white" was the more important boundary this rhetoric was meant to mark.

3 The Barrier of Good Taste

Avoiding *A Sojourn in the City of Amalgamation* in the Wake of Abolitionism

A double-sided painting from New England circa 1825 provides, on one side, a portrait of a well-dressed man in a bust-length form and, on the flip side, two very provocative vignettes entitled *Virginian Luxuries*. One vignette depicts the same man posed to strike with a long stick the bared back of man much more dark skinned than himself and the other depicts him kissing a woman also darker than himself (Figures 2 and 3).[1] The frame molding on the flip side of the portrait lacks the hardware typical of the backside of a painting, indicating it was meant to look as finished as the front. The topography of the painting thus seems to make the point that behind the respectable facade of "white" Virginia gentlemen lurk brutal desires; "black" men are subject to the white man's stick or whip and "black" women to the white man's sexual advances. This comment on Virginia life might mean the painting was a Northern critique of slavery and perhaps even an assertion that slavery should be eradicated. But the flip side of the portrait, what we would now term the "inter-racial" side, was also meant to be a secret side, only to be looked at by the owner or shown momentarily to special guests, as evidenced by the fact that the sole hook from which to hang the painting is on the flip side. That the critique was hidden might indicate that its creator and owner meant not to anger and thus potentially alienate Southern slaveholders.[2] On the other hand, that the inter-racial kiss was only meant to be viewed surreptitiously, even by white Northerners, might indicate that viewers were assumed to be improperly titillated by it. This would explain why the black woman was not shown desperately resisting. Part of the titillation would be that she seems to desire white men. Of course, it is also possible that the painting elicited both responses, a mixture of horror and titillation of the kind present in the Federalist poems about Thomas Jefferson and Sally Hemings. In 1820s New England, however, direct pictorial speculation about such relationships was felt too risqué for polite, everyday social life. Even the Akin print accusing Jefferson of being sexual

2. Unknown artist, obverse of *Virginian Luxuries*, ca. 1825. By permission of the Abby Aldrich Rockefeller Folk Art Museum, Williamsburg, Virginia.

partners with his slave pictorially depicts both of them as birds standing far apart from one another.

This encoding of pictorial images of inter-racial sex, as in the case of Akin, and secreting, as in the case of *Virginian Luxuries*, came to an end in the Northeast in the 1830s when a new kind of abolitionist came on the scene and called for immediate emancipation. Those who opposed this message of immediatism and who feared the quickness and capability with which the

3. Unknown artist, *Virginian Luxuries*, ca. 1825. By permission of the Abby Aldrich Rockefeller Folk Art Museum, Williamsburg, Virginia.

immediate abolitionists organized themselves repeatedly and vociferously called them "amalgamationists," which is to say that they accused them of being in favor of the "physical commixture of the white and colored race."[3] One argument was that if the immediate abolitionists wanted to free the slaves and live among them rather than sending them to Africa, then they must want to marry them. The conviction that the abolitionists could be foiled in these terms was so great that newspaper articles, political pamphlets, and even a novel took their anti-abolitionist stands on the basis of the horrors of amalgamation. So powerful was this rhetoric that as many as 165 anti-abolitionist riots broke out in the North over the course of the decade.[4] As historian Leonard L. Richards notes in his study of these riots, "anti-abolitionists repeated no charge with greater pertinacity than that of amalgamation, and none could more effectively stir up the rancor and the brutality of a mob."[5] By the end of the 1830s, lithographed prints of inter-racial couples flirting, kissing, and marrying was a popular form of anti-abolitionist political commentary. The term borrowed from metallurgy twenty years before to refer to the mixing of race blood had become a political flashpoint.

William Lloyd Garrison began the immediate abolitionist movement and his Massachusetts-based anti-slavery newspaper the *Liberator* as a challenge to the American Colonization Society, a group that, since its founding in 1816, had sought gradual emancipation and that relocated freed blacks to Liberia.[6] On January 1, 1831, in the first issue of the *Liberator*, Garrison retracted his own earlier support of "*gradual* abolition" in favor of "the immediate enfranchisement of our slave population." He also commenced in these pages a crusade against Northern race prejudice, condemning New England for its "prejudice more stubborn, an apathy more frozen, than among slave owners themselves."[7] In the second issue, he argued that the Massachusetts law dating back to 1705 that banned inter-racial marriage violated blacks' constitutional rights.[8] This was the first time anyone had publicly challenged the legal prohibition against inter-racial marriage.

By Garrison's generation, Americans generally considered marriage a private affair governed by conjugal affection and therefore believed that state intervention should be minimal.[9] Colonial nuptial laws, which had required banns, licenses, parental consent, and other public acts for legal marriage, had been significantly loosened after the Revolution, reflecting the state's new emphasis on individualism and freedom.[10] Indeed, the state went so far as to recognize common-law marriages, those undertaken without licensure or solemnization and requiring only the conspicuous adoption of the marital lifestyle. James Kent, whose 1826–39 *Commentaries* made him America's version of Sir William Blackstone, originated judicial recognition of common-law marriage in the 1809 case of *Fenton v. Reed* when he was chief justice of the New York Supreme Court.[11] In his later embellishment on his ruling in the second volume of his *Commentaries*, he gave the legal viewpoint that marriage was a private affair: "No peculiar ceremonies are requisite by the common law to the valid celebration of the marriage. The consent of the parties is all that is required; and as marriage is said to be a contract *jure gentium*, that consent is all that is required by natural or public law."[12] As it did in other areas, the state honored individualism and privacy, viewing marriage as a voluntary and contractual act between two people. Historian Daniel Scott Smith has termed this shift one from the colonial "parental-run marriage system," under which marriage was principally considered a means of property transferal and consolidation and therefore subject to the jurisdiction of the family and state, to a "participant-run marriage system."[13]

Marriage continued to be viewed by the state, however, as the foundation of social order and therefore was still required of those who wished to produce lawful heirs.[14] Even after the Revolution, when new means were created for legitimating bastard children who otherwise had none to few legal means of inheritance, maintenance, or custody, matrimony offered the most socially and legally acceptable means of legitimating children.[15] In the 1790s, when Connecticut Supreme Court Reporter Jesse Root wanted to explain why "one man should be joined to one woman in a constant society of cohabiting together," he argued that their marriage "is agreeable to the order of nature, is necessary for the propagation of their offspring, and to render clear and certain the right of succession."[16] Certain state controls were thought necessary for the production of lawful heirs and thus for economic and social order across generational time. Restrictions on nuptial freedom included age and kin limitations, as well as deeming sexual and mental incapacity grounds for disallowing or annulling a marriage. In many states, however, the biggest legal exception to marital freedom was the prohibition of inter-racial marriages.

Massachusetts, Pennsylvania, and all of the southern colonies passed statutes prohibiting inter-racial marriages between 1661 and 1725, when slavery became defined as the complete deprivation of rights for life in perpetuity.[17] In all of these slave states, inter-racial marriage laws and *partus sequitur ventrem* ensured that slavery would be a race-based system by stipulating that "white" men could have only "white" heirs and that any offspring born of slave mothers and masters would have no recourse to inherited freedom or wealth. The Massachusetts law, for example, made the offspring of any inter-racial couple bastards by declaring all inter-racial marriages "absolutely null and void."[18] Inter-racial marriage laws legally defined the progeny of inter-racial couples as bastards, with the result that white property remained in white hands through the legitimacy and inheritance rights that only white/white intra-racial marriage conferred.[19]

By 1804, when slavery was abolished in all the northern states, Massachusetts and Rhode Island (which passed a law forbidding inter-racial marriage in 1798) retained their inter-racial marriage legislation. (Pennsylvania's 1725 law was repealed in 1780.) Garrison protested the ongoing legal prohibition in Massachusetts of inter-racial marriage on the premise that it made "the wearing of a black skin a punishable offense."[20] The law also discriminated against blacks, he argued, by "violat[ing] one of the principles of our Constitution . . . the right of every individual to seek happiness."[21] One might argue that white men also had their happiness curtailed by the ban on inter-racial marriage, which would indicate that the ban does not discriminate against blacks.[22] But Garrison understood that, in a white-dominated society, the curtailment of white choices was comparatively inconsequential.[23] Laws banning inter-racial marriages discriminated against blacks by adding legal weight to the idea that blacks are socially inferior to whites. They made race a legal, not just a social, category, which could only hurt those at the bottom of the race hierarchy while protecting those at the top.

In 1831, Garrison's remarks about the Massachusetts marriage law were not widely known. The circulation of the *Liberator* was small and aimed primarily at black readers. The colonizationists only took notice of Garrison in 1833, following a year of widespread abolitionist organizing and nationwide pamphleteering, the likes of which dwarfed the efforts of the popular colonizationists. Garrison's movement had grown from four local societies in two states to forty-seven societies in ten states. He also published *Thoughts on African Colonization* in 1833, in which he provided racist excerpts from the writings of colonizationists and seventy-six pages of anti-colonization resolutions from free black groups. That same year, abolitionist Lydia Maria Child was garnering much attention with her *Appeal in Favor of That Class of Americans Called Africans*, the first anti-slavery work to be published in book form in the United States. In it, Child followed Garrison in condemning Northern racism. And in the last chapter, she cited as the very first "evidence" of prejudice against blacks "an unjust law . . . in this [Massachusetts] Commonwealth, by which marriages between persons of different color is pronounced illegal." She believed "the government ought not to be invested with power to control the affections. . . . A man has at least as good a right to choose his wife, as he has to choose his religion."[24] Seemingly aware that marriage is not a right specifically covered by the Constitution, Child invokes the First Amendment, the right to freedom of religion, arguing that choosing a wife is comparable and therefore should be protected. Garrison and his followers were getting their message out, and that message included the view that the Massachusetts law banning inter-racial marriage must be overturned. Concerned about the growing presence of his movement and having familiarized themselves with Garrison's position, the colonizationists began to attack Garrison with the label of amalgamationist, accusing him of trying to repeal the law so that he could himself marry a black woman.[25] Soon, they had accused almost every leading abolitionist of seeking political equality for blacks out of inter-racial desire. The anti-abolitionists believed that painting this particular picture would be the best way of garnering support.

A little more than six months after the formation in New York City of the American Anti-Slavery Society by Arthur and Lewis Tappan, amalgamation rhetoric was used against them as well in New York City's anti-abolitionist press.[26] On the morning of the Fourth of July 1834, James Watson Webb, the editor of the New York City *Courier and Enquirer*, published a list of the activities scheduled for the holiday that included an announcement that "At eleven, the Fanatics meet at Chatham-street Chapel, to have their zeal inflamed by the doctrines of abolition and amalgamation."[27] Independence Day had traditionally been a day of organizing and fundraising for the American Colonization Society. In linking the agenda of those who instead advocated immediate abolitionism without deportation to "amalgamation," Webb felt he could light a match to an already smoldering hostility toward the abolitionists. He was right. A mob broke into the chapel just as Lewis Tappan finished reading the American Anti-Slavery Society's Declaration of Sentiments to a racially mixed audience that included a choir drawn from three churches, two of which were black. One of the worst riots of the decade followed, lasting a total of eleven days. Mobs proceeded to break up other integrated abolitionist meetings with their menacing taunts. The homes and stores owned by leading abolitionists, both black and white, were attacked, as were the churches they attended. Lewis Tappan's house, for example, was sacked by the mob. A store owned by him and his brother, Arthur Tappan, the president of the American Anti-Slavery Society, was damaged. Henry Ludlow's church and the Reverend Samuel H. Cox's home were attacked.[28] Violence also occurred in the Sixth Ward, the home of a large black population and the location of the church headed by the first black Episcopal priest, Peter Williams, also a member of the American Anti-Slavery Society. His home and the inside of his church were demolished during the riots. Finally, on Friday, July 11, the mayor issued a proclamation ordering the mobs to disband. But the rioters of that evening were nevertheless so violent that even the 27th National Guard was unable to control them. Only on July 15 was it deemed safe enough for the militia to disband. New York would not see the likes of such violence again until the draft riots of 1863.

Almost every instance of violence that month was accompanied by rumors that the person targeted promoted amalgamation. In most cases, it is unclear from written sources whether the rumors instigated the violence or were circulated afterward to justify it. But most rumors were probably spread orally before being reported in the newspapers and other sources, which would indicate that they preceded the violence. Of course, more important than the timing is that the rioters equated a person's support of abolitionism with support of inter-marriage and viewed this as cause to physically attack them. Lewis Tappan was said to support inter-marriage.[29] It was said that Henry Ludlow promoted "amalgamation" and that he had married a white to a black in his church.[30] It was also reported in the papers that Peter Williams had married an inter-racial couple at his church.[31] Samuel Cox was reported in the *Morning Courier and New-York Enquirer* to enjoy flirting with black women and to want his children to marry blacks.[32] And Arthur Tappan was rumored to want to marry his daughter "against her consent, to a negro."[33] Considering that none of these leaders of the American Anti-Slavery Society had followed Garrison and Child in supporting the repeal of the Massachusetts inter-marriage law, why were they dogged in this way by the issue of amalgamation?

If we look at the anti-abolitionists' targets and the commentary about them, it is clear that one thing that deeply troubled those who rioted was the integrated nature of the abolitionist movement. The newspapers reported of the break-in at Chatham Street Chapel, where Lewis Tappan was presiding, that it was upon finding blacks and whites "obnoxiously mixed" inside the chapel that the unwelcome guests attempted to drown out the speeches and hymns with their taunts until the abolitionists were forced to withdraw.[34] News of other integrated meetings spurred riots in the days that followed. On July 8, when it was discovered that an integrated anti-slavery meeting was being held at Clinton Hall, a mob broke up the meeting. The next day, a mob waited outside Chatham Street Chapel in anticipation of another integrated meeting there. When it was clear that there would be no such meeting, the mob proceeded to break into the building anyway.

The integration of the abolitionist movement made it a radically new social formation in the United States at a time when men and women, and blacks and whites, were meant to stay in their respective spheres. Women were not invited to attend the first meeting of the American Anti-Slavery Society. But within days, many women who had been active abolitionists insisted on attending. In the years that followed, they attended this and other gender-mixed meetings, even as they continued to form hundreds of their own anti-slavery societies. Abolitionists and their opponents alike repeatedly termed the mixed meetings "promiscuous" ones, thereby noting their sense that such meetings were perhaps improper.[35] Later in the decade, women became delegates to the national conventions and some spoke from the platform at mixed meetings, even as they suffered intense ridicule from both within and without the movement for doing so.[36]

The movement was also racially integrated at a time when blacks were restricted to certain seats in churches, courtrooms, and theaters. At the formation of the American Anti-Slavery Society, for example, three of the delegates were black. One, James McCrummell, served as a presiding officer at a session, while six blacks were named to the society's board of managers, including Peter Williams. In the largest deviation from standard social practices, white women worked alongside these black men and women in the movement. In one instance, Lucretia Mott asked McCrummell, who was familiar with parliamentary procedure, to help preside over the Philadelphia Female Anti-Slavery Society, which she had formed in response to the initial exclusion of women from the American Anti-Slavery Society. In another, when the anti-slavery women convened in Philadelphia in May 1838, they elected three black female officers.

It was argued repeatedly that these integrated meetings were a welcomed opportunity for white abolitionist leaders to flirt with blacks. It was after he had spoken out against segregated church pews and attended the July 4 meeting at Chatham Street Chapel that Reverend Cox, for example, was rumored to have flirted with black women in the pews and to want his children to marry blacks. Webb's *Morning Courier and New-York Enquirer* reported of the Chatham Street meeting that Cox "particularly distinguished himself by his attention to the ladies, both ivory and ebony—seeming to be particularly alive to their accommodation even during prayers. . . . Many a matronly wench will have cause to remember the tender attentions of the Doctor upon this excellent anniversary."[37] That Reverend Cox was supposedly violating prayer time was meant to further indicate to readers that he had no sense of appropriate behavior.

The *Morning Courier and New-York Enquirer* continued to use terms more suitable for a romance novel in describing the integrated nature of the political meeting at the chapel: "One Reverend looking individual in black clothes and white cuticle, squired a couple of lampblack virgins to their pew and gallantly seated himself between them! Lewis Tappan sat in *alto relieve* in front of some six or eight colored damsels."[38] Because he was presiding over the integrated meeting, Tappan is said here to appear to the black women there in the form of the portrait of a beloved. And the anonymous Reverend who "squires" the virgins is said to be "gallant," even as this is meant to signify his bravery in sitting between black women. The inappropriateness of these inter-racial romances is indicated by the play here on "cuticle." A clergyman would wear "black clothes and white *collar.*" But at a time when whites insisted that whites and blacks were always distinguishable by the tinge of the half moons on their fingernails, it would be this clergyman's "white cuticles" that would indicate he is white and therefore should not be interested in black women.[39]

The article in the *Morning Courier* also implied that integrated meetings would lead to the break up of the white family when it stated of the meeting at the Chatham Street Chapel that "Mr. Cuffy Blinkumskite [sat] at one end of the pew, and the amiable Mrs. Motherwort and the Misses Motherwort at the other."[40] "Cuffy" was a generic name given to slaves. Here Cuffy is said to share a pew with a married white woman whose role of mother is indicated by the presence of her daughters as well as by her name. Presumably her "amiable" nature and abolitionist tendencies become a dangerous mix when she and her daughters are placed next to a single black man. The inter-racial flirting that supposedly transpired at abolitionist meetings might, it was argued, lead to the break up of married white couples and the corruption of their daughters.

In 1839, Edward W. Clay (1799–1857) also complained about the abolitionists' integrated meetings in a series of lithographs that depict such meetings as having inter-racial sexual results.[41] Clay was a prominent caricaturist, engraver, and lithographer who was born in Philadelphia and who moved to New York City in 1837.[42] The first print in the series portrays an integrated abolitionist meeting as an orgy of inter-racial desires and, not surprisingly, focuses specifically on the efforts begun by Garrison to overturn the Massachusetts ban of inter-racial marriage. *Johnny Q, Introducing the Haytien Ambassador to the Ladies of Lynn, Mass.* (1839) (Figure 4) depicts a meeting of the Lynn (Massachusetts) Female Anti-Slavery Society, which in 1839 was petitioning the Massachusetts legislature to overturn the law banning inter-racial marriage. Clay imagines black men and white women standing shoulder to shoulder to meet a completely fictitious black ambassador from the only black republic. All of the white women lean forward eagerly to see the dark visitor. Several make admiring and even sexual comments about him and are thus perhaps leaning forward out of a desire to embrace him. One white woman is made to remark, "How I should like to kiss his balmy lips!" Clay implies that their attraction must be to the ambassador's own heightened sexuality—he remarks to the women in garbled English that they "make vater in my mouse"—even as his appearance was meant to be laughable and only appealing to the deluded few who didn't mind a man boasting in broken English of salivating. That the women have this lascivious interest in the ambassador supposedly explained their fight for the right to inter-marry and their willingness to attend a meeting with so many black men in attendance. Clay means to make the accusation with his print that white abolitionists attend integrated meetings solely as a means of finding black spouses with whom to satisfy what he imagines are their strong inter-racial desires. Clay dedicates the print to "Miss Caroline [*sic*] Augusta Chase & the 500 ladies of Lynn who wish to marry Black Husbands."[43] Clay's portrayal of John Quincy Adams here as a kind of pimp was a comment on Adams's role fighting the gag rule in Congress that in 1836 had put the lid on petitions calling an end to slavery. Apparently only a man who wants the country to address the issue of slavery would attend a racially mixed meeting and, what is more, orchestrate a meeting between a hypersexual black man and equally hypersexual white abolitionist women.

4. E. W. Clay, *Johnny Q, Introducing the Haytien Ambassador to the Ladies of Lynn, Mass.*, 1839. Courtesy, The Library Company of Philadelphia.

Clay argued again that integrated political meetings would have sexual results in the next two prints in his amalgamation series: *Practical Amalgamation (Musical Soirée)* (1839) and *An Amalgamation Waltz* (1839) (Figures 5 and 6). That the men and women in these prints are abolitionists is indicated by the word "amalgamation" in Clay's titles with which the abolitionists had become associated. Also, most of them depict a man easily identifiable as Garrison.[44] In *Soirée*, abolitionists have moved from integrated abolitionist meetings to integrated socializing. Worse, in *An Amalgamation Waltz*, the white women have taken to the dance floor in the arms of black men. White abolitionist women in particular are the concern here because they should be the keepers of the domestic hearth and not pursuing roles in the public sphere. Like Webb and the other anti-abolitionist newspaper men in New York City, Clay believed an integrated political movement would lead to romantic interracial coupling. Or, knowing this would unsettle their audiences, Clay and Webb depicted as much so as to elicit disgust with the movement. Either way, the integrated nature of the abolitionist movement became linked to the

5. E. W. Clay, *Practical Amalgamation (Musical Soirée)*, 1839. Courtesy American Antiquarian Society.

inter-racial coupling that was imagined to result. According to the anti-abolitionists, blacks and whites must stay socially segregated. That white women otherwise would have improper sexual responses to black men was perceived as more than a compelling enough reason.

In addition to weathering abuse for participating in an integrated movement and for thereby promoting inter-racial sex, the abolitionists were attacked as amalgamationists for their stated opposition to race prejudice.[45] When the American Anti-Slavery Society formed in 1833, its third article dedicated the society to the eradication of racism: "This society shall aim to elevate the character and condition of the people of color, by encouraging their intellectual, moral and religious improvement, and by removing public prejudice; that they thus may, according to their intellectual and moral worth, share an equality with the whites, of civil and religious privileges."[46] Numerous other such articles followed as abolitionist societies sprang up across the Northeast.

The anti-abolitionists borrowed the rhetoric of practice from the Puritan tradition of the Covenant of Works to argue that the abolitionists could only

6. E. W. Clay, *An Amalgamation Waltz*, 1839. Courtesy American Antiquarian Society.

really fulfill their stated goal of "removing public prejudice" by making a "practical testimony" of their own lack of prejudice.[47] It seemed to the anti-abolitionists that if marriage is the greatest sign of social equality between two people and their families, a fact that anthropologists have since long corroborated, then the abolitionists must be seeking to inter-marry as a way of showing that they had no prejudice whatsoever.[48] Clay made this point by including the word "practical" in the title of his series *Practical Amalgamation.* If the abolitionists were not merely theorizing a world without race prejudice, but were intent on enacting or practicing their theories, they could be expected, according to Clay and others, to inter-mix romantically with blacks.

During the July riots, this particular accusation came in the form of rumors that the abolitionists were seeking black spouses. Arthur Tappan, for example, was rumored to have divorced his wife and married a black woman himself.[49] One popular form of these rumors were fabricated newspaper ads for spouses.[50] Three days after the initial clash at the Chatham Street Chapel, the *New-York Commercial Advertiser,* another paper very much opposed to the "principles and practice of the misguided fanatics," attempted to egg on the mobs with its insistence that the *Liberator* had published a white abolitionist's advertisement for a "Colored woman" who would help him end race prejudice by becoming his wife.[51]

A WIFE WANTED.—We have been requested to give the following advertisement for insertion in the Liberator. The author of it is serious in his proposal, and actuated by disinterested and generous motives. He is an estimable man and we believe will make a good husband. We presume the novelty of the advertisement will insure a wide circulation.

For the Liberator.

A Friend of equal rights is convinced that our colored brethren and sisters are entitled to all the rights and privileges which are claim[ed] by the whites; that prejudice against color is extremely absurd; and that as this prejudice exists, its victims will feel that yoke of oppression crushing them to earth. He takes the liberty also to state, (being himself what is termed a white man,) should he meet with a suitable opportunity, he is convinced that it is his duty, and it is his determination, to bear testimony against this prejudice by marrying a Colored Woman.

Information would be thankfully received of any young, respectable and intelligent Colored Woman, (entirely or chiefly of African descent) who would be willing to endure the insults and reproaches that would be heaped upon her for being the partner of a white man, and who is either in low circumstances or would be willing to cede all she has or may have of this world's goods to the American Anti-Slavery Society, that the mouths of gainsayers may be stopped. Information sent by letter (post paid) to E. K., West Chester, Pa., will meet due attention.[52]

According to the anti-abolitionists, the abolitionists viewed inter-racial marriage as an important step in ending prejudice and one that they were willing to take themselves, even as doing so would subject them to ridicule. After all, in the abolitionists' mind, all blacks are their "brethren and sisters" and their own whiteness merely a social fiction—the man says he is only "what is *termed* a white man" (emphasis added). The abolitionist in this case is even willing to wed a darker-skinned woman at a time when darker-skinned women were viewed as far less attractive than lighter-skinned women. But the author of this fictive ad, which never did appear in the *Liberator*, also makes it clear that the supposed abolitionist in question is still disgusted by the prospect of a black wife, as evidenced by his desire to marry solely out of a sense of "duty." The fact that he seems to have been completely brainwashed by the American Anti-Slavery Society indicates that in his right mind, the abolitionist would desire only a white wife. In short, the reader of the ad is never meant to be persuaded that inter-racial marriage is a good and natural thing, rather just the opposite.[53] If an abolitionist wanted to "bear testimony against . . . prejudice by marrying a Colored Woman" that was meant to be reason enough to believe prejudice has its rightful place in society.

According to their opponents, if abolitionists were not already married to black spouses as a means of "practically" combating prejudice, this only proved that, in addition to having radical and dangerous ideas, they were hypocritical. During the riots, the *New York Times*, which claimed "little sympathy for the deluded fanatics" being attacked on the street, printed a similar and equally fabricated ad, in this case presumably by a black man in search of a white spouse.[54] The paper noted above it that "the immediate abolition society . . . [should] give . . . [the advertiser] an introduction to their families. If they are sincere in their principles, they will be able to find a match for him among their own sisters and daughters."[55] Another paper also wondered at the same time why

certain *Professors*, (as the young chaps call themselves,) did not provide themselves with *sable* instead of white spouses, before entering upon their [abolitionist] mission. And as their leading editor, Garrison, sanctions the scheme, it is suggested whether the leaders [of immediate abolitionism] in this city ought not in their *family arrangements*, to bear *practical testimony* against the prejudice of color.[56]

If Garrison believed in the constitutional right to marry (although the article could be referencing instead Garrison's rumored search for a black wife) and was fighting not only for immediate emancipation but also the end of race prejudice, why had none of his fellow abolitionists crossed what many whites clearly considered the last barrier of prejudice? Opposition to prejudice, if it entailed a deep personal commitment, should mean making that "practical testimony" to racial equality. The anti-abolitionist press thus argued implicitly that the abolitionists must abort their aim to abolish prejudice, which it claimed was hypocritical anyway, or face serious opposition.

Jerome B. Holgate (1812–93) was twenty-two years old when he visited New York City from his home in Utica, New York, during the summer of the riots. Six months earlier, in late December 1833 and early January 1834, various meetings had been held at local Utica churches to debate colonization versus immediate emancipation. In his *Memorial History of Utica, New York* (1892), M. M. Bagg explains of this two-week period that the churches were "crowded to . . . utmost capacity. The speeches were bitter and intense and caused much excitement in the community."[57] Holgate had already participated in an 1833 debate about abolition at the Utica Literary Club for which he argued in support of colonization. He attended the new round of debates in Utica religiously, hearing much that would have recommitted him to his position.[58] Again and again, the meetings would end with resolutions in favor of the methods of the American Colonization Society.[59] After one such meeting, a crowd burned the effigy of abolitionist Beriah Green, president of Oneida Institute, a "manual labor school," who had spoken on behalf of immediate emancipation in Utica on the first of January and who was thus rumored to have married an inter-racial couple.[60] In Utica, as in New York City, abolitionism was perceived as linked to amalgamation and as deserving of violent opposition on that count. Holgate's experiences in Utica and his position in favor of colonization indicate that once in New York City, he would have paid close attention to and been in agreement with the anti-abolitionist commentary surrounding the July riots. That he felt particularly passionate about the issues is indicated by his response in the months that followed the July riots. Holgate penned an incendiary novel against amalgamation based closely on the ideas he heard promulgated by the likes of James Watson Webb. He privately printed and published the results under a pseudonym in February 1835.

A Sojourn in the City of Amalgamation in the Year of Our Lord 19– by *Oliver Bolokitten–Esq.* follows Bolokitten to a Northern city of the future, the "City of Amalgamation," where much as in the fabricated advertisements during the July riots of 1834, whites and blacks inter-marry solely as a means of combating race prejudice. The results are depicted as monstrous. A chapter is devoted to the story of one man who is suffering from a "war which took place in his own body, between the differently coloured particles of flesh" as a result of the marriage forced on his white mother by her "rigid amalgama-tionist" father to an African man as "homely as a broken jawed baboon" who has vowed to "achieve" her "by fair means or foul."[61] If readers were not dis-gusted enough at the thought of a white woman having to marry and have sex with a man who is essentially described as an ugly primate, they could pity their offspring for the impossible conditions of his physical life. Readers are also told of a white man who

did not marry . . . [his black wife] because he loved her, that was out of the question, but because an amalgamationist wished it. You must know, therefore, that she being rather of a jealous disposition, was constantly hectoring him with the cruel innuendo, that he loved some white lady more than her, and being provoked he left her. This jeal-ousy is natural and he ought to have borne with it, and lived a miserable life for the sake of philanthropy. (144)

In both instances, the inter-racial couples were forcefully married by aboli-tionists intent on using inter-marriage to end racial prejudice. And in both instances, the resulting marriages are unhappy ones. Not surprisingly, given his evil ways and ugly visage, the African man's white wife feels "unconquer-able disgust." And the white man who inter-marries a badgering woman probably did love a white woman more. In both cases, Holgate aims to fully naturalize the white aversion to the black spouse as the basis for arguing that prejudice is not really prejudice at all but rather a means of protecting one's self from untenable and even unhealthy situations.

It is with much trepidation that the reader next encounters the white Mr. Sternfast explaining to his white daughter Julia that "We must eschew all worldly ideas of love and romance when duty opposes. And I conceive that it is the duty of every one to unite in abrogating a prejudice so heinous [as race prejudice], whether male or female." He explains that "when my former wife expired, thereby leaving me free in this important matter, I instantly espoused a negress, thereby lending my feeble influence to the popular cause. Nor can I aver I love my present partner as my former; indeed, daughter, I do not love her at all. . . [which] is of no moment whatever, when a common good is con-cerned" (138–39). Holgate makes the point again here that inter-racial mar-riages can only possibly be formed out of political necessity, because true love is never inter-racial. Sternfast loved his deceased white wife but not his current black one. He "eschew[ed]" love in order to combat prejudice. He insists that his daughter also inter-marry in order to be "benevolent," even though she loves the white Albert Ossleton. In order to force the resistant young woman to comply, Sternfast and his new wife decide to drug her, for "are we not bound to curb prejudices? What's a dose of opium, when a holy benevolence requires it?" (188). The idea that a father would drug his daughter in order to force her to marry an undesirable man against her will is shocking enough. That the father equates such behavior with "holy benevolence" makes the point that the abolitionists are absolute madmen. In Holgate's mind and in those of many of the newspaper men covering the July riots in New York City, the abolitionists are overstepping the boundaries of decency when they attempt to overthrow race prejudice because the resulting inter-racial marriages that are imagined as part of that project are disgusting. For Holgate, that Julia could only marry a black man while unconscious means that the white preference for other whites was not a form of prejudice against blacks but rather a natural inclination.

Not surprisingly, Holgate's novel staunchly supported gradual colonization. At one point, Bolokitten is taken to hear a "colonizationist," a man Bolokitten describes as having "an eye bespeaking considerable astuteness of intellect" (97). The man asks

Is it philanthropy, to excite the longing fancy of an imprisoned wretch, hopeless as to immediate liberation, with blissful scenes and unrealizable hopes? Do you not aggravate instead of alleviating his misery? Were it not far more philanthropic to console and soothe him? To instruct him to endure patiently the grievous burthen that oppresses him, until a more congenial destiny meliorate his cares? (100)

The colonizationist views himself as every bit as sympathetic and philanthropic as the abolitionists, just far more realistic. Certainly, if "immediate liberation" is supposedly and for some unexplained reason an impossibility, promising it is cruel. The point is made again in the novel when a black man tells Bolokitten of a mole he found in a field that he took home and put in a cage for a time. When he went to release it, the mole died. From this he concludes that when blacks are free, "we be worse off, for we know not wat a do, we be in a strange lan' like de lettle mole me speak of" (114). "Wen we be slave we be appy, for we hab ebery ting dat we want" (111). Yes, American blacks would like to move to Africa, he asserts, but only if they will be taken care of. And when a white listener disagrees, the blacks tar and feather him. But certainly Holgate's biggest reason for supporting the colonizationists with his novel is that only they would remove from American soil the black bodies that the abolitionists supposedly would have him and other whites marry even in what he argues is the inevitable absence of any love whatsoever. His novel is thus devoted to portraying the unhappy and degrading inter-racial marriages that would result should the colonizationists not be allowed to carry out their plans.

The anti-abolitionists indicated that one of the reasons whites naturally prefer their own is because blacks are unattractive and the act of inter-mixing thus aesthetically repugnant. A *New York Times* article reported sarcastically of the July Fourth meeting at Chatham Street Chapel that "The pews presented a beautiful specimen of Mosaic work, composed of all colors and shades, from the hue of the lily to that of coal. Clear, red and white were placed in unctious [*sic*] communion with dingy black, and the rose of the West, and the coal-black rose of Congo, bloomed side by side."[62] That such a mosaic of blacks and whites, men and women is not at all "beautiful" is indicated by the descriptions of black as a "dingy" color and of the black communion with whites as "unctuous" or greasy. The term "Mosaic" invokes not just this mixture of colors but, because it is capitalized, the Biblical or Mosaic account of man's origins. The message here is that given the great color differences between the races and the ugly results when they are in proximity of one another, the different races cannot possibly have descended from the same couple, Adam and Eve, and therefore are separate species who should not try to intermix.

Clay's prints likewise present the act of inter-mixing as ugly by using two different and usually wholly incompatible means of representation in each print. On the one hand, he uses fine-line drawing to create many of the figures. These figures seem to have stepped out of either a Currier and Ives print or the lithograph Clay seems to be parodying in his *Amalgamation Waltz, The Dance* by E. B. and E. C. Kellogg (circa 1840), in which attractive and genteel couples move gracefully across the dance floor and thus express their whiteness as a kind of good taste. On the other hand, Clay provides rude caricatures of many of the figures. The faces of these figures are an unrealistically uniform pitch black, their lips are distended, and their hair is preposterous. These ugly figures belong on the covers of minstrel show sheet music and are thus read as black.[63] In short, for Clay the two different races belong to two different art forms. Anything else is a violation of aesthetics. And it is precisely through the mixing of these two different art forms that Clay strengthens the idea of racial difference itself.

Like Clay, Holgate imagines the abolitionists attending racially mixed balls and thus again makes the point that the integrated nature of their move-ment would have inter-racial romantic results. Of course, because the novel is written from Bolokitten's initially sympathetic point of view, his description of the ball is ostensibly a celebration of its many aesthetic charms. But Holgate is careful to show that the "blacks" in attendance are an unattractive lot and therefore only of interest to the "whites" because those "whites" aim to abol-ish prejudice. Bolokitten reports that there was

glittering company, black folks and white folks,—damsels, gentry! Here a tall black maiden, with red dress, her eyes sparkling like coals of fire, gallanted by a Mr. ———— living in Broadway, No. ***; there a white belle, charmingly lovely, paraded with a stal-wort negro, now living, called ***** *****, his nose crocked like a hawk's beak, but the benevolent self-denying damsels said, 'poor fellow, we will not reject him on that account,' and received him with the greatest pleasure. In fine, there was not a bandy leg, or mar face in that whole assembly unhonoured with the brightest glances; like worn out, old grey-haired veterans, honours, caresses, were poured upon them wher-ever they went. . . . The most uncouth had the best prospect of an heiress, while the handsome wight contemned and repudiated, (at least apparently) wandered unblessed by a lady's smile, and all because *prejudices must be abrogated.* (170)

The most attractive white men go companionless because the women are so intent on embracing the very ugliest race as a show of their benevolence. Left to their own devices, Holgate implies, whites would not be attracted to crocked noses, bandy legs, and marred faces and would instead pursue other whites because of their "charmingly lovely" appearance. In short, the anti-abolitionists, like Jefferson, looked to the realm of aesthetics to make their arguments against inter-racial mixing.

In addition to the visual pain for whites of partaking of or even witness-ing inter-mixing, there was the disgust generated by the supposed stench. There had been what Alain Corbin terms an "olfactory revolution" in the mid-eighteenth century. Prior to this revolution, smells whites later viewed as unacceptable were not only tolerated and even ignored but, in some cases, such as that of the smell of human and animal excrement, deemed salubri-ous.[64] During the reign of Charles II (1660–85), for example, London authori-ties ordered that all cesspools be opened so that the odor could ward off the plague. After the mid-eighteenth century, however, the bourgeoisie no longer had a high tolerance for stench. The place for defecation was separated from the rest of human life so that the smell would not invade the rest of the house. Catherine Beecher would advise in 1841 that "The privy . . . should have . . . [a]

window. . . . Keeping the window open, and the door shut, will prevent any disagreeable effects in the house."[65] As the middle and upper classes came to imagine themselves as clean and clean-smelling people, those who could not or were not imagined to comply with such standards were deemed repulsive. Most importantly for our purposes, those deemed repulsive for a myriad of other reasons were imagined to stink. As Corbin notes, the stigmatization of odors, even imagined odors, was a means of distinguishing one's bourgeois self from others and a means of justifying one's treatment of those others.[66] When Jefferson commented in his *Notes on the State of Virginia* that blacks have a "very strong and disagreeable odour," this served as part of his rationale for why blacks must not be allowed to mix with whites. That blacks were still used as personal servants makes the point that smell was an excuse used for only those effects that were convenient.

The smell argument was used in the 1830s to make the point that if abolitionists actually sought to socialize and perhaps, as was rumored, even couple with such bad-smelling people, this was another sign of their perversity. In Clay's *Johnny Q*, for example, one of the white women is made to remark of the black ambassador, "What a delightful perfume he has brought into the room with him." Because blacks supposedly smell bad, whites should not want to be anywhere near them. That the women of Lynn like this smell is, in large part, what makes them and their effort to overturn the Massachusetts ban of inter-racial marriage subjects of ridicule.

A later, circa 1845, lithograph by T. W. Strong slanders abolitionist women in the same way.[67] Entitled *Professor Pompey Magnetizing an Abolition Lady*, it depicts a white woman choosing, ostensibly as a part of her abolitionist agenda, to be physically intimate with a black mesmerist who she notes smells like a skunk (Figure 7).[68] The woman's decision to undergo mesmerism was itself a sign of her loose sexual morals. Many contemporaries felt that mesmerism, described in 1849 as an "induced somnolent state, [by which] the cerebral actions of the operator and the subject or subjects are one," violated the sanctity of women.[69] Nathaniel Hawthorne was one who believed this of mesmerism, worrying to his wife of her mesmeric treatment for headaches that "the sacredness of the individual is violated by it," especially when the "intruder" is "not . . . thy husband."[70] Strong seems to concur. In his print, the white woman is the subject of both the mesmerist's and another black man's desire. The mesmerist straddles her lap and has his hand on her breast, while another black man warns him, "Take care dar'fessor Pompey! I hab some notion arter dat young white Lady, myself." That the professor is using his mesmeric powers only to draw the white woman further into his sexual con-

7. T. W. Strong, *Professor Pompey Magnetizing an Abolition Lady*, ca. 1845. Courtesy American Antiquarian Society.

trol is indicated by her reply when he asks how she feels: "Oh, I seem to be carried away into a dark wood where I inhale a perfume much like that of a skunk." That this sexual dream space as well as her provocative position on the Professor Pompey's lap is repugnant and therefore naturally undesirable for whites is indicated by the foul smell.

Even children were schooled in the connection between how black's reputedly smelled and the inappropriateness of the abolitionists in supposedly promoting inter-racial coupling. In another one of T. W. Strong's works, *Boy's Own Book of Fun* (circa 1852–66) (Figure 8), one of the book's two hundred engravings depicts a corpulent mammy figure wrapped in the arms of a gaunt white man whose name in the text below reveals that Strong might have meant him to be abolitionist newspaper editor Horace Greeley: "'Every one to his liking, as Mr. Horace Squash said when he kissed a lady of color.' But I

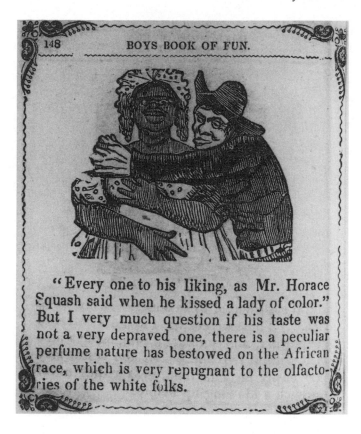

8. T. W. Strong, from *Boy's Own Book of Fun*, ca. 1852–66, 148. Courtesy American Antiquarian Society.

very much question if his taste was not a very depraved one, [for] there is a peculiar perfume nature has bestowed on the African race, which is very repugnant to the olfactories of the white folks."[71] Here again a white abolitionist's true motives are revealed to be inter-racial desire. And those whites with inter-racial desires are deemed "depraved" insofar as they can tolerate and might even prefer bad smells.

The articles on the Chatham Street Chapel meeting mention smell repeatedly. The *New York Times* noted that "There was a full and fragrant congregation, rendered double fragrant by the melting heat of the day. . . . There was no wasting of fragrance on the desert air, for the delicate aroma was inhaled by hundreds."72 Having remarked that the racially integrated meeting was the site of intense inter-racial flirting, the *Times* elicits the reader's further disgust by noting that the white abolitionists were romantically interested in foul-smelling people. The asides and puns on the bad smell of the blacks at this meeting were also many. The *Morning Courier and New-York Inquirer* reported that a hymn "was chaunted with great fervour as well as fragrancy by Mesdames of the ladies of colours."73 Yet another newspaper said, "we can compare the salt and pepper appearance of assemblage to nothing but a flock of—we won't say what—for . . . 'comparisons are *oderous*.' "74 In these cases, the authors demonstrate their superiority to the abolitionists by showing both their wit and their disdain for blacks because of their imagined smell.

The *New York Times* also focused on smell in its remarks about a supposed advertisement by a black man in search of a white wife:

When one gets to the windward of him, he is one of the sweetest fellows in the land — especially in cool weather. . . . In emulation of the white gentleman who sighs for the fragrant love of an oleaginous negress, he promises that after having possessed himself of her personal property, to support himself and family in genteel style. . . . It is not stated in the advertisement whether applications are to be made before cool weather comes.75

What shocks this newspaper and what will presumably shock its readers is that there are white abolitionist woman out there who would be willing to marry a man who clearly smells vile, just as there are supposedly "white gentlemen who sigh . . . for the fragrant love of an oleaginous negress." Readers learn that inter-racial desires mark whites as outcasts by indicating their preference for foul odors.

Holgate makes smell his principle theme in *A Sojourn in the City of Amalgamation*. When Bolokitten and the inter-racial couples he is following arrive at the City of Amalgamation, they proceed to an integrated church meeting of the type reported in the New York City papers during the July 1834 riots. Each of the couples Bolokitten follows is composed of a white man and a black woman. And each white man must have a machine next to him in the church that makes the smell of his black female partner tolerable for him. Each machine is

composed of fans and little vials, ingeniously intermingled. It whizzed round seemingly by a perpetual motion power, and with amazing swiftness: its object being to protect the husband from those disagreeable evaporations exhaling from the odiferous spouse, which it did by fanning off the offensive air, and at the same time dispensing, by means of the vials, a delightsome perfume. (17)

The second part of Holgate's title, *in the Year of Our Lord 19–*, makes clear that his novel is a futuristic one, taking place in the century following his own. If whites and blacks are to couple in that future, they will supposedly need all of the future's scientific ingenuity to do so. For when mixed couples are not next to a machine or the machines break down, the white partner experiences violent vomiting (20–21, 36, 54–55). One man in the vicinity of some black women is said to have "clapp[ed] a kerchief to his mouth, staggered to a casement near by, the door of which being a-jar; he seized from thence a crooked-necked bottle [of perfume], which he was in the act of conveying to his nose, when the stomachal tide gushed forth, bespattering all around him" (32). This kind of reaction is meant to indicate that inter-racial coupling is not just in bad taste, but because of how blacks smell and because whites are sensitive, is an unnatural act. And yet even though forcing such relationships brings upon whites grave physical illness, the abolitionists in the novel try again and again to inter-mix. The man whose "stomachal tide gushed forth" immediately apologies: "I feel ashamed of it; but these are diabolical weaknesses. I must overcome them" (32).

Bolokitten further narrates that if the two inter-racial couples he is following are to do more than just sit together in church, if they are to "amalgamate," they will need more than these machines. The black women are taken to a special site for "boiling" and "perfuming" where they are "bound upon a queer contrivance resembling a rack, in the middle of the floor, while . . . mettlesome elves hovering round, whipped them with their silver whips" (31). The overseer of this process, who has to often stop and vomit before the process is completed, explains that whipping "fractures the flesh just enough" so that the perfume can penetrate the women's bodies. The women are then placed in a thing that "resembled a coop, constructed about young trees; it was of sheet iron, circular, and perforated with small holes" (35–36). This is lowered into a vat of perfume suspended over a large fire. In this scene, the abolitionists end up treating black women the same way slave owners do. In both cases, as *Virginian Luxuries* reminds us, the women end up getting whipped as part and parcel of the same inappropriate desire to rule them sexually and otherwise. The abolitionists end up proving, according to Holgate, that they are just as sadistic and that blacks and whites are not meant to be together. To force togetherness is only to torture both parties. After all, the overseer has to stop and vomit; his body is telling him that his proximity to black women is unnatural.

For the white men in Holgate's novel, the process of preparing to amalgamate is entirely different. Because they are the ones who will have to endure any remaining odors, perfume bottles are affixed to their nose hairs. Indeed, nose hairs are said to exist because "Nature evidently intended that men should be bottled . . . and . . . intermingle, intermarry, amalgamate!" (42). Of course, no reader would find such logic remotely plausible. Holgate intends his readers to see the abolitionists as fools and as cruel ones at that.

Bolokitten soon finds, however, that perfuming and nose bottling are still not sufficiently potent to offset the smells that whites find so noxious. The abolitionists must further inure themselves to bad smells. Bolokitten reports of the City of Amalgamation:

Know then, O reader, that . . . hundreds in this sublime metropolis had ordure about their dwellings, for the purpose of whipping their olfactory nerves into the astonishing belief that manure is ambrosial, and not foul and disgustful, as their diabolical prejudices led them to imagine. . . . [They] do nocturnally slumber with a platter of this excrement smoking before their noses, in order so their olfactory nerves [will] not believ[e] . . . that manure is offensive, which, according to these obstreperous wights' creed, is a *hell-bent prejudice*, which no consideration whatever, not even that of a stomachal splitting and disgorging of vile and foul secretions should prevent from overcoming. (141–42)

It seems the abolitionists are so eager to overcome what Holgate insists are natural preferences that they are willing to constantly smell animal excrement served up on a plate. Their efforts must thus be termed both perverse and monstrous. In short, Holgate has the abolitionists reverse what had become standard bourgeois practice. Rather than avoiding the stench of bodily waste, the abolitionists seek it out, apparently under the impression that blacks smell like shit. The novel reiterates this point when the man whose own body is at war with itself is described as "white" from the waist up and "black" from the waist down, the latter a part of the body described repeatedly as "extremely odorous" because of "the depot of all the immense overflowings and drainings of the adjacent wilds" (87). Smell is a potent argument here because it is both a kind of aesthetic sensibility but also a physical sense. According to Holgate's logic, if whites cannot help but vomit in the presence of excrement,

then they really can't be expected to inter-marry with blacks. Holgate is arguing that more than good taste is at stake here. The very health of the human
body is said to be in jeopardy when a white inter-marries. Constant vomiting
would not exactly be the most salubrious terms upon which to live. And, of
course, that even the abolitionists equate the smell of blacks with the smell of
shit means that blacks are a very degraded lot indeed.

After his "sojourn," Bolokitten thus declares of the slavery question that
"The point to be settled . . . is not what concerns the abusing or maltreating of
a fellow creature, but what disinclines one to the companionship or presence
of a particular individual" (60). Presumably, everyone could easily agree that
the abuse and maltreatment of blacks must stop. The novel is not a proslavery
one. Rather, it wrestles with the question of what should be done in addition
to emancipation, in addition to halting the abuse. Bolokitten makes an analogy to convey his answer that summons forth the smell issue once again and
this time in the same way the print about mesmerism does: "Am I compelled
for the sake of a mere dogma to endure the ambrosial evaporations of a hol-
low tree ensconced skunk?" (60–61). For Holgate, a person should be free to
avoid "unpleasant sensations" such as bad smells and unattractive appear-
ances. In short, slavery must someday end but the kind of social equality evident at integrated meetings and that would lead to inter-marriage must not
follow. Holgate and his anti-abolitionist peers made the point that, as indicated by the unattractive nature of mixing and the intolerable smell of blacks, the
dismantling of race prejudice must only go so far. According to them, if the
abolitionists must usher in a new world, it must be one where marriage
remains strictly intra-racial for reasons that no properly educated white could
contest—namely aesthetics and smell, the latter of which is termed a defense
against physical illness, but both of which came under the auspices of good
taste.

Taste was an operative word in the press during the New York City riots
whenever the issue of amalgamation was addressed. Good taste was the barrier thought to normally prevent inter-mixing and thus that which the abolitionists were perceived as breaking down. The following are excerpts from
two different articles that spoke to taste in the *New-York Commercial Advertiser.*

We have long been of the opinion, and frequently expressed it, that the Abolitionists
are *the worst enemies* the blacks of this city have. They are holding out to them the
promise of amalgamation, feeding their pride with impracticable hopes, exclaiming

and denouncing the prejudice against color . . . inviting them to sit with the whites indiscriminately . . . in public assemblies and social parties, and thus attempting to break down the barrier which nature had set up between the races, and of which the guardian sentinel is TASTE.[76]

On a different day, the same paper noted that

For wise and good purposes the Creator of all the earth gave distinctive features and properties to those whom he appointed to inhabit its diverse territories. He also, at the same time, endowed his creatures with the faculty of TASTE, accompanying it with entire *freedom of choice*, thereby forming a perpetual and insurmountable barrier to the execrable amalgamation.[77]

The word "taste" is printed in all capitals in both articles to indicate its central role in keeping whites from desiring "execrable amalgamation" and perhaps, insofar as whites were meant to care deeply about taste, to draw the reader's eye to these articles. The first article deems taste the "guardian sentinel" of a "barrier which nature had set up" and the latter article naturalizes this "sentinel" by making it God-given. People are said to have "entire *freedom of choice*" in picking their mates. It is simply that their God-given and natural taste leads them to only pick others of their same race, presumably because blacks have "distinctive features and properties" that whites find unappealing insofar as they are different than their own. According to the anti-abolitionists' logic, then, it is not that whites are racist but rather that they are destined to simply prefer their own. Rarely, then, do the anti-abolitionists present the case that mixed-race offspring are what is to be feared of the abolitionists' efforts. Holgate's chapter devoted to the "war" raging in one such offspring's body is his only in-depth look at the physical results of inter-racial sex. For him and for his fellow anti-abolitionists in New York, "amalgamation" did not mean simply the inter-mingling of race blood. Rather, "amalgamation" had come to signify the loss of the good taste that was defined by the likes of Jefferson as preference for a certain set of physical traits associated with whiteness.

The ending of *A Sojourn in the City of Amalgamation* comes to rest squarely on this issue of good taste. Julia Sternfast seems to be wed to the black Wyming against her will, as her father had planned. But then, after the wedding ceremony, Wyming takes her into a small apartment where he proceeds to wash his face. Julia "suddenly beheld that dark face . . . most wonderfully changed; instead of the black brows and facetious look of the unaccountable Wyming, there shone through the pearly element upon her, the intelligent features, lit with a sweet smile, and sparkling eyes of Albert Ossleton!" (190). Albert's white skin is more desirable than Wyming's because Julia associates the former with intelligence, sweetness, vitality, and, as Cooper does in *The Last of the Mohicans*, cleanliness. Again, intra-racial attraction is said to be located in what are deemed understandable preferences for certain physical traits and distinctly not in prejudice. Because these preferences are for cleanliness and intelligence, they are deemed not at all prejudicial but a sign of good taste. In the arguments in the 1830s about abolitionism, white participants and onlookers convinced themselves that good taste was not a form of prejudice, even as their arguments prove that what the anti-abolitionists deemed "taste" was simply prejudice by another name insofar as it meant viewing blacks as ugly and thus unworthy. As Pierre Bourdieu notes in *Distinction: A Social Critique of the Judgement of Taste*, "Whereas the ideology of charisma regards taste in legitimate culture as a gift of nature, scientific observation shows that cultural needs are the product of upbringing and education."[78] The anti-abolitionists wanted to believe that taste was God-given but it was clearly a formation that resulted out of a perceived cultural need—the cultural need to maintain a race hierarchy.

Holgate seems to have circulated his novel among the members of the Utica Literary Club. At least seventeen out of the fifty-six young male members of the club had fathers who seem to have become so concerned about the so-called amalgamationists that when the abolitionists attempted to convene a meeting in Utica eight months after Holgate had his novel printed, they rioted.[79] A state anti-slavery convention had been planned and in the weeks and days prior to the scheduled meeting in Utica on October 21, numerous official and other meetings were convened to discuss whether the abolitionists should be allowed to meet in the Utica court room. After the anti-abolitionists held a large public meeting during which they denounced the rights of the abolitionists to convene, the city's Common Council denied the court room to the anti-slavery convention. Finally, on the appointed day, at the Second Presbyterian meetinghouse, the abolitionists were able to convene and form the New York State Antislavery Society before twenty-five men appointed by the anti-abolitionists broke up the meeting with "loud threats of violence."[80] That night, the offices of a newspaper that had supported the rights of the abolitionists to meet, the *Oneida Standard and Democrat*, was also attacked. The abolitionists suffered more threats and violence on their way to Peterboro, where they finally reconvened. It seems that like Webb Holgate succeeded in helping to rouse the ire of his townsmen.

In truth, despite their willingness to fight for the abolishment of slavery and the end of race prejudice, most of the abolitionists were not in favor of inter-marriage and certainly none of them is on record for ever inter-marrying in the antebellum period themselves.[81] They, too, believed that good taste should and always would attract white to white. Even Garrison never actually advocated inter-racial marriage for whites and, furthermore, seemed to be discouraging it on the grounds of good taste.[82] When one of Garrison's Southern opponents asked him to think through all of the implications of the Massachusetts law's reversal, his response, as reported in the *Liberator*, indicates that he was not entirely willing to dismantle the institution of intra-racial marriage even as so many racist structures were based on it. The question posed of Garrison is one that would crop up again and again in debates in the United States about racial equality: "How should you like to have a black man marry your daughter?"[83] It was a question rarely asked about sons. The gender bias in the question was undoubtedly the result of the deeply ingrained assumptions that white daughters need paternal protection and that black men are hypersexual, thus making the paternal protection of white daughters all the more necessary.[84] In other words, it is assumed by the questioner that the black son-in-law's supposed hypersexuality would ruin the white man's daughter and thereby demoralize her and her extended family. Clay and Holgate both took this tack of stressing the horror of white women in particular being with black men. Garrison and any white person of whom the question is posed is being asked if he could bear not only his daughter's ruin but also, insofar as marriage was the means of passing on familial wealth, to share his social and economic wealth with this black son-in-law and black grandchildren. In 1831, Garrison answered the question by showing the Southern man's supposed hypocrisy in asking such a question, but in doing so also refuses to answer it himself: "I am not married—I have no daughter. Sir, I am not familiar with *your* practices; but allow me to say, that slaveholders generally should be the last persons to affect fastidiousness on that point; for they seem to be enamored of *amalgamation*."[85] Of course, most of the mixing in the South to which Garrison refers is that which transpired between white male slave owners and their female slaves. We can assume the southern slave owner was also interested in protecting his white daughter, a point Garrison ignores even as he shares that interest as indicated by his implied answer to the question about his own hypothetical white daughter: no, he would not let her intermarry.

Garrison also chose to print in the *Liberator* a letter to the editor in which the correspondent argued, like Garrison, that the law must be overturned, but felt compelled to add, "I would not recommend the whites to marry blacks, or the blacks to marry whites; and still less should I recommend persons who are well-informed, polished and virtuous, to marry those who are rude, ignorant and degraded, whatever may be their complexion."[86] Of course the implication here is that whites are "polished and virtuous" and blacks are "rude, ignorant and degraded." As argued by the anti-abolitionists as well, the barrier that should not be crossed is the barrier of good taste. One should be, as Garrison put it, "fastidious."

Lobbyists of the Massachusetts legislature seeking to overturn the ban were also careful because of the taste issue not to endorse inter-racial marriage per se. In 1832, lobbyist John P. Bigelow referred to such marriages as "the gratification of a depraved taste."[87] Perhaps as a response to the likes of Clay's *Johnny Q* lithograph, Aroline Chase's supporters in the legislature also went to great lengths in 1839 to make clear that neither they nor the women petitioners condoned inter-racial marriages. The legislator who presented their petition to the House of Representatives declared that "Practically, by personal examination, and by the employment of all appropriate means, none in my judgment, would go further to discourage all intermixture of the Caucasian and African races, than the signers of these petitions. I believe them to be entirely opposed to such intermixture."[88]

The immediate abolitionists were forced to declare more vociferously that they were not amalgamationists once they became the targets of mob violence. In New York City, after 11 days of rioting in July 1834, the Executive Committee of the American Anti-Slavery Society wrote and submitted to the mayor a "Disclaimer," the first point of which was that "We entirely disclaim any desire to promote or encourage intermarriages between white and colored persons."[89] The disclaimer was published in the papers on July 14. Thus even as the mayor issued a second proclamation at the same time that called out the militia, its services were no longer needed. As the *New York Times* noted of the abolitionists under its printing of the disclaimer, "They have denied the principal charges alleged against them, and that denial will and must save them from further violence."[90]

Well after their disclaimer put a stop to the July riots, the abolitionists continued to assert their disinterest in inter-racial coupling and marriage. On August 5, 1834, for example, one of several refutations was printed, four of the eight items of which addressed amalgamation:

"IT IS NOT TRUE"

That any advertisement of a colored man for a white wife, or of a white man for a colored wife, has ever appeared in the N. Y. Evangelist, or in the Emancipator. . . .

Or—that a leading officer of society escorted one or two colored women into his pew—

Or—that *any* recent marriages are known to have taken place in this region between white and colored persons—

Or—that the scattered cases of such marriages or associations that do or may exist, in certain classes of society here or elsewhere—(we have never known any, except, some years ago, at the south,) have any manner of connexion [sic] to the anti-slavery movements. [91]

In refuting the charges absolutely and vehemently, the abolitionists aimed to dissuade more mob action and, presumably, to defend their own taste by concurring with their opponents that there must be limits to the dismantling of racial prejudice. Their refutations were undoubtedly also meant to reassure apprehensive abolitionist readers and thereby help build the abolitionist cause.

The abolitionists perceived no contradiction between their insistence on the naturalness of intra-racial marriage and their embrace of the doctrine of Christian love. This is evidenced in an article in the *Emancipator* in which they explain why they can leave the issue of inter-marriage off the table:

Neither the abolitionists nor the colored people have ever asked or desired any such thing [as inter-marriage]. Our plans and principles do not require us to do so. All we ask is that all men should love our neighbors as themselves, according to God's reasonable and just law, allow each other the enjoyment of our equal rights, and assist in promoting each other's moral elevation and happiness, here and hereafter. Does this make it necessary that white and colored people should intermarry? No. Abolitionists, at least, do not think so, and have never said so.[92]

Bolokitten argues similarly in the anti-abolitionist *Sojourn* that the Christian law to love one's neighbor does not mean one should inter-marry. He explains:

I do not believe that I am compelled, because bound to love my neighbor as myself, to give him by favourite horse when he has been so unfortunate as to lose his; and yet, if I loved him as myself, I would do so, for I would feel his afflictions as poignantly as my own, and be as desirous to meliorate them. . . . But is not my neighbor trammeled by the same ordinance? . . . He must restore me the animal, for he loves me as much as I him. There must then of course ensue, on every such occasion, reciprocal acts of benevolence, and what's this but abrogating the very purpose of the law? (65–66)

For Holgate's Bolokitten, Christian law fails the test of logic and thus is not meant to be followed to the letter. Scripture also tells us, he asserts, that one must not "injure a fellow creature." But does that mean one must "abuse one's self by those unpleasant sensations which that particular individual's presence creates within me?" (60). For the anti-abolitionists, as for the abolitionists, whites can follow the major Christian precepts without having to marry their neighbors if they are black. "[W]e all prefer some people over others," Bolokitten insists, "which means that God intended to create a 'diversified' world" (60). Holgate and other anti-abolitionists have made it impossible to discern any contradiction between loving one's neighbor as one's self and refusing to ever consider that neighbor a possible spouse. In other words, they successfully drove a rhetorical wedge between "preference" and what is distinctly prejudicial: disdaining one's black "neighbor" as a possible marriage partner. "Preference" is declared God's intention and one that, ironically, Holgate thinks he can claim brings a "diversified" society. Phrased this way, the white sexual race "preference" for other whites is no longer recognizable as disdain for blacks but is rather a form of good taste and even healthy precepts, the latter idea of which naturalizes taste.

Having thus positively stated their position against inter-marriage over and over, the New York abolitionists finally seemed to have made their agreement with the anti-abolitionists heard. In 1838, following repeated "disclaimers" by the abolitionists, the rioting fell off, although as Clay's prints prove, the name calling persisted for a time.[93] The abolitionists were at least able to recommence the effort to overturn the Massachusetts law, which had stalled in 1832 undoubtedly because the anti-amalgamation mob violence made attempts dangerous.[94] In February 1839, Aroline Chase was able to lead the Lynn Female Anti-Slavery Society in presenting signatures they had gathered to the Massachusetts State Legislature in support of repealing "all laws making distinction between people of color and white citizens."[95] The law was overturned in 1843. Ironically, only once the barrier of prejudice as good taste was agreed upon were the abolitionists able to dismantle the legal forms of prejudice, leaving an arguably more slippery form of prejudice intact. That the law banning inter-racial marriage in Massachusetts could be repealed was because the ideology of taste had been strengthened by anti-amalgamation rhetoric from the abolitionists and anti-abolitionists alike. Good taste, a euphemism for the prejudice of schooled sexual race preferences, ensured that no laws were deemed necessary in Massachusetts to keep whites and blacks apart. Furthermore, in 1840, the Tappans' branch of the American Anti-Slavery Society moved out of churches and into the political party system. As historian Lorman Ratner points out, whereas in the 1830s John Quincy Adams was alone in his support of free speech for abolitionists, by the 1850s Congressman Charles Sumner, Theodore Parker, and others took anti-slavery political positions. Formerly mobbed in the 1830s, Garrison found a large and sympathetic audience in the 1850s. And Harriet Beecher Stowe's *Uncle Tom's Cabin* (1852) attracted a large Northern audience, while novels that romanticized plantation life began to disappear. In short, the anti-slavery position was no longer a monstrous one. Rather than the abolitionists, the slaveholders and "slave power" had become the enemy.[96]

4 Combating Abolitionism with the Species Argument

Race and Economic Anxieties in Poe's Philadelphia

Philadelphia was the site of another one of the largest anti-abolitionist riots. In May 1838, a mob burned to the ground the abolitionists' newly built Pennsylvania Hall for Free Discussion, attempted to burn the Friends Shelter for Colored Orphans, and attacked a black church. The hall was built earlier that year by a joint stock company formed by the abolitionists when they had trouble hiring halls for their meetings. In addition to providing rooms for various "benevolent or moral societies" to meet, the hall was intended to serve as a headquarters for publishing abolitionist newspapers and tracts.[1] In spring 1838, this largest and most expensive building in the city was ready to house the abolitionists so they could further their cause in Philadelphia and beyond.[2] A three-day dedicatory celebration was planned and the program for it published in the Philadelphia papers on the day it began, May 14, 1838. Several national abolitionist leaders were on the program as featured speakers. Abolitionist David Paul Brown, a black Philadelphia lawyer, was chosen to give the dedicatory oration. William Lloyd Garrison, Alvan Stewart, and other prominent abolitionists gave speeches on the second day of dedicatory activity. Black and white abolitionists alike comprised the audience during the dedication and worked together at other racially integrated abolitionist meetings held at the hall in those first days of its existence. At the second Anti-Slavery Convention of American Women, for example, two black women were elected officers: Susan Paul as one of ten vice presidents and Sarah M. Douglass as treasurer. Grace Douglass, Sarah's mother, and Harriet Purvis, another black woman, also attended. There was no separate black gallery in the hall as there would have been at the time in theaters and churches for, as one abolitionist reported later, "we should have been false to our principles if we had refused to admit men of every sect, rank, and color, on terms of equality."[3]

The racial integration of such a lavish building elicited much comment from anti-abolitionists who, as they had in New York, viewed integration, in the words of the *Pennsylvanian*, as "a first step toward the amalgamation of the races."[4] One paper dubbed Pennsylvania Hall a "Temple of Amalgamation," another "a stately edifice, sacred to the cause of amalgamation."[5] A lithograph of the hall, entitled *Abolition Hall. The Evening Before the Conflagration at the Time More Than 50,000 Persons Were Glorifying in Its Destruction at Philadelphia May—1838. Drawn by Zip Coon*, brought these descriptions to life (Figure 9). The extremely large and, in the print, looming hall is portrayed as a place of unbridled and presumably extramarital passions between black men and white women, the latter of whose extreme degradation is evidenced both by these alliances and by their willingness to act in a

9. Unknown artist, *Abolition Hall. The Evening Before the Conflagration at the Time More Than 50,000 Persons Were Glorifying in Its Destruction at Philadelphia May—1838. Drawn by Zip Coon*. From a salt print photograph of an unrecorded lithograph, ca. 1850. Courtesy The Library Company of Philadelphia.

lascivious manner on the street. That abolitionists were to blame is indicated by a sign in the print's foreground: "Abolition by Brown David Paul [*sic*]." The reversal of Brown's name may have been a means of avoiding the charge of slander, but certainly also drove home that abolitionism was under the control of a black, or rather "Brown," man. According to its title, a black man was also the print's creator. Zip Coon was a minstrel name for a stock Northern dandy, the type who would have created such a print to memorialize his presumed enjoyment of the inter-racial scene. One shouldn't have been surprised that "50,000 persons were glorifying" in the hall's destruction.

By the second day of racially mixed meetings at the hall, placards were posted throughout the city calling on people to gather at the hall on the sixteenth at 11 A.M. in order to "interfere, *forcibly* if they *must*."[6] The menacing presence of the anti-abolitionists who convened prompted the women, white and black, to link arms upon exiting the hall as a means of self-defense.[7] This only disgusted their opponents even more. One eyewitness reported in a letter to a Georgia paper dated May 17 that

Yesterday, in the broad light of day, I saw many pairs and trios of different hues, from "jetty black to snowy white," arm in arm, emerge from its [Philadelphia's] spacious halls. There, sir, was the descendant of Ham or of Africa, linked, side by side, with some of the fairest and wealthiest daughters of Philadelphia, conversing as they went, no doubt strengthening each other in *the faith*, by their warm expressions of mutual assurance and hope that the period would soon arrive when they might become sisters-in-law.[8]

This commentator imagines that black and white women can only be talking about the presumably eagerly sought inter-racial marriages that they supposedly aimed for abolitionism to engineer. At the same time, a rumor began to circulate that, on the evening of that day, a white woman who had married a black man would give a lecture on abolition.[9] One newspaper reported of the rumor that it "was too much, and more than the high-spirited Philadelphians could bear."[10] An address was indeed planned for that evening, but the white female speaker was not married to a black man. It was widely known that, only days before, Angelina Grimké had married Theodore Weld, a white abolitionist and that the ceremony was officiated by two clergymen, one of whom, Theodore S. Wright, was black. Several black friends were also known to have attended.[11] Either the integrated nature of the wedding was thought so shocking that it might as well have been an inter-racial marriage and the rumors thus took shape accordingly, or the anti-abolitionists were looking to gather support for their mounting ire about amalgamation in the best way they knew how. Whichever the case, the rumor, coupled with the fact that Grimké was intent on addressing a "promiscuous assembly," put the whites congregating outside the hall over the edge. (In fact, many of the women attending the convention disapproved of a woman making a public address to an audience that included men; therefore, the convention did not endorse Grimké's speech.[12]) The mob threw brickbats, stones, and broken bottles through the new glass windows and, when Grimké finished her speech, assaulted a number of black attendees as they left the hall.[13] Once again, physical violence was the result of amalgamation hysteria.

The next day, on May 17, several thousand whites felt compelled to gather outside of the hall. Summoned to the spot, the mayor essentially urged them to act as they saw fit: "We never call out the military here! We do not need such measures. Indeed, I would, fellow citizens, look upon you as my police! I look upon you as my police, and I trust you will abide by the laws, and keep order. I now bid you farewell for the night."[14] Historians have argued of the Jacksonian era that rioters often felt entitled to violent and illegal activity because they reflected the views of the "respectable" majority.[15] In this case, when the mayor left the area after urging those gathered to serve as his police, the mob felt entitled to torch the hall. That other city officials also condoned this action is indicated by the fact that the fire company stood idly by, bothering only to keep nearby buildings hosed down.[16] The mob must also have felt justified in its actions by the fact that, the year before, in July 1837, the delegates to the Commonwealth's Constitutional Convention had voted overwhelmingly to restrict the vote to white men, arguing of blacks that "to incorporate them with ourselves in the exercise of the right of franchise, is a violation of the law of nature, and would lead to an amalgamation in the exercise thereof."[17] Furthermore, the electorate had given the constitution so revised its approval. Those Philadelphians concerned enough about amalgamation to riot were not only those, however, whose views merely seemed to reflect those of the people in authority but who were in authority themselves. As Leonard Richards has demonstrated of the anti-abolitionist/anti-amalgamation rioters in Philadelphia and elsewhere, they were so-called "gentlemen of property and standing" or, as Richards puts it, "men of means and influence."[18]

As they had so often since the mid-1830s, the white abolitionists denied vehemently that they sought to promote inter-marriages. Immediately after the burning of the hall, abolitionist Samuel Webb wrote a book about it, in which he explained that

It has been alleged . . . that it is part of the design of the abolitionists to promote inter-marriages between whites and colored people; and the false and absurd charge of advocating amalgamation, has been used perhaps more effectually than any other, in exciting and arraying against us the passions, prejudice, and fury of the mob. This charge has been so often denied, and from its first presentation has stood so entirely on the bare assertion of our calumniators, unsupported by proof, that nothing but its vociferous reiteration at the present time, and its injurious influence on the minds of the ignorant and misinformed, would induce us again to allude to it, as we now do, for the purpose of once more recording against it our explicit denial.[19]

Webb seems hardly surprised that the charge of amalgamation was successful in spurring violent opposition to the abolitionists. He argues not that it would be wrong to attack whites who advocated inter-marriage, but that the abolitionists shouldn't have been attacked because they didn't advocate any such thing. He thus sounds remarkably like the anti-abolitionist press, which acknowledged that mobbing was morally problematic, but which also claimed of the racially integrated meetings that "it was little short of insanity to fire the temper of the multitude by such public displays."[20] Likewise, the police committee charged with investigating the fire concluded that

it can be no matter of surprise . . . that the mass of the community, without distinction of political or religious opinions, could ill brook the erection of an edifice in this city, for the encouragement of practices believed by many to be subversive of the established orders of society, and even viewed by some as repugnant to that separation and distinction which it has pleased the great Author of nature to establish among the various races of man.[21]

Everyone accepted that the specter of amalgamation had and would continue to yield a violent response.

One of the concerns that spurred the anti-amalgamation rioters was the amount of black wealth in the city. There were 15,000 blacks in Philadelphia in 1830. One thousand of them held a substantial amount of wealth by the period's standards, at least some of which was spent on status-conferring luxuries.[22] A book published in 1841 by black Philadelphian Joseph Willson on the lifestyles of "the higher classes of colored society," described "parlors . . . carpeted and furnished with sofas, sideboards, cardtables, mirrors, . . . and in many instances, . . . a piano forte."[23] Many whites repeatedly expressed anxiety in the newspaper and elsewhere about these attempts at gentility. Consider a complaint in the *Pennsylvania Gazette* from 1828:

A joke of no ordinary magnitude was enacted last night, by getting up a Coloured Fancy Ball, at the Assembly-Room. . . . Carriages arrived, with *ladies* and *gentlemen* of colour, dressed in "character" in the most grotesque style. . . . It is worthy of remark, that many of the coaches containing these sable divinities were attended by white coachmen and *white footmen.* It is indeed high time that some serious attention was paid to the conduct and pursuits of the class of persons alluded to, and it may be well to inquire if matters progress at this rate how long it will be before masters and servants change places.[24]

That blacks should aspire to the status of "ladies and gentlemen" is considered not merely a "joke" but a matter of grave concern. Whites imagined that blacks were already beginning to switch places with them in the economic scheme of things.

Native Philadelphian Edward W. Clay drew on this status anxiety when he created a series of cartoons just prior to the advent of immediate abolitionism that mocked the status aspirations of the wealthy blacks of Philadelphia by depicting their attempts at proper dress and manners as misguided and laughable. In one of the prints in this series, Clay uses the ubiquitous idea that blacks smell to reassure his anxious audience that blacks will never achieve true gentility (Figure 10). Clay depicts an overdressed black man greeting a similarly dressed black woman. In response to his question, "How do you find yourself dis hot weader Miss Chloe?" she responds, "Pretty well I tank you Mr. Cesar only I aspire too much!" By punning on the word "perspire," Clay makes the point that Miss Chloe can never join the upper ranks of society, despite her "aspiration" and despite her fine clothes, because she "perspires" too much and thus presumably smells bad. According to Clay, those blacks who did achieve wealth were not deserving of the social privileges that attended it and thereby should not be granted such wealth in the first place. Immensely popular and even copied overseas, the title of the series, *Life in Philadelphia,* became a recognized short-hand way of referring to black aspirations throughout the late 1820s and '30s and thus served to remind white Philadelphians that the blacks of their city were supposedly a particularly striving bunch.[25] These prints must have been popular for the reassurance they provided whites but, in having done so, also reveal the anxious need for such reassurance in the first place.

In August 1834 and again at the riot at Pennsylvania Hall in May 1838, these economic and status anxieties culminated in violence aimed specifically at blacks and at the black centers of community power.[26] In 1834, a mob of

10. E. W. Clay, *Life in Philadelphia*, plate 4 [Miss Chloe], 1829. Courtesy The Library Company of Philadelphia.

whites spent three days attacking a Masonic hall, black churches, the homes of the more wealthy blacks, and some racially integrated establishments. In 1838, immediately after attacking blacks at Pennsylvania Hall and then burning the building down, the mob journeyed to the section of the city where most of the abolitionists lived and there burned the Friends Shelter for Colored Orphans before moving on to attack a black church.[27] According to historian Emma Jones Lapsanksy, any time white rioters attacked a black church, they were attacking "the seat of the black community's organizational strength, while simultaneously aiming at one of the symbols of black arrogance."[28] The black churches of Philadelphia were formed in the 1790s when black Philadelphians rejected the segregated seating at mixed churches. They quickly became the centers of the black community. And the influence of the black leaders they nurtured spread beyond religion into the business and political arenas as well, prompting at least one Philadelphian in 1830 to connect black churches to rising black status aspirations: "In the olden time, dressy blacks and dandy coloured beaux and belles, as we now see them issuing from their proper churches, were quite unknown. Their aspirings and little vanities have been growing since they got those separate churches."[29]

The series of anti-abolitionist lithographs published by Clay a year after the 1838 Philadelphia riots indicates that whites linked black aspirations to the threat of amalgamation.[30] Indeed, the series may have been inspired by the riots. Although Clay had moved to New York City after the *Life in Philadelphia* series, he surely paid close attention to the riotous events of his home town. Unlike the earlier *Life in Philadelphia* series, in his *Practical Amalgamation* series wealthy blacks achieve their status goals by linking themselves romantically with and then marrying white abolitionists.[31]

In two prints from Clay's 1839 series, *Practical Amalgamation (Musical Soirée)* and *An Amalgamation Waltz* (Figures 5 and 6), both discussed in the last chapter, "black" and "white" abolitionists socialize with one another and with the kind of proximity that would have been shocking to Clay's audience. The black figures are dressed in lavish and expensive fashions and thus atypically for most blacks in the 1830s. Indeed, these are exactly the same kind of clothes worn by the wealthy characters in the earlier *Life in Philadelphia* series. In *Soirée*, Clay is careful to show the mixed crowd socializing in rooms decorated with ornate picture frames, lavish carpets, rich draperies, and detailed moldings. There is even the piano forte that Joseph Willson revealed was a sure mark of having reached genteel and wealthy heights. Few, if any, blacks at the time could hope for such wealth that here seems to be a result of or at least is unquestioned by the abolitionists, even as whites are being harmed by it. Clay depicts the white men in an economically subordinate position to blacks in reverse of the status quo. In *An Amalgamation Waltz*, while white women cavort in the arms of black men, white men are relegated to working in the orchestra, at a great remove from the festivities. And in another print from the series, *Johnny Q* (Figure 4), also discussed in the previous chapter, there is a similar situation. While a black man has risen to the powerful position of ambassador, in part it seems, thanks to the lascivious white abolitionist women who desire him, the servants entering the room are white.

In another print from the series, entitled *Practical Amalgamation* (Figure 11), gentility and wealth are again central themes. Here the abolitionist women have moved from the racially integrated political activism of *Johnny Q* and the inter-racial socializing of *Waltz* and *Soirée* that followed to full-fledged inter-racial romance. This print depicts a black man and woman on a settee entertaining their respective lovers. The man's top hat and the woman's jewelry along with their lavish attire signal their aspirations to the rank of gentleman and lady. Perhaps the parlor in which they sit, with its richly detailed carpet and ornate picture frames, belongs to one or both of them. But rather than turning to each other on the settee they share, both entertain a white abolitionist lover. Again, that they are abolitionists is indicated by the term "amalgamation" in the title, for white abolitionists were said to promote amalgamation as the best means of eradicating race prejudice. Futhermore, the white man in the print looks suspiciously like William Lloyd Garrison. That one or more of the people in *Practical Amalgamation* are abolitionists is further indicated by the fact that they have on their parlor wall portraits of

11. E. W. Clay, *Practical Amalgamation*, 1839. Courtesy The Library Company of Philadelphia.

abolitionists and abolitionist supporters, namely Arthur Tappan, Daniel O'Connell, the Irish leader of the Catholic Emancipation movement and a loud supporter of American abolitionism, and John Quincy Adams, crusader against Congress's gag rule that, in 1836, put the lid on petitions calling for an end to slavery. While the white man has taken a subordinate position, as indicated by his position kneeling on the floor to a black woman, the black man has become the leader of gentility. His guitar is one sign of the position he has usurped. Black men were expected to play not guitars, but banjos. In *Notes on the State of Virginia,* Jefferson had explained that "the instrument proper to them is the Banjar [*sic*] which they brought hither from Africa" (266). It was just then beginning to appear in the burgeoning minstrel show tradition.[32] That this same guitar protrudes from the lap of the black man, between whose legs is the body of a white woman, might have signified to the print's audience that black men are sexually conquering quite amenable white women as a means of attaining class and status goals.[33] Amalgamation, the supposed goal of abolitionism, will usher in a world where "blacks" will gain wealth and "white" men will lose it. For Clay, the desires of white abolitionist women are particularly to blame.

In *Practical Amalgamation (The Wedding)* (Figure 12), the event so fearfully anticipated by James Watson Webb, Jerome B. Holgate, and other anti-abolitionists has come to pass in the wake of abolitionism: a man coded as black by his caricatured profile, nose, lips, hair, and bowed legs, and a woman coded as white in the print by the fine-line drawing that depicts her quite realistically, exchange wedding vows. The friends in attendance comprise a racially mixed group overseen by a man who looks much like Garrison. Garrison has his back to the reader, as if to signify how much he cares for their concerns, and is accompanied by a black woman. The officiating clergyman is carefully shown in profile with dark skin so as to be understood as "black." That a "black" clergymen has taken center stage is meant to show the reversal of the race hierarchy in the wake of abolitionism and amalgamation. As with *Johnny Q,* viewers would have imagined that the white women in the print joined the abolitionist movement out of their perverse desire for these ridiculous-looking black men. Anti-abolitionists believed white abolition women wished to marry black men as a "practical testimony" to their rejection of race prejudices that the print imagines as fully natural given the ugliness of the "blacks," although the abolitionists who did urge testimonies had far more minor gestures in mind. Indeed, the *Philadelphia Saturday Courier* had recently reminded readers in May 1838 that the women at the previous Anti-

12. E. W. Clay, *Practical Amalgamation (The Wedding)*, 1839. Courtesy American Antiquarian Society.

Slavery Convention of American Women had passed a resolution to "use all our influence in having our coloured friends seated promiscuously in all our congregations; and that as long as our churches are disgraced with side seats and corners, set apart for them, we will, as much as possible, take our seats with them."[34]

This conflation of economic, status, and sexual anxieties in the wake of immediate abolitionism is best evidenced in Clay's *The Fruits of Amalgamation* (Figure 13), the final print in his amalgamation series.[35] (Thus, though this series is not numbered, the prints comprise a natural order. A print that shows black and white abolitionists working together depicts a scene that comes before scenes of inter-racial socializing. These are, in turn, followed by inter-racial marriage and procreation.) Presumably the "fruits" of the inter-racial marriage in the previous print are the two children, both of whom are rendered particularly dark by Clay, reminding us that children of inter-racial

13. E. W. Clay, *The Fruits of Amalgamation*, 1839. Courtesy American Antiquarian Society.

couples were considered black. But it is important to note that Clay's concern in the rest of the amalgamation series is not with the perceived biological "fruits" of inter-racial reproduction. Even here the death of the white family is a death measured in the nonbiological terms of taste and status. The husband, whose profile, dark skin, and ridiculously ornate attire indicate his blackness, is in elaborate dress reclining on a sofa and reading the abolitionist newspaper the *Emancipator* while an ornately framed picture of Garrison hangs on the wall. The man's economic wealth and his attainment of a "white" wife are thus linked, as in Clay's previous prints in the series, to the efforts of abolitionists. And again we see what this will mean for white men. A white servant enters the room to serve tea to the guests, another inter-racial couple, perhaps Garrison and the same "black" woman who attended him in Clay's previous prints. The wife, whose whiteness is again identifiable by the fine-line drawings that depict her, is seated under a picture entitled *Othello & Desdemona*. By the 1830s, *Othello* was a popular play in the United States, giving abolitionist-supporter John Quincy Adams in 1835 a reason to declare the inter-racial marriage it depicted a "gross outrage upon the law of Nature," even as he insisted upon sitting through the performance, perhaps because he enjoyed his moral indignity.[36] In Clay's mind, as it would seem in Adams's, only a couple eager themselves to cross the color line would display a scene from *Othello* in their parlor. That the picture depicts Desdemona kneeling before her blackamoor husband, presumably pleading for her life, is a harbinger for what might lie in store for the white woman seated directly below in Clay's print upon whose lap rests the feet of her black husband and upon whose conspicuously bared white breast rests her baby's dark hand. If the black hand on her breast violates her female purity in racialized sexual terms, the feet of her black husband further indicate that she has become the welcome mat for black entrance into the genteel classes when she should have served as the gate keeper. Clearly, white womanhood has desecrated white middle- and upper-class sanctity by admitting these predators specifically into the parlor. To use Kathryn Kish Sklar's terms, this room was supposed to serve as a woman's "cultural podium" from which she could exert her moral beneficence on American society.[37] Karen Halttunen adds, "The parlor was the arena within which the aspiring middle classes worked to establish their claims to social status, to that elusive quality of 'gentility.' "[38] That the parlor in particular has been polluted makes the specific point that abolitionism's threat to "whites" is an economic and status threat even as it is a race threat and, indeed, that these are inextricable in the United States. And the cause of these problems, as Clay saw it, was not simply that white abolitionist women were willing to entertain the affections of black men in the parlor or anywhere else for that matter, but also that black men were successfully baiting these women in order to satisfy their economic and status ambitions. Their hook, according to Clay's prints, was phallic potency and hypersexuality.

By the nineteenth century, there was a long tradition of sexualizing black men. Clay taps this tradition when he invokes the play in which Shakespeare describes Othello's embraces as "the gross clasps of a lascivious Moor" (I, I, 127). Clay also draws on this tradition when he codes the "black" men in his amalgamation prints by their intense sexual arousal. In addition to the inappropriate embraces and the phallic potency revealed in the erect guitar, for example, he makes the black ambassador in *Johnny Q* state that political business is far from his mind. Further, Clay's exaggeration of most of the black men's profiles was meant to signify that the black men in Clay's prints are primates and therefore as dangerously venerous as these supposed relatives.

In the eighteenth century, Dutch anatomist Petrus Camper (1722–89) had used *linea facialis*, or "facial lines," to substantiate the perception that whites, blacks, and nonhuman primates are in a hierarchical relationship to one another. He explained and demonstrated with illustrations in a dissertation, translated into English in 1794 and widely cited in English-speaking countries thereafter, that "A line drawn from the forehead to the upper lip [of a person or animal in profile] would demonstrate the difference betwixt the faces of different nations, and likewise the resemblance betwixt the head of a negro and that of a monkey" (Figure 14).[39] According to him, "negroes," on average, have a facial angle of seventy degrees and apes of forty-two to fifty degrees, whereas the ideal profile of the gods in Greek statuary, at one hundred degrees, approached a vertical line. He argued that Europeans have an angle of eighty degrees and thus approach the ideal.[40] But, as Camper's drawings make clear, and in the recent words of scientist Stephen Jay Gould, these and other measurements of race were "fudged" quite unconsciously "in the clear interest of controlling a priori convictions."[41] Soon, blacks were repeatedly drawn in profile by scientists and artists alike with what are now recognized to be exaggerated facial angles in order to make the point that blacks are related to nonhuman primates, prompting historian Londa Schiebinger to conclude that Camper's drawings of facial angles became "the central visual icon of all subsequent racism . . . in the nineteenth century."[42] Clay's means of depicting black men in profile would have been quickly recognized as signifying their affinity to that animal which was most noted for its venerous nature and particularly for its interest in the female above it on the Chain of Being. As Buffon asserted in his *Natural History* (trans. 1781–85), orangutans are "equally ardent for women as for its own females," a point used to great effect in the late eighteenth century by Jefferson in his *Notes on the State of Virginia* and, in 1839, by Clay whose series *Practical Amalgamation* makes the point that abolitionism was pairing white women with dangerous animals.[43]

By the 1830s, white Americans knew a lot about non-human primates. Natural history was a popular field available for consumption in a variety of forms, including magazine articles, school textbooks, laymen's science books, engravings, newspaper reports, encyclopedia entries, and museum and other types of exhibits, all of which were littered with stories, studies, and pictures of simians.[44] Thus when a primate (variously called an orangutan and a chimpanzee) was available for viewing in Philadelphia in July of 1839, the *Philadelphia Gazette* assumed not only that people would want to view it but that people would already be familiar with the naturalists' descriptions of these animals:

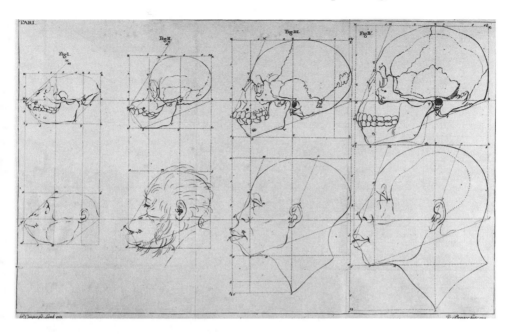

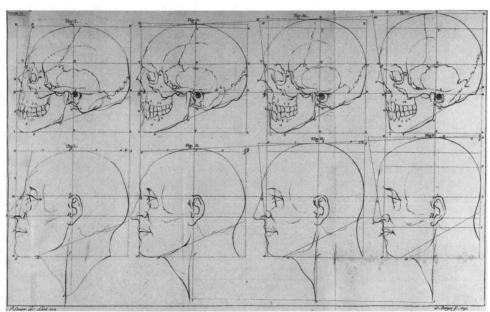

14. Petrus Camper, *Über den natürlichen Unterschied der Gesichtszüge in Menschen* (1792), figures 1 and 2. Courtesy Staatsbibliothek zu Berlin, Preußischer Kulturbesitz.

NOW exhibiting at the Masonic Hall, Chestnut street, from 8 o'clock, AM. to 6 o'clock, PM., the only living CHIMPANZEE, lately brought from Africa[.] This animal is the genuine "Troglodytes Niger" of Naturalists, or "Wild Man of the Woods," and is the finest specimen ever seen in this country. It bears a most striking resemblance to the human form, and in natural sagacity far exceeds the description of Naturalists.

Admittance 25 cents; Children half price. Tickets to be had at the door.[45]

White Americans were expected to be both fascinated with and educated about the orangutan's humanlike looks and behavior.

Many natural history texts of the nineteenth century repeated the popular myth about orangutans and women. *A Natural History of the Globe, of Man, and of Quadrupeds* (1833) insisted that orangutans "are passionately fond of women. . . . [T]here is no safety for them in passing through the woods they inhabit, as these animals immediately attack and injure them."[46] Indeed, any reference to primates instantly conjured up notions of inter-species rape. Charles Baudelaire explained in 1859 of a sculpture called "Ourang Outang Carrying Off a Woman Deep into the Woods":

Why not a crocodile, a tiger, or any other beast that might eat a woman? Because it's not a question of mastication but of violation. For the ape alone, the gigantic ape—at the same time more and less than a man—has sometimes demonstrated a human appetite for women. And in this the artist finds the means to astonish his viewer.[47]

According to Baudelaire, the artifact in question comprises a coherent narrative only if the viewer knows that orangutans have "sometimes demonstrated a human appetite for women," a common idea in early nineteenth-century natural history. That a woman might be sexually violated by this animal, "at the same time more and less a man," was a horror beyond all others. For inter-species sex was the least natural of all imagined couplings. In Clay's prints, this assumption works similarly. With their apelike facial angles, the black men seem to be committing not just an inter-racial but an inter-species atrocity. And if a species was comprised of those organisms capable of inter-breeding, as defined by Linneaus in the eighteenth century and understood by middle-class Americans, a group well versed in horticulture and animal husbandry, then organisms from different species would not naturally mate. That abolitionism was bringing together apelike black men with white women meant that it was violating the fundamental boundary of nature: that of species.

Edgar Allan Poe moved to Philadelphia sometime between the latter part of 1837 and the early part of 1838 and stayed until 1844.[48] While there, he wrote and published a short story that relies, as did the *Philadelphia Gazette*, on the general public's knowledge of simians, the display of which at Masonic Hall in 1839 coincided with Poe's stay.[49] The narrator of "The Murders in the Rue Morgue," which appeared in the April 1841 issue of Philadelphia's *Graham Magazine*, makes it clear that the mystery's solution only makes sense if one is familiar with natural history accounts of orangutans. After gentleman detective C. Auguste Dupin has solved the mystery for himself, he asks his companion, the tale's narrator, to read a passage from Georges Cuvier about which the companion says:

It was a minute anatomical and generally descriptive account of the large fulvous Ourang-Outang of the East Indian Islands. The gigantic stature, the prodigious strength and activity, the wild ferocity, and the imitative propensities of these mammalia are *sufficiently well known to all.* I understood the full horrors of the murder *at once.* (emphasis added)[50]

Poe had already attempted to capitalize on the interest in natural history, and had in the process familiarized himself with Cuvier, when he contributed to *The Conchologist's First Book* (1839) and helped write Thomas Wyatt's *Synopsis of Natural History* (1839), shortly before penning "Murders." According to Poe, for *The Conchologist's First Book,* he "translated from Cuvier . . . the accounts of the animals."[51] And the *Synopsis,* as stated on its title page, included substantial "additions from the work of Cuvier."[52] With "Murders," Poe put his knowledge of the well-known natural historian to scary effect. The orangutan in "Murder" displays all of the simian characteristics to which Dupin refers in the passage from Cuvier: "gigantic stature," "prodigious strength," "wild ferocity," and "imitative propensities." It is the last trait, however, that initiates the murderous turn of events. Madame L'Espanaye and her daughter Mademoiselle L'Espanaye are brutally murdered when the escaped orangutan enters their bedroom wielding a razor in imitation of a barber.

When Linnaeus placed humans in the same taxonomic order as simians, he noted that "Neither the face nor the feet, nor the upright gait, nor in any other aspect of his external structure does man differ from the apes."[53] Similar accounts of orangutans looking and acting like humans were popular in Poe's day. The following account of an imitative orangutan from Buffon was cited in virtually every antebellum book on the animal kingdom. This particular version is taken from an encyclopedia popular in the United States in the second quarter of the nineteenth century and owned by Poe's adoptive family, the Allans:

Buffon relates, that he had seen this animal offer its hand to those who came to see him, and walk with them; as if he had been one of the company; that he has seen him sit at table, unfold his napkin, wipe his lips, make use of his knife and fork, pour out his drink into a glass, take his cup and saucer, put in sugar, pour out the tea, and stir it, in order to let it cool; and that he has done this not only at the command of his master, but often without bidding.[54]

Not only can this nonhuman primate imitate humans but he can imitate genteel ways and does so even when his master has not commanded him to do so.

Like the orangutan described by Buffon, the animal in Poe's story wants to imitate its owner and even escapes from a locked closet in order to do so. The sailor explains, as recounted by the narrator:

Returning home from some sailors' frolic on the night, or rather in the morning of the murder, he found the beast occupying his own bed-room, into which it had broken from a closet adjoining, where it had been, as was thought, securely confined. Razor in hand, and fully lathered, it was sitting before a looking-glass, attempting the operation of shaving, in which it had no doubt previously watched its master through the key-hole of the closet. (564–65)

Poe's orangutan goes one step further here than Buffon's. It goes so far as to try to look like its so-called "master." For although the animal's use of a mirror can be construed as merely further imitation—indeed it is said only to sit before the glass, not necessarily to be looking in it—the use of the mirror can also be read as the sign of the animal's desire to find itself looking like and thus embodied as a man. For the orangutan imitates that particular ritual whereby men rid themselves of the facial hair that would more closely ally men with hairy or furry creatures. Indeed, less than twenty-five years later, Abraham Lincoln would be widely lambasted for growing a beard, with many anti-Lincoln men referring to him as the "Illinois Ape" and "the baboon."[55]

Upon discovery by its owner, the orangutan escapes the apartment with the barbering razor in hand, bringing it finally into the apartment of the L'Espanayes, where it again engages in imitative acts. The orangutan's owner reports what he sees there, as narrated by Dupin's companion: "As . . . [he] looked in [to the L'Espanaye apartment], the gigantic animal had seized

Madam L'Espanaye by the hair, (which was loose, as she had been combing it,) and was flourishing the razor about her face, in imitation of the motions of a barber" (566). But if the orangutan once sat before a mirror attempting to imitate an act "it had no doubt previously watched," here it is said to "imitate" a profession it seems to have never seen, at least as far as the reader knows. Even more remarkably, it is ultimately these barbering attempts, a seeming narrative inconsistency, that result in Madam's slit throat and almost total decapitation.

The barbering primate would have been less puzzling to local readers, many of whom would have visited Peale's Museum in Philadelphia where, since 1811, the Peales had been capitalizing on the widespread knowledge that nonhuman primates could behave in humanlike ways. A very popular exhibit showcased stuffed monkeys dressed in the outfits of various professions and arranged in occupational poses.[56] One exhibit that seems to have made a particular impression displayed the monkeys dressed and arranged so as to depict the life of a barber shop. In his *Memoirs*, Charles Godfrey Leland noted of his boyhood in 1830s Philadelphia, "I owe so very much . . . to old Peale's Museum. . . . How often have I paused in its dark galleries in awe before the tremendous skeleton of the Mammoth. . . . And the stuffed monkeys—one shaving another—what exquisite humour, which never palled upon us!"[57] This particular exhibit undoubtedly served to remind viewers not only of the oft-noted similarities between monkeys and humans, but that the barbers to the white men of Philadelphia were the supposed closest relatives to the simians who portrayed them at Peale's: blacks.

Blacks were perceived to be naturally good at barbering. In his study *The Colored Aristocracy of St. Louis* (1858), Cyprian Clamorgan asserts that "a mulatto takes to razors and soap as naturally as a young duck to a pool of water . . . ; they certainly make the best barbers in the world, and were doubtless intended by nature for the art. In its exercise, they take white men by the nose without giving offense, and without causing an effusion of blood."[58] Herman Melville has his protagonist in "Benito Cereno" (1856) voice sentiments similar to Clamorgan's about the naturalness of black barbering skills. On board the *San Dominick*, Captain Amasa Delano comforts himself that nothing is amiss when he watches the Negro Babo shave his master, Don Benito. The scene is described by Delano as follows: "There is something in the Negro which, in a peculiar way, fits him for avocations about one's person. Most Negroes are natural valets and hairdressers, taking to the comb and brush congenially as to the castinets, and flourishing them apparently with almost equal satisfaction." For Delano, "seeing the colored servant, napkin on arm, so debonair about his master, in a business so familiar as that of shaving too, all his old weakness for Negroes returned."[59] It seems whites felt comfortable and safe watching what they perceived to be the particularly capable hands of black barbers.

But if Delano momentarily envisions barbers as content servants or slaves, Clamorgan makes it clear that barbering was the chosen profession of those free blacks who wanted to rise. He notes that "a majority of our colored aristocracy [in St. Louis] belong to the tonsorial profession."[60] Of the thirty-one men whom Clamorgan describes as being of this aristocracy, census materials indicate that as many as eleven were barbers at some time. The next most prevalent job among this set of men is that of steward, of which only four of the thirty-one men worked as such. A coveted position at this time, many blacks were undoubtedly attracted to the entrepreneurial nature of the barbering business. Historian Roger Lane explains that "barbers could be classified as either skilled workingmen, if they worked for others, or as small capitalist entrepreneurs if they were in business for themselves. The line between the two was slight and often artificial. . . . [I]t is appropriate to think of black tradesmen more as real or potential entrepreneurs than as wage-earners."[61] As for Philadelphia, in his landmark study, *The Philadelphia Negro: A Social Study* (1899), W. E. B. Du Bois cites an 1849 study in which barbers are said to comprise roughly five percent of the total black workforce in Philadelphia.[62] As in St. Louis, it was a lucrative position. Du Bois and other African Americans at the end of the century lamented the encroachment of Germans and Italians on this traditionally black business, even as they noted the increasing disdain in the black community for a job in which the color line had to be respected.

The exhibit at Peale's seems to indicate that insofar as barbering was the chosen profession of those blacks who wanted to rise, it might have been a sore point for whites who would have therefore found relief mocking them. The wrapper illustration of Clay's *Life in Philadelphia* series is more obvious in its depiction of white anxiety about the lucrative nature of black barbering. In this contribution by Anthony Imbert to the series, a flamboyant black barber is shown working on a decidedly morose-looking white client (Figure 15). The barber sports the various accouterments he perceives signal affluence: an ornate collar and a fancy coat. Imbert labels the barber's razor "Magnum Don," or great gentleman, to underscore the barber's pretension in his dress and, perhaps too, in his choice of an entrepreneurial profession. In contrast, the white client wears simple garments. The rack supporting his equally unos-

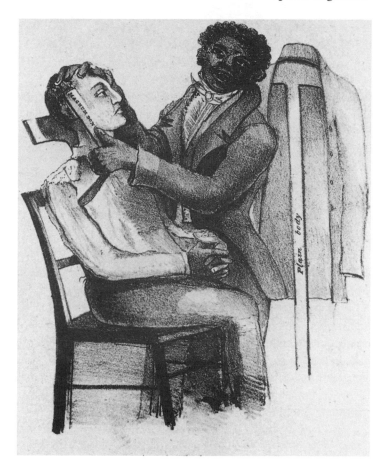

15. Anthony Imbert, wrapper illustration for *Life in Philadelphia*, ca. 1829–30, Bd 912 Im1 83. Courtesy The Historical Society of Pennsylvania.

tentatious coat is clearly labeled "Plain body." The Quaker-like garb indicates that Imbert may have wanted to portray the client as an abolitionist. In that case, the abolitionist's desire for equality—political, economic, and otherwise—would have paved the way for his own economic and perhaps literal bloodletting. One slip of the sharp razor and the white client is a dead man. Either way, Imbert associates the economic striving of free blacks in Philadelphia with both cultural and economic poaching on white society and connects that poaching with possible white extinction.

Clamorgan also reveals the nature of the black barber's terrible power, despite insisting that black barbers can take white men by the nose "without giving offense":

When one of these gossiping knights of the razor gets his customer under his hands, it would seem that his tongue keeps pace with his razor; they are dumb as mutes until they get a man's head thrown back on a level with his breast, his face, and especially his mouth, besmeared with a thick coating of lather, and the glittering steel flourishing in *terrorem* over his throat.[63]

The white customer is immobilized by the lather, by the blade "flourishing in *terrorem*" over his throat, and by the black man's voice, usually silenced in American life, but liberated here by his position as an entrepreneurial business man. Again, it was the economic element of the black barbering profession in particular that made it a great source of anxiety for whites. As Clamorgan and Du Bois demonstrate, barbering was the most visible profession of the propertied black class. This alone would account for the fact that it was singled out as a point over which whites felt it necessary to fret. Because barbering was an entrepreneurial and thus potentially white job and because the backbone of the barbering business was shaving beards, the barbershop put the bared necks of white clients in fearful proximity with aspiring blacks both literally and metaphorically.

So, too, in "Benito Cereno" does the potential for murder lurk in the barber's razor. Babo lathers only those areas of his master that do not sport beard, "the upper lip and low down under the throat," the latter a decidedly vulnerable spot. In the barber's chair, Don Benito does not manifest the same comfort expressed by Delano upon witnessing the barbering scene: "Not unaffected by the close sight of the gleaming steel, Don Benito nervously shuddered." Delano does not fail to notice this response, "nor, as he saw the two thus postured, could he resist the vagary that in the black he saw a headsman, and in the white a man at the block." Benito shudders again when the knife touches his throat: "No sword drawn before James the First of England, no assassination in that timid king's presence, could have produced a more terrified aspect than was now presented by Don Benito."[64] Babo nicks him but only draws a small amount of blood. Later, Melville justifies the white men's unease about the black barber by revealing that Don Benito was Babo's captive.

By making a barbering razor the chief murder weapon, Poe draws on the perceived similarities between blacks and simians in order to claim as dangerous the possibility of upward mobility that black barbering signaled for so many whites at the time. When Poe has the orangutan in "Murders" attempt to shave Madame in what will result in her beheading, he has stepped into the terms set up by Peale's Museum whereby monkeys are black barbers and thus barbering blacks are bestial. And yet, in doing so, he is not "humerous" (Leland's term for describing the museum), but instead plays out the anxiety at the heart of Imbert's barber print, Melville's "Benito Cereno," and the anti-black violence of 1834 and 1838; a throat is slit and blood shed. This is not to say, however, that Poe allows the orangutan to function in full allegorical manner. For, at the end, when the sailor is allowed to sell his orangutan "for . . . a very large sum at the *Jardin des Plantes*" (568), Poe, in effect, returns the orangutan to Cuvier and to the realm of natural history more generally where it is less easily allowed to function as a symbol. In this way, Poe ultimately disavows any connection in his tale between orangutans and blacks. It is this disavowal which has long made "The Murders in the Rue Morgue" seem so very distant for scholars from the historical context that shaped it.[65] Rather, Poe continually draws on the perceived similarities between blacks and nonhuman primates in order to create a comparison between the two in the reader's mind.

But if orangutans were thought to look and act like blacks who had not recently shaved and even to be related to them, nothing made the two seem more similar, as we have seen, than the type of desire they each supposedly had for the women above them on the Great Chain of Being. Poe's 1841 tale, like Clay's 1839 *Practical Amalgamation* prints and the other commentary on the riot at Pennsylvania Hall, raises the specter of inter-racial sex, reminding us that his stay in Philadelphia also coincided with the 1838 riots there. The orangutan kills the two women not only while they are in their bedroom, but as they are making preparations to retire for the evening. The sailor is careful to recall that the women have let down their hair and are "habited in their night clothes" (566). Further, as literary critic Judith Fetterley notes, "One of the bodies has been forcibly thrust up a chimney, an image evocative of rape; hair, traditionally associated with feminine sexuality and allure, and described in the newspaper accounts of the event as 'tresses,' has been pulled from the head of one of the women."[66] At a time when abolitionist women were reviled for interacting and perhaps more with black men, white readers would have read the orangutan's assault, not as Baudelaire did of the statue as merely typical of orangutans, but as a point of comparison to inter-racial rape. White women were at risk when in proximity to black men because these men were animals who, like the animal to whom they were supposedly related, had monstrous sexual desires. And that black men were arguably like orangutans gave the threat of inter-racial sex its terrifying nature.

Also like Clay, Poe firmly links the specter of amalgamation to the possibility of black upward mobility when he has the instrument of that mobility for many free blacks, the barber's razor, serve as the means of violating the bodies of two cloistered white women. It seems, then, that Poe's tale is a direct reflection of the same concerns, also seen in Clay's prints, that had earlier fueled riotous whites in the late 1830s. That abolitionists were reviled for the amalgamation it was thought they championed had much to do in Philadelphia with the concern that amalgamation would be a means to, or otherwise tandem with, the rise of blacks into the genteel classes where they would usurp the position of those who were truly genteel: other whites. Indeed, in carrying the Imbert scene to a bloody conclusion, Poe not only reflects the very fears circulating in antebellum Philadelphia in the wake of immediate abolitionism, but he attempts to heighten them, thus seeming to want to justify or exacerbate those very tensions that had earlier erupted in mob violence at Pennsylvania Hall. In his tale, the threat of amalgamation not only comes to pass but results in murderous extinction. To the extent the abolitionists were reviled, it seems Poe would have the level of hatred increased several fold.[67]

It must be noted, too, however, that Clay's prints and Poe's tale are not simply attacks on free blacks and white abolitionists. Clay's work also must have provided titillating entertainment with its sexual content. And although the white bared breast and the amorous embraces he depicts would have undoubtedly provided certain pleasures without the added inter-racial elements, such pleasures were only heightened when black men, the most sexualized men of all for white culture, were placed in physical proximity to white women.[68] In fact, it is the proximity of black men that provides the occasion for depicting the bared breast and amorous embraces in the first place. The irony of the prints, then, is that in visually rendering anti-abolition sentiments, Clay provided his audience with a form of pornography, literally that which stages sex and thereby might elicit sexual arousal.

Poe's tale, much as it offers a stern warning, provides a similar erotic spectacle. The detective genre, which Poe is credited with inventing here, serves to keep the scene of sexualized violence center stage, providing the reader with various accounts of it as Dupin and others discuss it. And when the sailor finally provides an eyewitness account of the attack, it is from the position of the window, the classic position of the voyeur and one that the reader is made to share with the sailor. But the detective genre also ensures that the reader, the sailor, and Dupin will never have to confront their involvement in the violent and erotic spectacle from which they cannot avert their eyes. For in solving the mystery of who murdered the two women, Dupin absolves the reader, the sailor, and himself for indulging the titillation that presumably kept all riveted to the scene. If it is all the orangutan's fault, then those desires can go unexamined and even unacknowledged. Readers can maintain their respectability because a surrogate has been found to both enact and take the blame for their titillation.[69] Indeed, the reflection and instillation of inter-racial desires here that are then purged from the narrative and the reader might have served as a kind of safety valve that helped whites to go ahead with the purely intra-racial desires the culture was demanding of them.

When Poe and Clay brought the perceived relationship between blacks and orangutans to the anti-abolitionist campaign, they were also wielding a more powerful ideological weapon than they might have foreseen. For if blacks were viewed as related to apes and were thus perceived to be a separate species from whites, contrary to Linnaeus's argument in *Systema Naturae* (1740) that all men comprised one species, then by virtue of the most common definition of species, sexual contact between blacks and whites was arguably wholly unnatural. Not surprisingly, then, in the wake of abolitionism, the unity school of ethnology came under increased pressure. Fearful of amalgamation, white Southerners and anti-abolitionist Northerners alike felt hardpressed to prove an absolute and immutable species difference between the races as a means of proving inter-racial sex a deviant, unnatural practice.[70]

In 1843, Dr. Josiah Clark Nott (1804–73) of Mobile, Alabama, became the first American scientist to draw the conclusion that the different races most certainly comprise wholly different species that had thus been created separately.[71] His inspiration, as indicated by the subtitle of his essay, seems to have been the abolitionists' imagined support of amalgamation. Indeed two years later, Nott confirmed that his aim was to provide his readers with a weapon against abolitionism.[72] "The Mulatto a Hybrid—probable extermination of the two races if the Whites and Blacks are allowed to intermarry" was published in the *American Journal of the Medical Sciences.* Rather than argue the impropriety or class and status risks of inter-marriage, as the anti-abolitionists of the 1830s did, Nott argues that inter-marriage would be a biological catastrophe. He explains that mulattoes are shorter lived than whites or blacks, that mulatto women are "bad breeders" and "bad nurses," and that when blacks and whites inter-marry they are "less prolific."[73] He concludes that there "may have been distinct creations" and that "*at the present day the Anglo-Saxon and Negro races are . . . distinct species.*"[74] By the late 1840s, such leading figures in science as Dr. Samuel George Morton and Dr. Louis Agassiz (1807–73) concurred with Nott, despite the risk of being characterized along with him as infidels for disputing the Biblical account of creation.[75]

In November 1846, Morton published "Hybridity in Animals considered in reference to the unity of the Human Species" in the *American Journal of Science*. In it, he notes that "hybridity" had typically been the test of "species character":

according to this supposed law of nature, . . . if mankind embraced several species, the intermixture of these would go no further than to produce a sterile hybrid variety. But since all the races are capable of producing, with each other, a progeny more or less fertile, it is inferred that they must all belong to one and the same species. This is the question at issue. (39)

Because he cannot deny that the races are inter-fertile, Morton looks else-where for evidence of species distinction. He finds what he is looking for in the second edition of James Cowles Prichard's *Researches into the Physical History of Mankind* (1813), a book that went through multiple editions and that was widely read by American scientists during the first half of the nineteenth century. Morton quotes Prichard at length:

It is manifest that there is some principle in nature which prevents the intermixture of species, and maintains the order and variety of the animal creation. If different species mixed their breed, and hybrid races were often propagated, the animal world would present a scene of confusion. By what method is this confusion prevented? The fact seems to be, that the tribes of wild animals are preserved distinct, not only by the steril-ity of mules, but that such animals are never, in the state of nature, brought into exis-tence. The separation of distinct species is sufficiently provided for by the *natural repugnance* between individuals of different kinds. This is, indeed, overcome *in the state of domestication*, in which the natural propensities cease, in a great measure, to direct their actions. (Morton's emphasis)[76]

Repugnance becomes the key, in Morton's thinking, to species distinction. He writes:

The same phenomena [as repugnance], moral as well as physical, takes place, to a certain extent, among men as among animals; for the repugnance of some human races to mix with others, has only been partially overcome by centuries of proximity, and, above all other means, by the moral degradation consequent to the state of slavery. Not only is this repugnance proverbial among all nations of the European stock among whom negroes have been introduced, but it appears to be almost equally natural to the Africans in their own country, towards such Europeans as have been thrown among them; for with the former a white skin is not more admired than a black one is with us.[77]

The theory of repugnance allows Morton to conclude that inter-fertility is "no proof of the unity of the human species."[78] Rather, innate feelings of repugnance are evidence of species distinction. The corollary here is that those humans without this repugnance are violating the norms of Nature itself, as evidenced by their supposed "moral degradation."

The so-called American school of ethnology, namely scientists who argued in favor of polygenism, was not immediately and widely embraced because, as I have noted, it seemed to undermine the Biblical account of creation. Its acceptance was only signaled in 1854 with the success of *Types of Mankind*, Nott's and George R. Gliddon's compendium of the materials that aimed to prove the species diversity of mankind.[79] Only a few reviewers took issue with the book's position on polygenism, which had otherwise and finally found wide acceptance. At least two of the negative reviewers reveal the concern that to continue championing the doctrine of unity meant being mistaken for an abolitionist or more particularly as an amalgamationist.[80] This was apparently enough to quiet most of the dissension. Polygenesis was clearly the answer for those who wished to prove that the races must not be allowed to mix as they certainly would, it was feared, should abolitionism succeed. In short, with polygenism, scientific racism was born, its existence called into being by the perceived necessity of proving inter-racial sex unnatural and thereby demonizing it with all of the authority that, by then, was invested in science.

The leap from taste to instinct was thus short and swift. Recall that during the Philadelphia riots, white abolitionist women were, as in New York, castigated for their bad taste. The *Pennsylvanian* insisted that "disgusting associations are matters of taste. If white ladies will parade arm in arm with negroes, will make them companions at their tables, and their boudoirs, we may lament the degeneracy of the times, but the evil must correct itself."[81] The

Philadelphia Saturday Courier asserted that "we have wholly misunderstood the taste of our fair countrywomen, if they are ready to carry out the doctrine of 'promiscuous amalgamation.' "[82] But when Clay and Poe paired white women with primates and primate-like black men who were thus, by definition, a wholly separate species than whites, these women are shown to have committed a far bigger crime, a biological crime against nature. Following the success of this primate or species approach, science stepped in to teach whites to experience their repugnance for blacks as fully instinctual. The door to social equality in the face of possible political equality was closing fast.

5 Making "Miscegenation"

Alcott's Paul Frere and the Limits of Brotherhood After Emancipation

In the years leading up to and during the Civil War, there were radical abolitionists who continued to champion the right to inter-racial marriage. Most prominent were the anti-slavery women of Massachusetts, who between 1838 and 1843 petitioned their state legislature to overturn the law banning inter-racial marriage as part of their effort to "obtain for . . . [blacks] equal civil and political rights and privileges with the whites."[1] They and their supporters stated publicly and persistently that marriage should be strictly a matter of personal preference.[2] A few radical abolitionists also argued not only that inter-marriage should be a right, but that inter-marriages between whites and blacks would be uplifting for the nation. In the beginning of 1863, for example, Louisa May Alcott published a story in the *Commonwealth*, an anti-slavery weekly newspaper based in Boston, that celebrated an inter-racial marriage for the way in which it began to open the racist eyes of the couple's community. That same year, Wendell Phillips went even further when he seemed to argue that people should seek out inter-marriage. He declared in a speech, "Remember this, the youngest of you; that, on the 4th of July, 1863, you heard a man say, that in the light of all history, in virtue of every page he ever read, he was an amalgamationist to the utmost extent." His only hope of the future, he explained, was "in that sublime mingling of races which is God's own method of civilizing and elevating the world."[3] One year later, in 1864, Moncure Daniel Conway argued similarly that because blacks have exactly those traits he viewed as deficient in the European race, namely "simple goodliness, kindliness, and affectionateness," "the mixture of the blacks and whites is good" for society.[4] While such statements were themselves patronizing, if not built on racist assumptions, they indicate that not everyone was opposed to inter-marriage.[5]

Most of the Northern middle class, however, believed that those who engaged or seemed to want to engage in "amalgamation" were violating not only the precepts of what was termed "the faculty of taste,"[6] but what one scientist termed "the natural repugnance between individuals of different kinds" or species.[7] That these beliefs were almost thoroughly naturalized in the North by the time of the Civil War is evidenced by the fact that they were mobilized there for political effect in the 1864 presidential election. In other words, enough people believed "amalgamation" was a violation of natural law that political operators could hope to tap that conviction on a wide scale. And so it was that in the final days of 1863, two New York Democrats intent on foiling Abraham Lincoln's bid for reelection wrote and published anonymously in New York City a seventy-two page pamphlet entitled *Miscegenation: The Theory of the Blending of the Races, Applied to the American White Man and Negro*, in which they posed as Republicans who advocated inter-racial marriage between "the white man" and "Negro," or what the authors named "miscegenation," as "indispensable to a progressive humanity."[8] The aim of David Goodman Croly, an editor of the New York *World*, one of the most influential Democratic journals in the country and the principal organ of the Democrats in New York, and George Wakeman, a reporter there, was to attribute to all Republicans the supposed views of the abolitionists, of whom it was so often claimed, as we have seen, that they wholeheartedly supported inter-marriage. "[B]ehold!" Croly and Wakeman write, "the great Republican party has merged into the little abolition party" (50). The pamphlet culminates in a chapter on "Miscegenation in the Presidential Contest" in which Croly and Wakeman argue that a vote for Lincoln and his party is a vote for "miscegenation."

The *Miscegenation* pamphlet was extremely popular, eventually going through a second printing and garnering lots of attention in the press both across the political spectrum and across the country.[9] It addressed a question on the minds of many in the wake of the newly made Emancipation Proclamation. As posed in the pamphlet, that question was: "What will you do with the negro when he is free?" (53). Croly and Wakeman's answer to this pressing question was that "When the President proclaimed Emancipation he proclaimed also the mingling of the races. The one follows the other as surely as noonday follows sunrise" (49). Of course, Croly and Wakeman did not really want "mingling" to occur, nor did they necessarily believe that it would. What they are implying here is that the Republicans are to be reviled for supposedly opening the door to the possibility. As we have seen, the anti-abolitionists had used such rhetoric against the Garrisonians in the 1830s. More recently, the Democrats had already attacked Lincoln as a supporter of inter-racial marriage in June 1858, following his "house divided" speech in Springfield, Illinois, in which Lincoln argued for arresting the further spread of slavery and for its ultimate extinction. As Lincoln noted in his first debate against Stephen A. Douglas for the Illinois senate seat, Douglas had inferred from that speech that Lincoln must thus mean to "set the negroes and white people to marrying one another."[10] Lincoln felt compelled to devote time in four of his seven debates with Douglas to refuting this charge: "I am not, nor ever have been," he argued, "in favor of bringing about in any way the social and political equality of the white and black races. . . . I am not nor ever have been in favor of making voters or jurors of negroes, nor of qualifying them to hold office, nor to intermarry with white people."[11] Now, in 1864, with emancipation a reality, Croly and Wakeman carefully spell out the logic behind the fear that there might be a link between the "social and political equality of the white and black races":

To free them [the slaves] is to recognize their equality with the white man. They are to compete with the white man in all spheres of labor. They are to receive wages. They are to provide for themselves. Therefore they will have the opportunity to rise to wealth and high position. Said a speaker at the Cooper Institute, in New York: "If the time ever comes when a majority of the people of this State desires a negro Governor, and elect him as such, I believe he ought to be Governor." It was a statement that commended itself to the common sense of the audience, and they did well to applaud. And the argument goes further. If a white woman shall prefer this black Governor, or any black man of wealth or distinction, for her husband, rather than an ignorant or drunken white man, she certainly ought to have him. (50–51)

With the possible riches born of political equality and thus economic opportunity, black men, it is feared, would also achieve "distinction." And insofar as "a white woman" will find such "distinction" attractive, especially when compared to "the ignorant or drunken white man," she will presumably marry the black man. After all, what woman with social aspirations or simply with the quintessential American admiration for a job well done, would not want to marry a governor? Referring to Lincoln's enlistment of black troops in the Union army, Croly and Wakeman argue similarly that because equality in the army is another form of political equality, it will also lead to social mingling and, from there, to "miscegenation": "If he [the black man] may fight to protect our homes and firesides, why may he not enjoy a cordial association in our families and social circles? Shall the fair, whose smiles are the proverbial reward of bravery, discriminate as to color where merit is equal?" (51). Again, where new opportunities allow black men to demonstrate equal "merit," who is to say "the fair" won't fall in love with them? Croly and Wakeman count on their readers to see both the reasonableness of these speculations and yet to register such disgust at the possibility that they will hopefully aim to hinder the Republicans from supposedly starting the country down this path. The degree to which Croly and Wakeman's logic resonated can be measured, in part, by the fact that Democrats took to calling the Emancipation Proclamation, the "Miscegenation Proclamation."[12]

One month after the *Miscegenation* pamphlet appeared, Ohio Congressman Samuel Sullivan Cox was as unaware as most were that the pamphlet was a hoax. He attacked it during a congressional debate on the Freedman's Bureau bill as a means of buttressing his entirely similar argument that the political equality that would presumably be sought by the Freedman's Bureau would be a step on the way to inter-mixing.[13] His critical remarks about the pamphlet and its supposedly Republican authors became widely known when the Democrats printed Cox's speech in pamphlet form as *Miscegenation or Amalgamation: Fate of the Freedman* (1864). Cox argued that the Republicans

used to deny, whenever it was charged, that they favored black citizenship; yet now they are favoring free black suffrage in the District of Columbia, and will favor it wherever in the South they need it for their purposes. . . . The Senate of the United States is discussing African equality in street cars. All these things . . . culminating in this grand plunder scheme of a department of freedmen, ought to convince us that that party is moving steadily forward to perfect social equality of black and white, and can only end in this detestable doctrine of—Miscegenation![14]

Of course, Cox was arguing precisely along the same lines as Croly and Wakeman, sure that black suffrage and "equality in street cars" would result in "perfect social equality" and therefore in this "detestable doctrine of—Miscegenation."

That this perceived link between political and social equality was the precise issue at stake in the pamphlet that resonated with readers is indicated by two political cartoons issued in order to capitalize on it. The two prints spell out in great detail the feared link between political and social equality and, in both, the term "miscegenation" is used as a scare tactic against the Republicans in signaling a sexual and marital outcome of that link. In *Political Caricature No. 2. Miscegenation or the Millennium of Abolitionism* (1864) (Figure 16), Lincoln and his fellow Republicans are attacked on the basis that their efforts as abolitionists will lead to "miscegenation." The print depicts several clusters of people in a park. In the far left section of the print, a black woman, Miss Dinah Arabella Aranintha Squash, is being presented to Abraham Lincoln by abolitionist Senator Charles Sumner, the latter of whom firmly holds the hand of his "dear friend." It appears Miss Dinah Squash has embellished her commonplace slave name (or at least this minstrel version of one) with what she perceives to be elegant English names but which become laughably garish when strung together next to the name she shares with a vegetable. Lincoln, the only one of the three to remove his hat in deference, says, "I shall be proud to number among my intimate friends any member of the Squash family, especially the little Squashes." That there are little Squashes is surprising considering that *Miss* Squash is not married, until the reader finds that despite her respectable attire, she, in her words, "gallevant[s] 'round wid de white gemmen!," enjoying "de hebenly Miscegenation times," a declaration punctuated with telling giggles. To the right, in the foreground of the center of the print, and yet less prominent in the frame than the Lincoln grouping, a man named Horace enjoys ice cream with a black female companion. Horace Greeley was

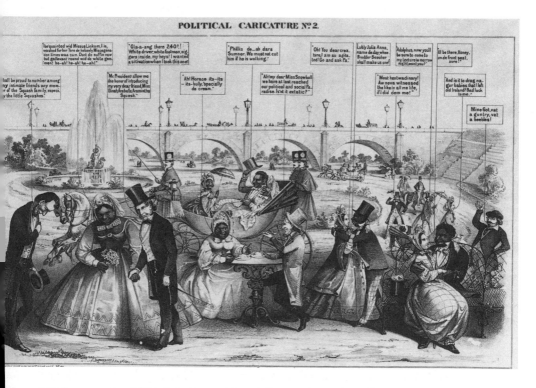

16. Unknown artist, *Political Caricature No. 2. Miscegenation or the Millennium of Abolitionism*, 1864. Photo courtesy Prints and Photographs Division of the Library of Congress.

the abolitionist editor of the New York *Tribune*. Croly and Wakeman had declared in their pamphlet that Greeley's "devotion to the negro race" was the result of Greeley's own romantic love for them (27). He is similarly attacked here for his positive review of the *Miscegenation* pamphlet, in which he wrote that "If a white man pleases to marry a black woman, the mere fact that she is black gives no one a right to interfere or prevent or set aside such marriage."[15] Greeley is made to say to his companion, "Ah! my dear Miss Snowball we have at last reached our political and social Paradise. Isn't it extatic?" The Democrats here proclaim him stupid by having him term a black woman as white as snow and thus perhaps, if one considers this metaphorically, as pure. Consider that she is calling him by his first name and is perhaps even declaring her sexual desire for white-colored men when she responds to his conflation of "political" and "social Paradise" with "its bully, 'specially de cream." Behind Greeley, also in the center of the print, a black couple, the only intraracial one in the print, is riding in a carriage with a white driver and two white footmen. The father lifts his hat to Charles Sumner, noting to his wife, "Phillis de-ah dars Sumner. We must not cut him if he is walking." The depiction of the carriage and its occupants indicates that the Republicans will usher in a world not just of racial equality, but one with a flipped race hierarchy, where blacks have more money and social status than whites. Indeed blacks would have the ability to make or break the lives of whites, one of whom is here left walking—even though a senator—while the blacks ride. As Croly and Wakeman also assumed, the rise of black men, say to the position of governor, will surely result in the fall of white men. The repulsive nature of the situation is registered in the print by the white driver who reminds the print's audience that blacks are not really gentlemen and ladies but rather "niggers." To the right of this grouping, two inter-racial couples embrace. One black man pleads to the white woman pressed up against him, "Lubly Julia Anna, name de day, when Brodder Beecher shall make us one!" She replies, "Oh! You dear creature. I am so agitated! Go and ask Pa." The Reverend Henry Ward Beecher, or "Brodder Beecher," was the former editor of the abolitionist *Independent*, the same paper that had recently, like Greeley, declared of the *Miscegenation* pamphlet that if a black and a white chose to marry, it was "nobody's business but their own."[16] A prominent Brooklyn minister and abolitionist, Beecher had been accused by Theodore Tilton in a sensational and much publicized trial in 1860 of having an adulterous affair with Tilton's wife Elizabeth. That Beecher would supposedly marry a white woman to a black man is thus supposedly just one more indication of his aberrant sexual views. Next to them, another white woman sits on the lap of a black man while reminding him, "Adolphus, now you'll be sure to come to my lecture tomorrow night, wont [*sic*] you?" She has been identified by scholars as Anna Dickinson.[17] Twenty years old in 1864, Dickinson was one of the more popular abolitionist orators. She was rumored to have authored the *Miscegenation* pamphlet or at least to support it.[18] When she was late to make a speech at the Cooper Institute, the New York correspondent for the London *Times* repeated the Democratic gossip that in order to "to pacify her audience," ads for the miscegenation pamphlet "were handed round for their perusal—a circumstance which suggested to many that the lecturer was either author of the book or peculiarly interested in its sale."[19] That the other white woman near her in the print is named "Julia *Anna*" (emphasis added) would have helped the audience make the connection. While this portion of the print makes the once more typical point that black men will couple with white women in the post-emancipation world, the print in its entirety depicts inter-racial coupling also occurring between white men and black women.[20] Finally, to the far most right, representatives of various white immigrant groups comment disfavorably on this racial chaos that has overrun the world, culminating in the parting conclusion at the edge of the frame, "Mine Got, vat a guntry, vat a beebles!"

Lincoln is thus situated squarely within the terrain of a new world where, now that class positions have presumably been reversed by the Republicans' success in achieving political equality for blacks, "miscegenation" is free to flourish. Because readers typically read from left to right, they would most likely conclude that Lincoln's political acknowledgment of blacks as freemen and fellow workers has set off a chain of events whereby the reversal of racialized economic fortunes, depicted in the left and background of the print, lead to the inter-racial couplings in the front and right of the print. But the print also makes the point that Lincoln's allies have made certain political changes precisely because they desire to effect sexual inter-racial liaisons. If Lincoln no longer employs Miss Squash, this is because her "white gemmen" friends, undoubtedly also Republican, have freed her from the necessity of earning a wage. And if Horace Greeley has insisted that marriage is a private matter, this is because he defines ecstasy as flirting with black women. In this way, too, the print attempts to persuade its readers that abolitionism will lead to miscegenation and that the Republicans must thus be opposed. That the "blacks" are grossly caricatured in the print and the "whites" are not, a tactic Clay had used to make race in his prints, heightens the sense that "miscegenation" would be a truly disgusting outcome of abolition.

In *Political Caricature. No. 4. The Miscegenation Ball* (1864) (Figure 17), a

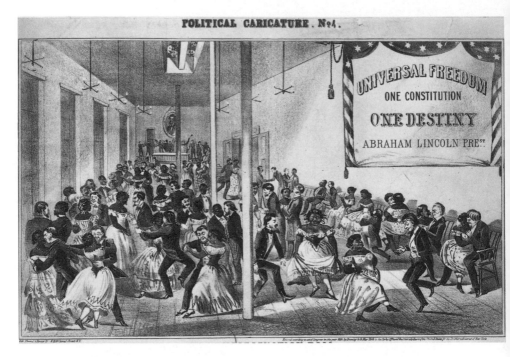

17. Unknown artist, *Political Caricature No. 4. The Miscegenation Ball*, 1864. Photo courtesy Prints and Photographs Division of the Library of Congress.

connection is also forged between political and social equality. The idea for the print was born after the Democratic press charged that a Lincoln rally attended by both blacks and whites was actually for the purpose of creating, as the *World* asserted on September 23, 1864, in the title of an article on the rally, "Miscegenation in Earnest." Part of what the *World* wrote is incorporated into the print itself (not shown above), the bottom of which reads:

The Miscegenation Ball at the Headquarters of the Lincoln Central Campaign Club, Corner of Broadway and Twenty Third Street New York Sept. 22d. 1864 being a perfect fac simile of the room &c. &c. (From the New York World Sept. 23d. 1864.) No sooner were the formal proceedings and speeches hurried through with, than the room was cleared for a "negro ball," which then and there took place! Some members of the "Central Lincoln Club" left the room before the mystical and circling rites of languishing glance and mazy dance commenced. But that MANY remained is also true. This fact WE CERTIFY, *that on the floor during the progress of the ball were many of the accredited leaders of the Black Republican party,* thus testifying their faith by works in the hall and headquarters of their political gathering. There were Republican OFFICE-HOLDERS, and prominent men of various degrees, and at least one PRESIDENTIAL ELECTOR ON THE REPUBLICAN TICKET.

Following the anti-abolitionists of the 1830s, the Democrats raise here the Puritan tradition of a Covenant of Works when they declare that the ball is the Republican means of "testifying to their faith by works." They reason that if the Republicans are like the Puritans in believing that only good works will testify to their faith, in this case to their faith in race equality, then they must inter-marry to prove that faith, otherwise they are not being sincere or even Christian. That the Republicans are supposedly more interested in the dancing than in the political principles that presumably lead to the dancing—they "hurried through" the speeches so as to start the "negro ball"—indicates that any such testimony on their part would be wholly sincere. Indeed, according to the Democrats' logic, the desire to enter into lascivious proximity to black women may have motivated the Republicans' political views. That this might be the case is indicated by the depiction of the dance as sexually pleasurable. White men dance with and embrace big-bosomed black women, many of whom lift up their daring off-the-shoulder dresses to reveal their ankles, a shocking sight at the time. That sex will result is also proclaimed by the embraces that continue off the dance floor and onto the sidelines, about which an advertisement for the print in the *Day-Book* said that the Republicans were "on the sofas . . . squeezing and ogling thick-lipped Phillises."[21] This print thus seems to be a direct descendant of E. W. Clay's 1839 *Amalgamation Waltz* (Figure 6) and of his 1845 *An Amalgamation Polka* (Figure 18), both part of the series of lithographs discussed in the previous two chapters in which Clay makes the case that abolitionism will be followed by inter-racial dancing and ultimately by what was then still termed "amalgamation." (Note that in the earlier of these two Clay prints, only white women dance with black partners and that, by 1845, Clay shows both white men and women dancing with black partners.) Finally, many of the white men in the print are bearded, as Lincoln was at the time, so as to pictorially make the point that, as stated in the *World*, "at least one Presidential Elector on the Republican Ticket" attended the ball. To the right of the stage, a banner proclaims, "Universal Freedom, One Constitution, One Destiny. Abraham Lincoln Prest." Lincoln's stance on

18. E. W. Clay, *An Amalgamation Polka, 1845.* Courtesy Nancy Burkett.

slavery is linked to inter-racial sex and perhaps to procreative inter-racial sex insofar as blacks and whites will share "One Destiny." The Democrats meant to turn the country against the Republicans by declaring that Lincoln's party has thus gone too far in advocating political equality because there might be these kind of social and even biological results.

The *Miscegenation* pamphlet reminds readers of all the most popular reasons voiced in the previous five years that black political equality must not coincide with social equality with whites and thus with the ultimate signifier of social equality: marriage. They thus begin *Miscegenation* with the by then largely debunked assertion that all humans share a "common father" (1). They then devote chapter 1, "Physiological Equality of the White and Colored Races," to supporting this claim. They argue that "The teachings of physiology as well as the inspiration of Christianity settle the question that all the tribes which inhabit the earth were originally derived from one type." They remark that "the most popular books" have pointed to skull shape, skin color, and "structural peculiarities" as evidence of "the unity of the [human] race" (3). They proceed in the chapter to cite the work of several well-known scientists, particularly James Cowles Prichard (1786–1848). Prichard's books were extremely popular. His *Researches into the Physical History of Man* was expanded and reprinted several times between 1813 and 1847. In his attempt at a popularized version of the ideas outlined there, *The Natural History of Man: Comprising Inquiries into the Modifying Influence of Physical and Moral Agencies on the Different Tribes of the Human Family* (1843), Prichard argued, as correctly characterized in the pamphlet, that "it is probable that all mankind are the offspring of one family" (quoted on lviii).[22] From here, Croly and Wakeman will go on to argue not only that inter-racial sex is natural—for the definition of species is that its members can and will procreate—but that inter-racial mixing is highly beneficial. Of the ten conclusions listed at the end of the *Miscegenation* pamphlet, the first is that the races comprise "one family," from which Croly and Wakeman deduce, in conclusion six, that "the mingling of diverse races is a positive benefit to the progeny" and, in conclusion ten, that "in the millennial future, the most perfect and highest type of manhood will not be white or black, but brown, or colored" (65).

That Croly and Wakeman base their entire mock argument in favor of "miscegenation" on monogenesis, the idea that whites and Negroes share a "common" origin or "father," was clear to readers, as evidenced by a response to the pamphlet by Dr. John H. Van Evrie of New York, the editor of the weekly *Day-Book*, a Democratic paper. Van Evrie wrote a pamphlet in response to *Miscegenation* with the same cover, number of pages and chapters, as well as its own neologism. He begins *Subgenation: The Theory of the Normal Relations of the Races; An Answer to "Miscegenation"* (1864) with the passage from Croly and Wakeman on this point that "The teachings of physiology as well as the inspiration of Christianity" prove "the tribes which inhabit the earth were originally derived from one type." Van Evrie notes that "it is this premise, thus audaciously assumed, which is the foundation of his [Croly's] whole argument." "The theory... that there is but a single human race, and that all man-kind, of whatever color, or mental or moral powers, are derived from it, is the very foundation and starting point of the entire Abolition and Miscegenetic doctrines."[23]

Croly and Wakeman's approach seems to stem from their awareness that radical abolitionists used the theory of monogenesis to argue that if whites and blacks shared one creation, one "common father," then blacks must be the same species as whites and therefore be equally as human and as deserving of human rights. In 1861, for example, the *Anti-Slavery Standard* published a review of *L'Unité de l'Espèce Humaine,* by M. de Quatrefarges, professor of natural history and ethnology at the Museum of Natural History in Paris. Quatrefarges declared that all of mankind was one species. Any differences between the races, he claimed, was purely a result of environmental conditions.[24] Abolitionists also cited the British ethnologist Dr. R. G. Latham, the French geographer Dumont d'Urville, Buffon, and Alexander von Humboldt. It was Humboldt's work on human species that prompted Charles Sumner to write that "Science is enlisted for the Equal Rights of All."[25] Only the rare radical abolitionist, however, made the leap from monogenesis to actually advocating inter-marriage. Sumner was one of those rare few. Five years after the appearance of the *Miscegenation* pamphlet, he gave a lecture in which he concluded that there must be a "blending" of the European and the African: "The pioneer intelligence of Europe going to blend with the gentleness of Africa will be a blessed sight, but not more blessed than the gentleness of Africa returning to blend with the same intelligence at home."[26] Croly and Wakeman would have the public believe that such a leap, as made in their own pamphlet, was common among the Republicans.

The invocation of Prichard and numerous other scientists—including Dr. John William Draper, author of an 1856 book on human physiology and president of the medical school at the University of the City of New York, Dutch anatomist Camper, and Buffon—gave the *Miscegenation* pamphlet scientific clout at a time when science had gained vast amounts of authority to determine what race is.[27] When it was revealed in the United States shortly after the presidential election that the pamphlet was a hoax, the New York *World* noted that the public had been compelled to take the pamphlet seriously because it was "full of scientific facts and learned questions which gave it an air of great plausibility."[28] And even as the paper that broke the story in London that the pamphlet was a hoax disparaged the *kind* of science invoked by the question of miscegenation, it made the point that the pamphlet was received as a scientific document:

The Miscegenation question turns out to have been a hoax of two gentlemen of New York, who little thought when they started it that learned professors and doctors, anthropologists and ethnologists, and all the class who go groping about in the dark believing themselves the only true lights of science, would have given Miscegenation a literature of its own.[29]

Of course, Croly and Wakeman were really aiming to marshal scientific evidence *against* inter-marriage insofar as they were aiming to convince readers of the opposite views to those they were pretending to advocate. Croly and Wakeman thus quote only those scientists who believed in monogenesis when, by 1864, and as discussed in the previous chapter, the so-called American school of ethnology had had much success in refuting the theory of monogenesis in favor of polygenesis. In other words, Croly and Wakeman quote those scientists whose views on the origins of humankind had already been devalued in the hopes of convincing readers that the Republican support of inter-racial mixing was built on false reasoning. Thus Croly and Wakeman do not, for example, quote Josiah C. Nott. Nott had argued in his 1843 article "The Mulatto a Hybrid—probable extermination of the two races if the Whites and Blacks are allowed to intermarry" that mulattoes have "been produced by a violation of nature's laws."[30] Instead, in their second chapter, "The Superiority of Mixed Races," Croly and Wakeman argue the opposite of Nott's conclusion: "If any fact is well established in history," they write, "it is that the miscegenetic or mixed races are much superior, mentally, physically, and morally, to those pure or unmixed" (8–9). As evidence, they note that the various nations of Europe are great because of their various degrees of inter-mixture, when, of course, the various nations of Europe were not considered different races at all. As one reviewer noted of the imagined single author of the pamphlet:

He argues about one thing and then jumps to the conclusion that this proves something very different and contradictory. He tries to convince us that because two and two make four, therefore two and three make four, also . . . that because the blending of certain races is beneficial, therefore the blending of the white and black races is "essential to American progress." This is the simplest nonsense, if it be not a trick to delude the thoughtless. All through the pamphlet we find the same sophistry.[31]

At a time when polygenesism was in vogue, Croly and Wakeman counted on their invocation of the largely debunked theory of monogenesis and the obviously inappropriate parallels they drew to Europe to convince readers that the supposed Republican belief in the benefits of "miscegenation" was a dangerous one because racial mixing meant violating a species difference and thus one of Nature's laws. That this approach worked is again evidenced by Van Evrie's response. In *Subgenation*, he countered their use of Prichard with Louis Agassiz's work as evidence that blacks and whites are separate species, from which he could conclude that "there should be severe laws passed punishing any sexual intercourse between the races" so that there will be no "weaker or hybrid race." "Mingling," he insisted, "leads to social decay and national suicide."[32]

While Croly and Wakeman's strategy required readers to infer, as Van Evrie had, the unnaturalness and dangers of race mixing, other Democrats were carefully spelling out very overtly all of the ways implicit in the *Miscegenation* pamphlet that breaching the supposed species divide was a monstrous act. In "God Bless Abraham Lincoln!: A Solemn Discourse by a Local Preacher" (circa 1863), the same terms used by Edgar Allan Poe in "The Murders in the Rue Morgue" are employed to argue that inter-racial sex is abhorrent because it breaches the species divide. The Democratic author of this pamphlet reports that Republicans are plotting to kill or castrate all Southern white men and then breed Northern white men with black women and Southern white women with black men. Any white women who resisted would be "flung out" for "the use of the unbridled and unbroken-in Black Ourang-Outangs," who would "deal with them according to their natural instincts." As in Poe's tale, an equivalence is made between black men and orangutans as a means of emphasizing not only the imagined animal-like nature of lustful black men, but the supposed species divide that accounts for that animalistic behavior. The same pamphlet contains a play that also refers to black men as orangutans. Entitled "Uncle Tom's Drama," it depicts white women with "snow-white bosoms, that ever throbbed in angelic purity" suffering "untold outrage, woe and wrong" at the hands of "black Ourang-Outangs" who use them to "gratify their brutal instincts." All of the white children of the South are then murdered with their "brains dashed out and bodies ruthlessly gashed and bleeding," while their fathers are "chained erect" to "behold the heart-rending outrages perpetrated" on the "Murdered Innocents."[33] If black men are really, as this pamphlet argues, orangutans, then sex between them and white women is across the species divide, which for most readers would mark inter-racial sex as monstrous and unnatural, as evidenced by the rape and murder with which the pamphlet associates it. Croly and Wakeman's readers would have extrapolated similar visions of orangutans and other monstrosities from the authors' ostensible championing of monogenesis and the leap then made in the pamphlet to championing "miscegenation."

Croly and Wakeman also made extensive use of the commonplace idea that racial mixing happens at the level of the blood. Chapter 3 of the *Miscegenation* pamphlet is entitled "The Blending of Diverse Bloods essential to American Progress," and chapter 17, "The Bloods of All Nations find their Level." Here, in arguing for a "blending of diverse bloods," they do sound remarkably like the radical abolitionists they are attempting to imitate. For blood was the means by which the few radical abolitionists who favored widescale race mixing imagined that the best qualities of "the African race" would be "infused" into the "Caucasian." This was sometimes referred to implicitly with the rhetoric of "mingling," a term through which both those in favor of and those disgusted by inter-racial sex and reproduction asserted that it was a biological event that happened on the level of human fluids. James Russell Lowell went this route in 1845 when he wrote:

We have never had any doubt that the African race was intended to introduce a new element of civilization, and that the Caucasian would be benefited greatly by an infusion of its gentler and less selfish qualities. The Caucasian mind, which seeks always to govern at whatever cost, can never come to so beautiful or Christian a height of civilization, as with a mixture of those seemingly humbler but truly more noble qualities which teach it to obey.[34]

For Lowell, "infusion" and "mixture" describe the means by which "the Caucasian mind" will be elevated. Although it is not clear if he necessarily means by a physical injection of blood, other abolitionists were clear on that point. In his addresses of 1854 and 1855, for example, Theodore Parker pointed specifically to the role of blood when he argued that "strong, real, Anglo-Saxon blood" needed to be mixed with the other American races "just enough to temper" it, thereby "furnish[ing] a new composite tribe, far better I trust than the old."[35] In 1862, Moncure Daniel Conway wrote an article for the Boston *Commonwealth* in which he argued that blacks have fertile imaginations and a warmth that whites must physically incorporate through blood mixture: "In our practical, anxious, unimaginative country, we need an infusion of this fervid African element, so child-like, exuberant, and hopeful."[36] For these radical abolitionists, just as for most Americans, racial differences were physical differences located in the blood. The only divergence in views was that, for the radical abolitionists, these physical differences could and should be bridged for the good of whites and the nation.

To make the case convincingly that a mixture of bloods is superior to "pure" blood, Croly and Wakeman draw upon the terminology of "grafting" and "crossing" used in horticulture and animal husbandry, as these are fields in which plants and animals are often hybridized to create superior traits. "All that is needed to make us the finest race on earth," they insist, "is to engraft upon our stock the negro element which providence has placed by our side on this continent. Of all the rich treasures of blood vouchsafed to us, that of the negro is the most precious, because it is unlike any other that enters into the composition of our national life" (11). They add that "a continuance of progress can only be obtained through a judicious crossing of diverse elements" (14). Without mixture, "The white man is going to seed; the black man is adding vigor and freshness to the trunk" (35). Mid-nineteenth-century readers, even urban ones, could be expected to understand, if not the mechanics, at least the importance of hybridizing plants and animals for longevity, superior yields, and other improvements. That Croly and Wakeman were using the terms of hybridization thus lent their argument an air of scientific authority. They sound perfectly reasonable, on one level, when they employ the principles of plant hybridization to human beings. "By crossing and improvement of different varieties, the strawberry," they reason, "or other garden fruit, is brought nearest to perfection, in sweetness, size, and fruitfulness." So, too, then, is made "a ripe and complete woman, possessing the best elements of two sources of parentage" (36). Of course, their readers would have recognized that such an argument mistakenly posits whites and Negroes as merely separate "varieties" when instead they were usually believed to be separate species, Croly and Wakeman's insistence at the outset of the pamphlet that all of the races comprise one family to the contrary. Indeed, that Croly and Wakeman here posit "the negro element" as a "rich treasure . . . of blood" is undoubtedly meant to remind readers that blacks are more than a separate "variety." And thus once the rhetoric of "grafting" and "crossing" what is here termed different "blood" reminded readers of the supposed species distinctions between the races, they would feel fully justified in imagining that, as Nott argued, mulattoes have "been produced by a violation of nature's laws." Indeed, it is precisely the invocation of blood that makes race mixing a violation at the deepest, because fully internal, level.

Croly and Wakeman also address the issues of taste and beauty in the *Miscegenation* pamphlet. They argue quite extensively in their mode as pretend Republicans that "negroes" are particularly attractive. In a chapter on "The Miscegenetic Ideal of Beauty in Woman," for example, they ask, "In what does beauty consist? . . . Her cheeks must be rounded, and have a tint of sun, her lips must be pouting, her teeth white and regular, her eyes large and bright; her hair must curl about her head. . . . But all these characteristics belong, in a somewhat exaggerated degree, to the negro girl" (36). Of course, for readers, the "exaggerated degree" made all the difference in the world. While those known as "mulattoes" and "quadroons" were often perceived as very beautiful at the time, it was their supposedly European traits that were appreciated. Recall Harriet Beecher Stowe's description of Cassy in *Uncle Tom's Cabin*: "Her straight, well-formed nose, her finely-cut mouth, and the graceful contour of her head and neck, showed that she must once have been beautiful."[37] Conversely, thicker lips and a thicker nose, as well as darker skin and tightly curled hair, were viewed as specifically black traits and as unattractive. Thus, these traits were meant to be distasteful to cultivated whites. Croly and Wakeman knew full well, indeed counted on the fact, that most members of the middle class believed that attraction to such traits was a sign of very bad taste, as stated in countless newspaper articles from the same year that also linked the issue of inter-racial marriage to taste. For example, the New York *Journal of Commerce* would declare of the Republicans in the wake of the *Miscegenation* pamphlet that "To persons of cultivated minds, refinement of feeling, and purity of taste, this [Republican] desire for black companionship in the household and in the endearing relations of married life seems strange and inexplicable."[38] And in an article "Practical Miscegenation in New York," the Democratic New York *World* quoted a letter written to the Philadelphia *Press* about two society women who, presumably under the influence of Republicans, supposedly had relations with black men, even parading with them down a busy avenue. The paper commented that it was not surprising to find women "with tastes so depraved," but it was "astonishing" that they were "women of wealth and refinement."[39] While these articles do not overtly link taste to beauty, it is implied that part of what makes the idea of "black companionship" distasteful is that blacks are ugly. Croly and Wakeman thus aimed to raise the idea that the Republicans have bad taste as a means of turning the public against them.

As we saw in the previous chapter, scientists had recently helped naturalize taste as instinct. And so it was that when the *New York Times* attempted to sum up the precise issue that was causing so much hysteria around the *Miscegenation* pamphlet in the midst of an overwhelmingly destructive civil war, they focused on "beauty" and "natural instinct":

We are in the middle of a gigantic war, with an enormous debt accumulating . . . nearly a million of men . . . in the field before the enemy, and death reaping them every . . . hour, with thousands of women weeping in their homes . . . with . . . most tremendous [political problems] . . . to solve, and all of a sudden our ears are assailed by writers of the two great parties, with cases of conscience, bursts of holy indignation, long wrangles on points of morals, points of psychology, points of ethnology, *and all about the possibility of the whites of this continent losing their admiration for their own women, repudiating the standard of beauty furnished them by natural instinct, and intermarrying with Negroes.*[40] (emphasis added)

The tone makes it clear that, for the author of this piece, there was no impos-

sibility, despite the seeming necessity of endless and even scientific speculation, that "the whites of this continent" would lose the good taste for white
beauty the *New York Times* equates with "natural instinct" and that had thus
far kept "whites" and "Negroes" from "intermarrying." That this should even
be an issue as men die and debt accumulates seemed ridiculous. The *New York
Times* insisted that "the notions of the Caucasian race, and particularly of the
Anglo-Saxon branch of it, on the subject of personal beauty during the last
2,000 years were so set . . . it was not at all likely they would undergo any
material change during the approaching Presidential campaign."[41] Implicit in
these comments is the idea that if a "Caucasian" married a "Negro," he or she
was not only guilty of bad taste but an aberration of Nature itself. Readers of
the *Miscegenation* pamphlet would have brought this idea to bear on their
reading of it. And so we see in *Subgenation* Van Evrie insisting that inter-racial
sex was "the gross violation of natural instincts."[42] The purported Republican
admiration of "Negro" beauty in the pamphlet meant the party was attempting to go against human instincts so fundamental that these instincts had
shaped two thousand years of history.

The *New York Times'* confidence level in taste as a means of ensuring
intra-racial attraction was so great that the paper felt free to make an extended
joke about it. The *Times* reported with tongue firmly in cheek that a group of
people, afraid the Republicans had lost their good taste in advocating "intermixture," convened and resolved that "there was but one way of preventing
this horrible consummation, and that was by the circulation of tracts, and of
plaster casts, calculated to enlighten the public as to the probable effects of an
intermixture of races, and to recall to their minds the standard of beauty, both
male and female, which existed at the time of the Revolution." It was reported, the *Times* added, that "an Italian gentleman, whose name we are not permitted to mention, has been engaged to furnish the association with 50,000
busts of the Medicean Venus and Apollo Belvidere, at one cent a piece, for
distribution."[43] The *Times* wanted to insist that attempts to school "the
Anglo-Saxon branch" in good taste are ridiculous because the ideal of beauty
that ensured intra-racial attraction and thereby presumably allowed the
Founding Fathers to safely instill liberal democracy "at the time of the Revolution" could not possibly have changed. The *Times*, too, then, saw taste as a
kind of instinct in that it was incorruptible. Indeed, that these ideas could not
have changed is precisely what allows the *Times* to make a joke about tracts
and plaster casts. The article did not elicit a sympathetic response to its sar-
casm, however. In a follow-up article, the author was forced to apologize for
taking what many found too "jocular" a tone.[44] It seems some readers did not

want to joke about the possibility of massive inter-racial attraction or about the possible difficulties of schooling "Caucasians" in the proper taste if, in fact, taste was not instinctual. These were, for many, serious matters.

So long as blacks were deemed physically unattractive, it could be argued that they were of a different and lesser sort than whites and thus undeserving of political equality. Louisa May Alcott recognized as much, as illustrated by her short story "M. L.," in which Alcott champions black rights by countering the standard taste argument. She shows that inter-racial marriages can occur between two genteel people with the good taste to recognize each other's attractiveness. That the story was first rejected by the abolitionist *Atlantic Monthly* before finding a home three years later says something about how risky such a tack was. But for Alcott, precisely because they dismantle the standard ideas of taste, inter-racial marriages are a necessary step in overcoming society's racism. The story centers around Claudia, an orphaned white woman living alone. Claudia is "gifted with beauty, opulence and position," but lives on a "Mont Blanc of cool indifference" when it comes to suitors, refusing to "make a worldly marriage or . . . to cheat her hunger into a painted feast."[45] Upon meeting the talented singer Paul Frere, she falls passionately in love for the first time, as unaware as the reader is at this point that Paul was born of a "Quadroon" slave mother (17). On the eve of their nuptials, Jessie Snowden, a jealous friend of Claudia's who once loved Paul unrequitedly, forces Paul to reveal his history. It turns out the self-inflicted scar on his hand is meant to hide the initials "M. L." that were once branded there to mark him as the property of one Maurice Lecroix. Unfortunately for Jessie, this cruel attempt to end Paul and Claudia's relationship fails. For while Paul fully expects Claudia's "abhorrence" after he has revealed his family history to her (17), she still loves him, even as "all the prejudices born of her position and strengthened by her education . . . assailed her with covert skill" (23). Despite prejudices that Alcott is careful to depict here as learned and not innate, Claudia proceeds to marry Paul. And despite the racism they first experience, Claudia finds great happiness as Paul's spouse. The narrator reports that the marriage transforms Claudia and leads her to a better society. The experience of being the target of prejudice is said to have "taught . . . [Claudia] the value of true friendship, showed her the poverty of old beliefs, the bitterness of old desires" (26). In short, she and her husband do not descend into the kind of depravity that the Philadelphia *Press* imagined of inter-racial couples. On the contrary, Claudia is lifted out of her life of meaningless parties and into loftier ambitions. Paul's own goodness makes her regret that her years have not been "fairer in aspirations, fuller of duties, richer in good deeds " (9). The narrator also reports that "In this new world . . . [Claudia] found a finer rank than any she had left, for men whose righteous lives were their renown, whose virtues their estate, were peers of this realm, whose sovereign was Truth, whose ministers were Justice and Humanity, whose subjects all 'who loved their neighbor better than themselves' " (27). Indeed, she and Paul are described as having made it to the Celestial City (27). Thus, when Claudia's old friends are ready to re-embrace her, she refuses, answering with the stipulation that forms the last line of the story: " 'Put off the old delusions that blind you to the light, and come up here with me' " (28). How these old friends are to get there is unstated but clear: either through engaging in the kind of inter-marriage that Claudia and Paul have or by embracing the inter-racial romantic love of others. These are the only ways that Paul can claim the political and social status of brother that comprises his last name, Frere. "Brother" was the term around which the abolitionist movement had rallied since 1787 when, in England, the Committee to Abolish the Slave Trade invented the emblem of the supplicating, enchained slave with the motto, "Am I Not a Man and a Brother?"[46] For Alcott, the black man's complete acceptance by whites as a brother and thus political equal is contingent on his full acceptance by whites as a lover and husband as well.

Alcott knew the acceptance of blacks as brothers would require an end to the belief that an attraction to a black person is a sign of a white person's bad taste. This is evidenced by the fact that except for Paul's unmasking, the story is comprised not of actions, but mainly of long passages describing the nature and strength of Claudia's attraction as a kind of good taste. At the outset of the story, prior to seeing Paul, Claudia is thrilled by his beautiful singing. By thus separating one of Paul's most attractive qualities from his body and his racial ancestry, the latter of which has not yet been revealed to either Claudia or the reader, Alcott attempts to counter the idea that passion is kindled only by physical beauty so that what is later read as inter-racial love cannot be considered solely physical and therefore debased. Claudia loves Paul's singing and later Paul solely because she has an educated ear and a good aesthetic sensibility. When Claudia does see Paul, she does not think to consider that what is described as "bronze" skin is a sign of black ancestry, nor is the reader necessarily suspicious. Indeed, Paul's racial status is revealed to us much later, at the same time it is revealed to Claudia. Alcott makes skin so irrelevant that it fails to serve as a signifying text except in hindsight. Early in the story, Claudia's attraction is understood to be only of the loftiest kind.

But even as Paul's voice is meant to prove that there can be a kind of spiritual attraction between men and women, Alcott also insists that the passions thus ignited are physical ones. Indeed, the effects of Paul's singing on Claudia are described in terms akin to sexual arousal: "Claudia's thirsty spirit drank in the silver sounds that . . . wrapped her senses in a blissful calm. . . . [The voice's] . . . energy stirred her blood . . . for this mellow voice seemed to bring to her . . . the ardent breath of human lips" (3–4). Claudia's nerves and blood are affected in the same way the proximity of ardent lips would affect her. That his effect on her is a sexual one is made all the more clear by Paul's understanding that his is a "dangerous power" (8). He thus seldom agrees to sing to Claudia when they are alone. But again, Alcott is careful to explain that this physical passion is of the most honorable kind insofar as it is the means to a greater spiritual good. When listening to Paul sing, for example, Claudia listens "with drooping lids and lips apart . . . till on the surges of sweet sound her spirit floated far away into that blissful realm where human aspirations are fulfilled, where human hearts find their ideas, and renew again the innocent beliefs that made their childhood green" (10). In short, through Paul's voice, Claudia's spirit is renewed and revivified. Indeed, all of Paul's listeners are affected by "something nobler than . . . [they] knew . . . [E]ye met eye with rare sincerity, false smiles faded, vapid conversation died abashed" (3). Claudia experiences his song as "a melody devout and sweet as saintliest hymn, for it had touched the chords of that diviner self" (4). Alcott thus redefines passion as a kind of noble force that can strip society of its various facades and reintroduce Christian goodness. This allows her to insist through the later developments of her story that passion imagined as inter-racial is not debased. Precisely because readers will only experience Claudia's attraction as an inter-racial one in hindsight, they are forced to see that they already experienced as good taste what they might have otherwise dismissed as disgusting.[47]

Alcott also counters the argument that whites have an innate distaste for blacks by opposing the idea, still circulating as pervasively as it had in the 1830s, that whites cannot tolerate the proximity of blacks because of their supposedly foul odors. She does this by associating Paul with good smells, even if just metaphorically. For example, she writes of Paul's voice that "its passion thrilled along . . . [Claudia's] nerves like south winds full of an aroma fiery and sweet" (3). Paul is said at other points, too, to bring something akin to a sweet smell into Claudia's life: "Through the close-scented air of the conservatory where she lived a solitary plant, there came a new influence, like a breath of ocean air, both strengthening and sweet" (7). And when Paul sings to her on her twenty-sixth birthday, "the west wind turned its leafy orchestra to an airy symphony, and every odorous shrub and flower paid tribute to the happy hour" (10). Once Paul's ancestry is revealed, the reader is thus forced to unlink blackness from foul odors. Finally, after it is revealed that the coupling is inter-racial, we are informed that Claudia becomes "rich in the virtues that 'Smell sweet, and blossom in the dust' " (27). Paul's acceptance as a brother to white men and a husband to a white woman will not be precluded, Alcott argues, by some kind of innate distaste for how blacks supposedly smell.

The argument that blacks smell bad and that bad smells are physically intolerable was a large part of the miscegenation debate in 1864. A year after Alcott was combating the smell argument in "M. L.," rumors spread by the Democrats of a Republican inter-racial ball slandered the Republicans by emphasizing their perversity in tolerating the smell of black participants. Van Evrie closed a pamphlet in which he plagiarized the *World*'s account of the same "negro ball" depicted in *Political Caricature. No. 4. The Miscegenation Ball* with the following lines about the supposed ball:

Full a hundred and fifty of coal black wenches
   Tripped gracefully on the fantastic light toe;
Some on the platform and more on the benches,
   Each damsel squeezed tightly her Republican beau.
On the rostrum they sat, both ogling and teasing,
   And some waddled lazily around the hall;
The smell was so strong that it set us a sneezing
   So we started away from the Miscegen Ball.[48]

While the Republicans may enjoy dancing and flirting with "coal black wenches," the Democrats, Van Evrie argues, are physically unable to tolerate such transgressions themselves because of the "strong" smell, as evidenced by their "sneezing." That the Republicans not only tolerate but presumably find these smells enjoyable is what brands them a monstrous party. The Democrats also distributed a "Black Republican Prayer" in which they pose as Republicans asking God to make "the blessings of Emancipation extend throughout our unhappy lands and the illustrious sweet-scented Sambo nestle in the bosom of every Abolition woman. . . . Amen."[49] Here, if the inter-racial coupling that supposedly results of emancipation is abhorrent, it is abhorrent because "Abolition women" have laid aside their good taste, as evidenced by their willingness and perhaps even eagerness to take to their bosoms "Sambos" who are distinctly not "sweet-scented." The New York *Daily News* noted similarly that "delicately organized" white women are disgusted at the idea of contact with "Negroes" because "the negro's body is disagreeably unctious [*sic*], especially in warm weather, and when under the influence of the strong 'emotional' excitement so certainly produced on his animal nature if permitted to follow her with lascivious glances, and to lay lascivious hands upon her."[50] The smell of Negro men is directly linked to their imagined sexual potency and proclivity for sexual violence. White women should want to avoid them not only because they smell bad, but because they are sexual "animals." Smell, in short, is coded here as a warning to be heeded at all costs.

Sometimes the commentary on smell came in the form of seemingly offhand or throw-away asides. But even these did the work of disparaging inter-racial liaisons and of thereby naturalizing white intra-racial coupling in the process of criticizing the Republicans. In the pamphlet *What Miscegenation Is! and What We Are to Expect Now that Mr. Lincoln is Re-elected* (circa 1864–65), it was argued that the doctrine of miscegenation "was wafted from Maine to Oregon."[51] And the *World* reported on September 23, 1864, of the supposed Republican inter-racial ball that "In came the colored belles into the Twenty-third Street Republican headquarters, arrayed in all that gorgeous and highly colored, not to say highly scented, splendor for which the dark daughters of the Aethiop race are aesthetically distinguished."[52] If "miscegenation" was unnatural, it was unnatural because whites could not be expected to tolerate foul odors. Again, that this reasoning was central to the arguments that blacks should not be the "brothers" of whites is evidenced by Alcott's attempt to counter it.

Other prominent abolitionists stated their support of inter-marriage after Croly and Wakeman sent them advance copies of the *Miscegenation* pamphlet in the hope that they could use the abolitionists' responses in newspaper ads for the pamphlet. Angelina Grimké (Weld) responded, for example, that she and her sister Sarah were "wholly at one" with the ideas in the pamphlet.[53] Parker Pillsbury, editor of the *National Anti-Slavery Standard*, the official journal of the American Anti-Slavery Society, wrote to the authors that the pamphlet had "cheered and gladdened a winter morning." He expressed his hope that the divorce laws would be "so modified that new marriages among the American races might even now take place where unfruitful, or unhappy unions (or disunions) are recognized."[54] His paper also printed a glowing review of the pamphlet, agreeing with its authors that "there will be progressive intermingling and that the nation will be benefited by it." The reviewer was certain that "many will agree with us in finding the pamphlet interesting and instructive, and in thanking the unknown author[s] for it."[55] These are some of the responses Croly and Wakeman reprinted as evidence of the dangers of the Republican party.

As made clear by those who responded favorably to the *Miscegenation* pamphlet in their private letters to its authors, most abolitionists felt, however, that the political stakes in arguing publicly for inter-marriage were too high. Angelina Grimké asked the authors, "will not the subject of amalgamation so detestable to many minds, if now so prominently advocated, have a tendency to retard the preparatory work of justice and equality which is so silently, but surely, opening the way for a full recognition of fraternity and miscegenation?"[56] For her and most abolitionists, the answer was yes, advocating amalgamation would "retard" their efforts. Thus Lucretia Mott made a point of noting in her response to Croly and Wakeman that while the Massachusetts Anti-Slavery Society had fought to repeal the law making inter-racial marriages a crime, they had never advocated "such unions."[57] Indeed, barring a few of the most radical abolitionists, abolitionist support of the ideas in the pamphlet was muted at best. Wendell Phillips, Charles Sumner, and Abby Kelly Foster did not even reply to the copies of *Miscegenation* they were known to receive.[58] What made the championing of "fraternity and miscegenation" risky, it appears, was precisely that doing so opened one to the charge of bad taste and thus to monstrous proclivities. Lincoln himself had insisted in an 1857 speech on *Dred Scott* that "there is a natural disgust" at the idea of inter-marriage.[59] And he

protested that counterfeit logic which concludes that, because I do not want a black woman for a *slave* I must necessarily want her for a *wife*. I need not have her for either, I can just leave her alone. In some respects she is certainly not my equal; but in her natural right to eat the bread she earns with her own hands without asking leave of any one else, she is my equal, and the equal of all others.[60]

In his fourth debate with Douglas, Lincoln asserted similarly, "I do not understand that because I do not want a negro woman for a slave I must necessarily want her for a wife. My understanding is that I can just let her alone. I am now in my fiftieth year, and I certainly never have had a black woman for either a slave or a wife."[61] In advocating emancipation, Lincoln felt it necessary to also make the point that his taste for white women had prevailed for fifty years and would thus continue to prevail in himself and others. There is nothing attractive, he implies, about a black woman when he repeatedly insists that he "can just let her alone." In other words, Lincoln is relying here on the same discourses of taste which the Democrats claimed he lacked. He bases his insistence of non-interest on a belief in black physical inferiority.

Even in Massachusetts, where what we now term "inter-racial" marriage became a political right in 1843, legislators made clear that the social barriers against such marriages must remain. The text of the repeal of the Commonwealth's ban on inter-marriage stated that such marriages are in "bad taste": "It is cruel, unjust and improper to . . . punish that as a high crime, which is at most evidence of vicious feeling, bad taste, and personal degradation."[62] In other words, taste was perceived as that social barrier. Inter-marriage must continue to be deemed abhorrent in its name.

Most radical abolitionists never attempted to explode the idea of white taste. Rather, they implicitly based their argument for the right to inter-marry on the idea that there might be exceptions to the rule. On the one hand, Theodore Tilton argued in a speech to the American Anti-Slavery Society on May 12, 1863, that "When a man and woman want to be married it is *their* business, not mine, nor anybody's else."[63] The implication here is that there are whites and blacks who will want to marry someone outside of their race and that, therefore, it cannot be the case that whites necessarily and in all cases prefer other whites. But, on the other hand, such remarks were almost always tempered with a capitulation to the standard taste argument. Thus, the radical abolitionists usually ended up equating good taste with the desire to intra-marry, if just to protect their reputations. The *Tribune* illustrated this tendency in March 1864 when it asserted that "We do not say such union [between black and white] would be wise; but we do distinctly assert that society has nothing to do with the wisdom of the matches."[64] So even as the *Tribune* advocated personal freedom to exercise one's taste, it distanced itself from the kind of taste that was construed as aberrant by insisting that inter-racial unions are not "wise." That the *Tribune* was furthering the same conservative project as the Democrats is indicated by other comments in the same editorial as well: "If a man can so far conquer his repugnance to a black woman as to make her the mother of his children, we ask in the name of the divine law and of decency, why he should not marry her."[65] Here the same urging that marriage should be a private affair is coupled with the assumption that no white with good taste will choose inter-racially because of an unquestioned "repugnance" for black women.

Despite making one of the few attempts, Alcott also failed to fully take on the standard taste argument, either because to do so would alienate her audience, even if they were abolitionists, or because the taste argument was so ingrained at that point that she could not fully see past it. Whatever the case, Alcott almost completely evacuates Paul Frere's body from her text. While literally not present in the opening scene, at which point Claudia only hears his voice, Paul finally has to enter the story as a man so light-skinned that his blackness can go unrecognized. Of course, this is precisely what allows Claudia to fall in love before her prejudices can take over. But Paul's lightness also allows Alcott to avoid arguing that so-called racial blackness is attractive. It seems Paul is a reasonable love interest only because he looks white. So even in such attempts to further the cause of abolitionism by arguing against the naturalness of prejudice, taste remained an important barrier to the idea of inter-marriage.

Croly and Wakeman's lasting contribution to the question about the link between political and social equality was that they provided a means of summoning with one word all of these scientific and aesthetic justifications against the inter-mixing that would supposedly result from a link. That word was "miscegenation," a word they coined at the outset of the pamphlet and which thus carried within it all of the pamphlet's arguments against inter-marriage. From then on, use of the term invoked all of the reasons inter-mixing was monstrous. That such an intervention was perceived as needed and useful is evidenced by the fact that the neologism caught on right away and, furthermore, became the most popular means used to refer to racial mixing for the next one hundred years and more. By March 1864, the New York *Tribune* was sure its readers were well aware of the neologism and its meaning. It asserted of the new word that "By this, as most of our readers know, is meant the intermarriage of different races."[66] By November, the word had been used so often over the course of that year that it was clear it was here to stay. In revealing the pamphlet as a hoax, the London *Morning Herald* declared that "Whatever good or evil the authors of 'Miscegenation' may have done in a political way, they have achieved a sort of reflected fame on the coining of two or three new words—at least one of which is destined to be incorporated into the language. Speakers and writers of English will gladly accept the word 'Miscegenation' in the place of the word amalgamation."[67] The authors of the pamphlet had insisted that "amalgamation" was a "poor word" because "it properly refers to the union of metals with quick silver," whereas "miscegenation," from the Latin *miscere* (to mix) and *genus* (race), "express[es] the idea with which we are dealing, and, what is quite as important, . . . nothing else" (2). As we have seen, "the idea with which we are dealing" was really the set of interrelated ideas implicit in a pamphlet only pretending to support the idea of inter-mixing. Readers were reminded that "Negroes" and "whites" are different species who have different blood and that "Negroes" are aesthetically on a different plane than "whites." The term "miscegenation" thus implies that whites with good taste will shun blacks romantically and sexually and that inter-racial sex is a violation of Nature's biological laws. Individually, these ideas were hardly new. Croly and Wakeman drew on all that inter-racial sex and marriage had come to signify in the years since the Revolution when the issue first became one of great concern because of the inception and initial attempts to expand liberal democracy. What was new was the crystallization of these ideas in one term. By the middle of a civil war termed a "war of amalgamation" because emancipation and thus political equality were more at stake than ever before, the urgency to summon these complex assumptions had become so great that what Karl Marx called in the *Grundrisse* (1857–58) a "simple abstraction" was needed to name those complex assumptions in shorthand.[68] Of course, Marx was referring to when Europeans began to use the term "class" as a means of invoking without elaboration what had become a complex social structure. The shorthand signaled that everyone had a fairly deep understanding of that structure so that it no longer had to be elaborated in every instance. So, too, with "miscegenation." It was widely perceived that with the end of the "slavery problem" as a result of the Emancipation Proclamation, there was now what the New York *World* and others referred to repeatedly as the "Negro question" and "the negro problem."[69] It is clear from the remarks reviewed in this chapter that the so-called problem was deemed by those who identified as white at both ends of the political spectrum to be both a highly complex one and extremely urgent. What exactly would emancipation entail? Did equality mean political equality and political equality only? Or was social equality necessary as well? Would social equality spell the end of "white" economic prosperity? And what would the results of that social equality be? The word "miscegenation," as anatomized in the pamphlet, implicitly provided answers to all of these questions.

That the neologism does the work of impeding a link between political and social equality is evidenced by the fact that any use of the term "miscegenation" demonizes inter-racial coupling precisely by reminding Americans of this idea that "whites" should have the instinct to recognize that "blacks" are physically different from and inferior to them, unattractive, and therefore socially unacceptable. The term "miscegenation" thus also impedes a link between political and social equality by consolidating whiteness as an identity available to those willing to demonstrate and internalize such sexual race preferences. Consider the pamphlet *What Miscegenation Is! And What We Are to Expect Now that Mr. Lincoln is Re-elected.* The Democratic author of the pamphlet, one "L. Seaman," like Croly and Wakeman, only pretends to advocate "miscegenation" so as to make the point that the Republicans are dangerous. He shows certain couplings to be a violation of aesthetics and, furthermore, makes this the featured, although implicit, argument against "miscegenation" on his cover (Figure 19). There, he portrays a woman and a grossly caricatured man kissing, about which he notes that

the different shades of complexion of the two contrast . . . beautifully and lend . . . enchantment to the scene. . . . [The] sweet, delicate little Roman nose of the one does not detract from the beauty of the broad, flat nose, with expanded nostrils, of the other—while the intellectual, bold majestic forehead of the one forms an unique, though beautiful contrast to the round, flat head, resembling a huge gutter mop, of the other.[70]

Readers were reminded here that light-colored skin, a slim nose, and a vertical facial angle are far preferable to a head "resembling a huge gutter mop." As we've seen, much of the Democrat's anti-Lincoln propaganda did its work by reminding readers that social proximity between "whites" and "blacks" was a violation of aesthetic taste that thus proved Lincoln a crass man. The propaganda thus also served as a reminder to readers of those aesthetic standards that would ensure intra-racial attraction. The pamphlet makes clear that whiteness is not the result of this intra-racial attraction and reproduction and is thus not a biological category, but rather is the understanding constantly being reinforced by the likes of this pamphlet that certain features imagined as "white" are more attractive than others.

Only a few of those who had been radical abolitionists would continue to advocate inter-marriage after the coining of "miscegenation" made the work of damning inter-racial coupling far more easy than before.[71] Gilbert Haven, a Methodist clergyman in Massachusetts, argued in 1869 that insofar as blacks comprise the superior race, "The daughters of those haughty Southerners, who have shrank from their touch as leprous, shall gratefully accept the offers of the sons of their fathers' slaves."[72] In her novel *A Romance of the Republic* (1867), Lydia Maria Child makes the point that inter-racial marriage must be America's destiny if racism is to be abolished. Haven was generally dismissed as an extremist, however. And Child's abolitionist colleagues virtually ignored her book.[73] Far more typical were the views of the members of the American Freedmen's Inquiry Commission. Comprised of three white anti-slavery men, the commission submitted its final report to the War Department on the future of blacks and their relations to whites in May 1864, five months after the *Miscegenation* pamphlet appeared. The commission ruled that "amalgamation of these two races is in itself a physical evil injurious to both . . . [and is thus] a practice which ought to be discouraged by public opinion, and avoid-

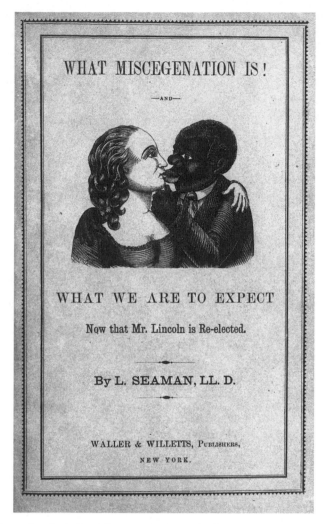

19. Cover illustration for *What Miscegenation Is! And What We Are to Expect Now that Mr. Lincoln is Re-elected*, ca. 1864. Brown University Library.

ed by all who consider it a duty, as parents, to transmit to their offspring the best conditions for sound health and well-being."[74] The commission had no doubt that what was coming to be termed "miscegenation" was biologically problematic. So without the barrier of slavery to preclude it, "public opinion" was left to "discourage" it. As I discuss next in my epilogue, the term and its successor, "inter-racial," continue to be a means of conveying and putting these assumptions in play as the racism inherent in the terms continues to go largely unrecognized.[75]

Epilogue: "Miscegenation" Today

A look at recent discussions about race and sex in everything from the popular press to science articles and historical scholarship reveals that many Americans still believe there is a special category of sex that is "inter-racial." We imagine that race is produced through sexual reproduction such that sex across imagined race lines must have its own term, must be marked as outside not only the social but the biological norm. In short, we hold on to biology when faced with the issue of race and sex even in the face of our many claims that race is purely a social fiction.[1]

Consider the entry for "miscegenation" in *Africana* (2000), the encyclopedia on African and African-American experience, edited by Kwame Anthony Appiah and Henry Louis Gates, Jr. Richard Newman, the author of the entry, describes "miscegenation" as "sexual relations across racial lines," as "sex across the color line," and as "interracial sex." Even as he notes that the term "miscegenation" is a "racist" one, he still believes, in other words, that it names a certain kind of sex. That he imagines this category of sex to be a biologically real one is evidenced in his two-column entry by his focus on topics as disparate as "black-white sex" during the Middle Passage and slavery, "the emergence of mulattos," and the legal prohibition in the United States of "interracial marriage." Readers of *Africana* learn that there is a special category of sex that exists outside the boundaries of historical periodization and thus in what is presumably biology. For him, "interracial" is just a less racist word for the same thing named by "miscegenation." That there could be no "miscegenation" before the term's coining, which he duly notes happened in 1864, does not occur to him.

A close reading of a 1994 article by an accomplished scientist attempting to claim that there is no biological race reveals how old ideas about the imagined relationship between race and sex keep him from accomplishing his stated task. Pulitzer Prize–winner Jared Diamond is an ecologist and physiologist at the University of California at Los Angeles. In this article for *Discover*, a science magazine for lay people, Diamond declares that "the reality of human races is another commonsense 'truth' destined to follow the flat Earth into oblivion."[2] He then proceeds to show that neither the sickle-cell gene, the enzyme lactase, finger print patterns, nor gene distinctiveness have been able to account for common race classifications. He concludes that

The traits we traditionally use [to classify people racially] are the ones subject to sexual selection, which is not really surprising. These traits are not only visible at a distance but also are highly variable; that's why they became the ones used throughout recorded history to make quick judgments about people. Racial classification didn't come from science but from the body's signals for differentiating attractive from unattractive sex partners, and for differentiating friend from foe.[3]

Here we can see still in play all of the ideas I have covered in this book that were developed in the antebellum period. For while Diamond may want to assert that various political alliances governed the development of a set of traits that were later used to signify race, his reliance on the role of "the body's signals" "throughout recorded history" implies that inter-racial sex is not just socially but also biologically abnormal. Furthermore, science is firmly grounded in a prejudice of which he is absolutely unaware. According to Diamond, there has always been a drive to sexually couple with another person who supposedly looks like oneself, someone with the same "traits," so that through sexual reproduction one can supposedly continue one's racial group. Despite Diamond's attempt to finesse his terms (to say, for example, "racial classification" rather than "race"), we are back to the idea that race is a biological category on some level. Through sexual reproduction, certain traits are perpetuated that he may say are just used to classify people racially but which, because they are still imagined as biologically produced and importantly, as more or less attractive, might as well be race. The moment sexual desire and reproduction enter the picture, Diamond ends up standing on the flat Earth. According to his principles of "sexual selection," if you are with someone who is of a different "race," that is because you did not receive your "body's signals," perhaps a message from your DNA, that your partner is "unattractive" and thereby a biologically unnatural choice for you. In other words, implicit in the idea that intra-racial coupling is biologically natural is the prejudical belief that other supposed races than one's own are rightly perceived as "unattractive."

Diamond argues that his findings are "not really surprising" if we consider that "throughout recorded history" people have used race traits to "make quick judgments about people." Of course, the history of Anglo-Americans having sex with their slaves refutes this claim easily enough. If Anglo-

Americans have used race traits to "make quick judgments," the judgments made have been related only to who makes an acceptable marriage partner. The recent "intra-racial" marriage rate of 97 percent among those who identify themselves as white only makes intra-racial desire *seem* natural, *seem* like "the body's signals."[4] The history of sexual racism covered in my book reveals that the feelings imagined by Diamond to be "the body's signals" are not from the body but from the culture's message that other "races" are "unattractive," messages that *Discover* is reproducing. Indeed, the message in *Discover* that inter-racial desire is against Nature is a particularly insidious form of prejudice because it attempts to masquerade as science.

Newman declares that the term "miscegenation" is "no longer in use" because it is racist. While this may be true in some communities, one still finds the term "miscegenation" used in the popular press. Just recently, a book review in *USA Today* described a novel about "the daughter of a white mother and an African-American father" as "a refreshing, nuanced look at miscegenation."[5] To be sure, nowhere in his article does Diamond use the term "miscegenation." Nonetheless, his ideas are clearly grounded in this concept, as evidenced by his insistence that desire within racial categories is instinctual. As I have shown of Diamond's article and of numerous texts produced between the Revolution and the Civil War, the insistence on the naturalness of intra-racial desire resulted from the prejudicial view that "blacks" are a biologically distinct group, are "unattractive," and are therefore inferior to those who imagine themselves as "white." So whether the particular word "miscegenation" is used today is irrelevant. The idea that there is a special kind of sex that is "inter-racial" is just as much a racist social fiction as the idea that there is something namable as "miscegenation."

Notes

Introduction

1. Michel Foucault discusses the intersection of sexuality and racism in the last two sections of *The History of Sexuality, Volume I: An Introduction*, trans. Richard Hurley (New York: Vintage Books, 1978). Later, he called this "the fundamental part of the book" and noted that "no one wants to talk about the last part" (quoted in Stoler, 21). Since then, Ann Laura Stoler has written a book on "the consequences for his treatment in the making of the European bourgeois self" (vii). Ann Laura Stoler, *Race and the Education of Desire: Foucault's* History of Sexuality *and the Colonial Order of Things* (Durham, N.C.: Duke University Press, 1995). My book, like Stoler's, follows Foucault in considering "the 'instrumentality' of sexuality in the making of race" (20), but moves the inquiry to the U.S. and back many decades from Foucault's dating of the emergence of racism to the late nineteenth century.

2. [David Goodman Croly and George Wakeman], *Miscegenation: The Theory of the Blending of the Races, Applied to the American White Man and Negro* (New York, 1863–64), 53.

3. On the timing of the first colonial statutes prohibiting inter-racial marriage, see Edmund S. Morgan, *American Slavery, American Freedom* (New York: W. W. Norton, 1975), 333–36; and Winthrop Jordan, who explains that "Indications of perpetual service, the very nub of slavery, coincided with indications that English settlers discriminated against Negro women, withheld arms from Negroes, and—though the timing is far less certain—reacted unfavorably to interracial sexual union" (80). Winthrop Jordan, *White over Black: American Attitudes Toward the Negro, 1550–1812* (New York: W. W. Norton, 1968). See also Peter W. Bardaglio, *Reconstructing the Household: Families, Sex, and the Law in the Nineteenth-Century South* (Chapel Hill: University of North Carolina Press, 1995), 50–55. He argues that "southern authorities took a decisive stand against racial amalgamation following the legislative enactment of slavery in the late seventeenth century" (50).

4. *Loving v. Virginia* (1967). The Supreme Court's decision is reprinted in *Lesbians, Gay Men and the Law*, ed. William Rubenstein (New York: Columbia University Press, 1993).

5. In *Northern Altitudes Towards Interracial Marriage: Legislation and Public Opinion in the Middle Atlantic States and the States of the Old Northwest, 1780–1930* (New York: Garland Publishing, 1987), David H. Fowler argues of New York's failure to pass laws prohibiting inter-racial marriage that "The reduction in the proportion of

Negroes to whites, the apparent slowing of Negro immigration, the comparative scarcity of Negroes in rural areas, and the segregation of Negroes by occupation all help to account for legislators' lack of concern" (162). He also argues that Pennsylvania's 1726 inter-marriage law, which had been repealed in 1780 under the act that initiated the gradual abolition of slavery, was not reinstated after the 1838 race riots in Philadelphia in part because a suffrage barrier to black citizenship there was deemed a certain level of protection against inter-racial marriage. I am arguing that literature and language also did the work of satisfying legislators in New York, Pennsylvania, and Massachusetts that inter-racial marriage was considered so disgusting by whites that it was unlikely to occur on a wide scale.

6. Thomas Jefferson, *Notes on the State of Virginia*, in *Thomas Jefferson Writings*, ed. Merrill D. Peterson, 123–325 (New York: Library of America, 1984), 265.

7. The *Liberator*, July 19, 1834.

8. [Croly and Wakeman], 2.

9. Most literature does not include a hyphen in the term "inter-racial." I use the hyphen in this book to make more easily visible when I am using the term "inter-" as opposed to "*intra*-racial." Intra-racial is a term not often seen because it is the normative case. The hyphens are thus also meant to help remind us of the socially constructed nature of *both* concepts.

10. James Fenimore Cooper, *The Last of the Mohicans* (New York: Penguin Books, 1986), 258.

11. [Jerome B. Holgate], *A Sojourn in the City of Amalgamation in the Year of Our Lord 19– by Oliver Bolokitten–Esq.* (New York, 1835), 60.

12. The *New-York Commercial Advertiser*, July 7, 1834.

13. Quoted by Samuel G. Morton, "Hybridity in Animals, considered in reference to the question of Unity of the Human Species," *American Journal of Science*, 2nd Ser., 3 (1847): 39–50, 203–12, 210.

14. Louisa May Alcott, "M. L." (1863), in *Louisa May Alcott on Race, Sex, and Slavery*, ed. Sarah Elbert, 3–28 (Boston: Northeastern University Press, 1997), 28.

Chapter 1

1. Josiah Quincy, "Journal of Josiah Quincy Junior, 1773," *Massachusetts Historical Society, Proceedings* 49 (June 1916): 424–81, 463.

2. The Massachusetts law against inter-racial fornication and marriage was enacted in 1705. In 1786, the part prohibiting fornication was eliminated. The remaining law banning inter-marriage was challenged by William Lloyd Garrison beginning in 1831 and was finally overturned in 1843; see Chapter 3. See also Louis Ruchames, "Race, Marriage, and Abolition in Massachusetts," *Journal of Negro History* 40.3 (July 1955): 250–273.

3. On the Quincys, see Linda K. Kerber, *Federalists in Dissent: Imagery and Ideology in Jeffersonian America* (Ithaca, N.Y.: Cornell University Press, 1970), 59–62.

4. The Richmond *Recorder*, September 1, 1802. For a reprinting of the entire article, see Sidney P. Moss and Carolyn Moss, "The Jefferson Legend in British Travel

Books," *Journal of the Early Republic* 7 (fall 1987): 253–74, 255. James T. Callender switched to the Federalist party when Jefferson passed over him for a federal job. On Callender and Jefferson, see Michael Durey, *"With the Hammer of Truth": James Thomsom Callender and America's Early National Heroes* (Charlottesville: University Press of Virginia, 1990); *Thomas Jefferson and James Thomsom Callender, 1798–1802*, ed. Worthington Chauncy Ford (Brooklyn, N.Y.: Historical Printing Club, 1897); Annette Gordon-Reed, *Thomas Jefferson and Sally Hemings: An American Controversy* (Charlottesville: University Press of Virginia, 1997), 59–77; and Fawn Brodie, *Thomas Jefferson: An Intimate History* (New York: W. W. Norton, 1974), 315–23.

5. Sally Hemings's full name was made known to the general public in 1873 when Madison Hemings, her son, gave a statement to an Ohio newspaperman. See Gordon-Reed, 7–58. Winthrop Jordan also notes that the published discussion about Jefferson and Hemings signaled a change in the amount of attention focused on inter-racial sex. He writes, "Given a new nation, with slavery now recognized as a national concern, the omnipresent fact of miscegenation was perforce seen in a somewhat different light than in earlier years. Cases of intermixture once of only local pertinence had now become ingredients in the larger problem of the integrity of the blood of the national community." Winthrop D. Jordan, *White over Black: American Attitudes Toward the Negro, 1550–1812* (New York: W. W. Norton, 1968), 470. On the way in which Callender moved "the rumor of Jefferson's interracial sexual affairs from private gossip to public discourse," see Joshua D. Rothman, "James Callender and Social Knowledge of Interracial Sex in Antebellum Virginia," in *Sally Hemings and Thomas Jefferson: History, Memory, and Civic Culture*, ed. Jan Ellen Lewis and Peter S. Onuf (Charlottesville: University Press of Virginia, 1999), 87–261, 106. Rumors of a presidential relationship with a slave woman made it into the press once prior to Callender's pronouncement in the form of speculation about certain mulattoes at Monticello when, during the campaign of 1800, Jefferson's death was reported in the press. When the rumor proved unfounded, the mistake was attributed to the fact that a Monticello slave supposedly called Thomas Jefferson had died. See Charles Warren, *Odd Byways in American History* (Cambridge, Mass.: Harvard University Press, 1942), ch. 7.

6. On Callender's error that Jefferson and Hemings had an oldest child named Tom, see Rothman, 102–3; and Gordon-Reed, 67–75. In addition to noting Tom's sable skin, Callender also terms the Jefferson-Hemings offspring a "yellow litter" (Richmond *Recorder*, December 15, 1802). But the slaves on Jefferson's plantation were noted by visitors and locals to be so light-skinned as to be of the same skin color as the legitimate Jefferson family. Traveling to Monticello in 1796, the Comte de Volney noted of the slaves there that they are "as white as I am" (quoted in Rothman, 87). Having pumped the local gossips for information about Monticello, Callender would have known of the slaves' coloring. Skin color differences, always subjective, had to be invented first by Callender and later by the other Federalists as an absolute difference in order to make Jefferson's crime one of a supposedly real biological difference that could be understood as "race."

7. Rothman, 106, 96. Jefferson went on to win reelection in 1804 based on the strength of his first term, which most people compared favorably to John Adams's presidency. (Adams had presided over new taxes, mounting public debt, Indian wars,

alien and sedition laws, oppressive armies, and restrictive trade wars.) In an article that traces the many attacks on Jefferson by the Federalists, Charles O. Lerche, Jr., concludes that "Based upon the experience of 1800 and of later campaigns of the same sort, it seems highly questionable whether the smear is ever effective in determining the outcome of a presidential election." Charles O. Lerche, Jr., "Jefferson and the Election of 1800: A Case Study in the Political Smear," *William and Mary Quarterly* 3.5 (1948): 466–91, 490. Robert M. S. McDonald concludes similarly that "rumors of a Jefferson-Hemings affair neither lasted long nor caused much damage" to Jefferson's reputation. Robert M. S. McDonald, "Race, Sex, and Reputation: Thomas Jefferson and the Sally Hemings Story," *Southern Cultures* 4.2 (summer 1998): 46–63. But these articles thus beg the question of what cultural work the rumors did do even as they failed to hurt Jefferson's bid for re-election.

8. Poems were published about Jefferson and Hemings in the *Port Folio* on October 2, 1802, October 30, 1802 (two poems), November 6, 1802, November 13, 1802, December 4, 1802, December 18, 1802, January 22, 1803, March 19, 1803, and April 9, 1803. On the *Port Folio*, see William C. Dowling, *Literary Federalism in the Age of Jefferson: Joseph Dennie and* The Port Folio, *1801–1811* (Columbia: University of South Carolina Press, 1999).

9. James C. Kelly and B. S. Lovell attribute the print to Akin and date it to circa 1804 in Newburyport, Massachusetts. James C. Kelly and B. S. Lovell, "Thomas Jefferson: His Friends and Foes," *The Virginia Magazine of History and Biography* 101:1 (January 1993): 133–57. Akin was born in South Carolina in 1773. The date he came to Philadelphia is not certain but he begins to appear in the city directories in 1799. Maureen O'Brien Quimby argues that "he apparently left Philadelphia in 1803, and was in Newburyport by January 1804." Maureen O'Brien Quimby, "The Political Art of James Akin," *Winterthur Portfolio 7*, ed. Ian M. B. Quimby (Charlottesville: University Press of Virginia, 1972), 59–112. I would argue that Akin produced the engraving in Philadelphia in spring 1803 at the latest, when the commentary of Jefferson and Hemings began to die out. But whatever its city of origin, what we do know about Akin's residence, as well as the content of the print, indicates that the engraving probably was a result of discussion in Philadelphia's Federalist press in 1802 and 1803.

10. On subscription rates for the *Port Folio*, see Ellis Paxson Oberholtzer, *The Literary History of Philadelphia* (Philadelphia, 1906), 168; and Linda K. Kerber and Walter John Morris, "Politics and Literature: The Adams Family and the *Port Folio*," *William and Mary Quarterly*, ser. 3, vol. 1, 23 (1966): 450–76, 450.

11. On the popularity of "A Song Supposed to Have Been Written by the Sage of Monticello," see Merrill D. Peterson, *Thomas Jefferson and the New Nation: A Biography* (New York: Oxford University Press, 1970), 708. On "Yankee Doodle" and the parodies of it, see Thomas Bailey, *Voices of America: The Nation's Story in Slogans, Sayings, and Songs* (New York: The Free Press, 1976) and Vera Brodsky Lawrence, *Music for Patriots, Politicians, and Presidents: Harmonies and Discords of the First Hundred Years* (New York: Macmillan, 1975).

12. The boy poet was William Cullen Bryant. Never included by Bryant in his collected works, "The Embargo; or, Sketches of the Times, A Satire; by a Youth of Thirteen" is reprinted in William Cullen Bryant, *The Embargo, or Sketches of the Times: A Satire* (Gainesville, Fla.: Scholars' Facsimiles and Reprints, 1955).

13. The *Port Folio*, July 10, 1802, reprinted in the *Recorder*, September 1, 1802.

14. On the Federalist fear of democracy, see Kerber, *Federalists in Dissent*, 174–83; and Dowling, *Literary Federalism*.

15. For the Federalists' views on slavery, see ch. 2 in Kerber, *Federalists in Dissent*, and Dowling, 16-20.

16. Quoted in Alexander O. Boulton, "The American Paradox: Jeffersonian Equality and Racial Science," *American Quarterly* 47.3 (September 1995): 467–92, 471.

17. Quoted in Boulton, 471.

18. On the Great Chain of Being, see Arthur O. Lovejoy, *The Great Chain of Being: A Study of the History of an Idea* (Cambridge, Mass.: Harvard University Press, 1966).

19. Stephen Jay Gould characterizes Linnaeus's ordering as horizontal in "The Geometer of Race," *Discover* (November 1994): 65–69. Douglas R. Egerton notes that in the tenth edition (1758), Linnaeus still described the different categories of humans in relative terms even as he did not rank them on a scale. Africans, for example, were said to be "ruled by caprice." Douglas R. Egerton "Thomas Jefferson and the Hemings Family: A Matter of Blood," *The Historian* 59.2 (winter 1997): 327–45.

20. Quoted in Robert E. Bieder, "Scientific Attitudes Towards Indian Mixed-Bloods in Early Nineteenth Century America," *The Journal of Ethnic Studies* 8.2 (summer 1980): 17–30, 17.

21. The *Port Folio*, April 9, 1803.

22. The Federalist poets believed they could protect themselves from the mud they were slinging by stating their various criticisms of Jefferson in the form of imitated Horatian satires. Horace had used satire to correct Roman society in the first century BC, attacking the vice and folly around him gently and playfully. As it had for Dryden and Pope in Augustan England, Horatian satire could thus expose the problems of the day while protecting the writer from any appearance of involvement in those problems. As long as the imitator was couching his comments in ancient forms, he was culling the virtue of ancient times and therefore not sullying himself with the dirt of the present. On the use of imitation as a means of protecting the poet, see Ian Jack, *Augustan Satire: Intention and Idiom in English Poetry, 1660–1750* (Oxford: Clarendon Press, 1966), 144. The use of classical verse in the *Port Folio* was also in keeping with its interest in classical literature in general. The first issue, for example, devoted three of its eight pages to a translation of the Thirteenth Satire of Juvenal, published anonymously by John Quincy Adams and printed in the magazine alongside the original. At the time, imitations of the best classical writers were expected at schools and universities. Throughout the eighteenth century, college applicants were only tested in Latin and Greek. Jefferson, however, had succeeded in getting William and Mary to drop ancient languages as an admission requirement. For the Federalists, this signaled a future citizenry without the requisite virtue culled from the Ancients. So, by drawing on their classical schooling to make their attacks, the Federalists were also furthering their case for traditional education in the wake of Republican calls for more "practical" education, understood by the Federalists to be a means of dumbing down the population. They were also implicitly insulting the Republicans who, they argued, might not understand their numerous classical allusions or the importance of certain classical forms. One contributor to the *Port Folio* of August 15, 1801, quoting Plautus, noted, "I subjoin a free translation, for the benefit of the young gentlemen of William and Mary

College, who may never have ventured beyond Terence" (quoted in Kerber, *Federalists in Dissent*, 112 n. 41). On the Federalist commitment to classical literature, see Kerber, *Federalists in Dissent*, ch. 4, "Salvaging the Classical Tradition."

23. Horace (Quintus Horatius Flaccus), *The Complete Works of Horace*, trans. Charles E. Passage (New York, 1983), 185–86.

24. For attributions, see Randolphe C. Randall, "Authors of the *Port Folio* Revealed by the Hall Files," *American Literature* 11 (1940): 379–416; and Kerber and Morris.

25. The *Port Folio*, October 30, 1802.

26. On the success of *Notes*, see Jordan, 429.

27. The *Recorder*, September 22, 1802.

28. Quoted in Kerber, *Federalists in Dissent*, 43.

29. On facial angle, see Schiebinger, 149–51; and my Chapter 4.

30. The *Port Folio*, October 2, 1802. This poem also parodies the lyrics of Henry Carey's (1692–1743) well-known song "Sally in our Alley," the chorus of which proclaims "of all the girls that are so smart, there's none like pretty Sally." For the complete lyrics of "Sally in our Alley," see William Chappell, *The Ballad Literature and Popular Music of the Olden Time: A History of the Ancient Songs, Ballads, and of the Dance Tunes of England, with Numerous Anecdotes and Entire Ballads; also, A Short Account of the Minstrels* (New York: Dover Publications, 1965), 645–48. For a history of the ballad, see Chappell and the entries on Carey in various editions of *The New Grove Dictionary of Music and Musicians*. A search of the *National Union Catalog* reveals that new words were often adapted to this song throughout the nineteenth century.

31. Thomas Green Fessenden, *Democracy Unveiled* (1806), 2: 21.

32. The *Port Folio*, November 6, 1802.

33. See P. J. Staudenraus, *The African Colonization Movement, 1816–1865* (New York: Columbia University Press, 1961).

34. Thomas Jefferson, *Notes on the State of Virginia* in *Thomas Jefferson: Writings*, ed. Merrill D. Peterson, 123–325 (New York: Library of America, 1984), 264. Hereafter, page numbers will be cited in the text. In an appendix to *Notes*, Jefferson included his proposed revision of Virginia's constitution, which would have also provided for the gradual abolition of slavery coupled with deportation.

35. By "Oranootan," Jefferson and his contemporaries meant the gorilla or, perhaps, the chimpanzee, both of which live in Africa. In actuality, orangutans are from Borneo and Sumatra.

36. See Jordan, 28–32; and Londa Schiebinger, *Nature's Body: Gender in the Making of Modern Science* (Boston: Beacon Press, 1993), 75–114.

37. Quoted in Jordan, 495.

38. Quoted in Jordan, 35.

39. Winthrop Jordan argues conversely that race and racism preceded slavery. This was later contested by Edmund S. Morgan in *American Slavery, American Freedom: The Ordeal of Colonial Virginia* (New York: W. W. Norton, 1975) and by others who argued that racism was invented to justify slavery. Most recently, Boulton has argued that "The question of which came first, racism or slavery, should be answered unequivocally. Slavery has existed in some form since the very beginnings of complex

human societies. Race, as either an emotional perception or a scientific category, conversely, can be definitively identified only by the late eighteenth or early nineteenth century, although its roots can be traced back earlier" (468).

40. The *Port Folio*, December 18, 1802.

41. On the times and reasons that the story about Jefferson and Hemings has cropped up in the U.S. since Callender first publicly broached it, see Gordon-Reed; Brodie; Scot A. French and Edward L. Ayers, "The Strange Career of Thomas Jefferson: Race and Slavery in American Memory, 1943–1993," in *Jeffersonian Legacies*, ed. Peter S. Onuf (Charlottesville: University Press of Virginia, 1993): 418–56; Merrill D. Peterson, *The Jefferson Image in the American Mind* (New York: Oxford University Press, 1960); and B. R. Burg, "The Rhetoric of Miscegenation: Thomas Jefferson, Sally Hemings, and Their Historians." *Phylon* 47.2 (1986): 128–38.

42. The results of DNA testing were published in *Nature*. See Eugene A. Foster et al., "Jefferson Fathered Slave's Last Child," *Nature* 196 (November 5, 1998): 27–28. See Gordon-Reed on the ways historians ignored African-American oral history about Sally Hemings.

43. For a different, and I would argue incomplete, view on why "Jefferson's rumored sexual relations with a slave mistress would become a favorite topic of Federalist satire," see Dowling, *Literary Federalism*, 18–19. Dowling argues that, for the Federalists, the relationship with Hemings proved the "biological equality" between blacks and whites that Jefferson had denied in *Notes* and that such slave owners were unfairly increasing their representation in Congress through the three-fifths rule.

Chapter 2

1. On the popularity of *The Last of the Mohicans* over time, see Martin Barker and Roger Sabin, *The Lasting of the Mohicans: History of an American Myth* (Jackson: University Press of Mississippi, 1995).

2. James Fenimore Cooper, *The Last of the Mohicans* (New York: Penguin Books, 1986), 78, 183–84, 121. Hereafter, page numbers will be cited in the text.

3. Quoted in Thomas Laqueur, *Making Sex: Body and Gender from the Greeks to Freud* (Cambridge, Mass.: Harvard University Press, 1990), 38.

4. Alighieri Dante, *The Divine Comedy: Purgatory*, trans. Dorothy L. Sayers (Harmondsworth: Penguin, 1955), 264.

5. Laqueur, 35.

6. Quoted in Laqueur, 56.

7. T. Salvi's *Il Chirugo: Trattatobreve* (1650); quoted in Piero Camporesi, *Juice of Life: The Symbolic and Magic Significance of Blood*, trans. Robert R. Barr (New York: Continuum, 1995), 14.

8. Camporesi quotes from, among other texts, I. Bosio's *La trionfante e gloriosa Croce* (1610): "Such is the efficacy and the virtue of the Blood of Christ—to restore life, to rejoin and reunite to their body any smitten, infirm, done to death, mutilated, and even altogether dead members" (quoted on 16). Camporesi concludes that "the blood

of Christ acquired the precious thaumaturgical value of a magic ointment that could annihilate the stench of sin, the fetor of the excremental human being, the acrid, fusty stench of the polluted community, the miasmas of malignity" (72).

9. Robert Hendrickson's *QPB Encyclopedia of Word and Phrase Origins* (New York: Facts on File, 1997) notes that neither *Bartlett's* nor the *OED* lists the phrase. Hendrickson traces the saying to 1672 when it was collected in a book of proverbs (81). On the assumption that "blood is thicker than water," see David M. Schneider, *A Critique of the Study of Kinship* (Ann Arbor: University of Michigan Press, 1984), especially chapter 14.

10. R. Howard Bloch, *Etymologies and Genealogies: A Literary Anthropology of the French Middle Ages* (Chicago: University of Chicago Press, 1983), 66.

11. Ibid., 69.

12. David M. Schneider, *American Kinship: A Cultural Account* (Englewood Cliffs, N.J.: Prentice-Hall, 1968), 93.

13. Pierre Bourdieu, *Outline of a Theory of Practice* (Cambridge, Mass.: Harvard University Press, 1997), 36. Only recently have social scientists such as Kath Weston, Schneider, and Bourdieu argued that blood rhetoric merely posits inherited identity as something biologically real in the blood rather than pointing to something really there, a dynamic made clear to them by the fact that certain non-Western cultures do not recognize so-called biogenetic kinship. Kath Weston, *Families We Choose: Lesbians, Gays, Kinship* (New York: Columbia University Press, 1991).

14. For Dr. Samuel Stanhope Smith's assertion in 1787 that blackness is a "universal freckle," see William Stanton, *The Leopard's Spots: Scientific Attitudes toward Race in America, 1815–59* (Chicago: University Press of Chicago, 1960), 5. I am somewhat simplifying the shift from a climatological account of race to an inherited account. On theories of racial inheritance that preceded the eighteenth-century shift away from a climatological account of race, see Conway Zirkle, "The Early History of the Idea of the Inheritance of Acquired Characters and of Pangenesis," *American Philosophical Society Transactions, n.s.,* 35, pt. 2 (1945), 91–151.

15. In 1578, Englishman George Best wrote in a piece printed by Richard Hakluyt in his *Principal Navigations*:

I myself have seen an Ethiopian as black as coal brought into England, who taking a fair English woman to wife, begat a son in all respects as black as the father was. . . . Whereby it seems this blackness proceeds rather of some natural infection of that man, which was so strong, that neither the nature of the Clime, neither the good complexion of the mother concurring, could anything alter. And therefore, we cannot impute it to the nature of the Clime. (In *The English Literatures of America, 1500–1800,* ed. Myra Jehlen and Michael Warner [New York: Routledge, 1997], 54–58, 55)

16. Quoted in Stanton, 9.

17. Sir William Blackstone, *Commentaries on the Laws of England* (1768), 2: 203.

18. Quoted in Werner Sollors, *Neither Black Nor White Yet Both: Thematic Explorations of Interracial Literature* (Oxford: Oxford University Press, 1997), 113–14. He reports being unable to find the source other than its date of origin (457, n. 4).

19. See Sollors, 120, 246.

20. Richard Slotkin, *Regeneration Through Violence: The Mythology of the Ameri-*

can Frontier, 1600–1860 (Middletown, Conn. Wesleyan University Press, 1973), 493.

21. Forrest G. Robinson, "Uncertain Borders: Race, Sex, Civilization in *The Last of the Mohicans*," *Arizona Quarterly* 47.1 (spring 1991): 1–28, 8.

22. William Cobbett, *The American Gardener* (1819), 66.

23. His choice of epigraph from *The Merchant of Venice*—"Mislike me not, for my complexion, / The shadowed livery of the burnished sun"—may seem to belie Cooper's rejection of the climatological argument, but Cooper seems only to want to imply with it that Chingachgook and Uncas deserve white respect.

24. On Cooper's role in justifying Indian removal, see Philip Fisher, *Hard Facts: Setting and Form in the American Novel* (Oxford: Oxford University Press, 1987).

25. Nina Baym, "Putting Women in Their Place: *The Last of the Mohicans* and Other Indian Stories," in *Feminism and American Literary History: Essays by Nina Baym* (New Brunswick, N.J.: Rutgers University Press, 1992), 19–35, 28.

26. Robinson, 21–22. Nina Baym also reads Cora's identity as static and reinscribes Cooper's blood rhetoric to say as much. She argues that Cora cannot couple with an Indian, not because she is functionally white at this point, but because her "already mixed blood, were it to be mixed again with an American Indian's, would produce tri-racial children—the 'e pluribus unum' of the American national seal" (27).

27. Claude Lévi-Strauss, *The Elementary Structures of Kinship* (Boston, 1969), as quoted in Gayle Rubin, "The Traffic in Women: Notes Toward a Political Economy of Sex," in *Toward an Anthropology of Women*, ed. Rayna Reiter (New York: Monthly Review Press, 1975), 157–210, 174.

28. Letter to Benjamin Hawkins, Feb. 18, 1803, in *Thomas Jefferson: Writings* (New York: Library of America, 1984), 1113–16, 1115. On Jefferson's attitude toward the Indians, see Richard Drinnon, *Facing West: The Metaphysics of Indian-Hating and Empire-Building* (Minneapolis: University of Minnesota Press, 1980), 78–98; and Bernard W. Sheehan, *Seeds of Extinction: Jeffersonian Philanthropy and the American Indian* (Chapel Hill: University of North Carolina Press, 1973).

29. Quoted in Robert E. Bieder, "Scientific Attitudes Toward Indian Mixed-Bloods in Early Nineteenth Century America," *The Journal of Ethnic Studies* 8.2 (summer 1980): 17–30, 20.

30. See Mary Young, "Racism in Red and Black: Indians and Other Free People of Color in Georgia Law, Politics, and Removal Policy," *The Georgia Historical Quarterly* 73.3 (fall 1989): 492–518, 493.

31. On those laws prohibiting Indian/white marriage that were aimed principally at excluding whites from marrying blacks, see David Fowler, *Northern Attitudes Towards Interracial Marriage: Legislation and Public Opinion in the Middle Atlantic and the States of the Old Northwest, 1780–1930* (New York: Garland Publishing, 1987), 106–7. On how Maine and Rhode Island simply copied Massachusetts' legislation, see Martyn, 224, 322. As Byron Curti Martyn notes in "Racism in the United States: A History of the Anti-Miscegenation Legislation and Litigation" (Ph.D. diss., University of Southern California, 1979), "Borrowing miscegenation laws among the colonies and later among the states was a common phenomena" (137–38).

32. Winthrop Jordan, *White over Black: American Attitudes Toward the Negro, 1550–1812* (New York: W. W. Norton, 1968), 163.

33. See Alden T. Vaughan, "From White Man to Redskin: Changing Anglo-American Perceptions of the American Indian," *The American Historical Review* 87 (October 1982): 917–53, 925–26.

34. For an example of this belief, see William Byrd, *William Byrd's Histories of the Dividing Line betwixt Virginia and North Carolina,* ed. William K. Boyd (Raleigh: The North Carolina Historical Commission, 1929), 4, 120–22.

35. In Puritan New England, however, inter-marriage was discouraged on the grounds that religious and economic differences were insurmountable. The 1680 Synod of Congressional Churches, for example, decreed against marriage to infidels. See David D. Smits, " 'We Are Not to Grow Wild': Seventeenth-Century New England's Repudiation of Anglo-Indian Intermarriage," *American Indian Culture and Research Journal* 11.4 (1987): 1–32, 21–22.

36. John Rolfe, "Letter of John Rolfe, 1614," in *Narratives of Early Virginia: 1606–1628,* ed. Lyon Gardiner Tyler (New York: C. Scribner, 1907), 239–44.

37. See Vaughan, 939. Scholars are in agreement that a shift occurred, but they locate the shift in white perceptions at slightly different times: Vaughn to the eighteenth century, Bieder to the 1820s, and Susan Scheckel to the War of 1812. Susan Scheckel, *The Insistence of the Indian: Race and Nationalism in Nineteenth-Century American Culture* (Princeton, N.J.: Princeton University Press, 1988), 4.

38. Quoted in Reginald Horseman, *Race and Manifest Destiny: The Origins of Racial Anglo-Saxonism* (Cambridge, Mass.: Harvard University Press, 1981), 119–20.

39. See Vaughan.

40. Samuel George Morton, *Crania Americana; or, A Comparative View of the Skulls of Various Aboriginal Nations of North and South America. To Which is Prefixed an Essay on the Varieties of the Human Species* (Philadelphia, 1839), 6.

41. Vaughan, 953.

42. Martyn, 326 n. 191.

43. Quoted in Bieder, 21.

44. Sheehan, 178.

45. Timothy Flint, *Recollections of the Last Ten Years in the Valley of Mississippi,* 1816, ed. George R. Brooks (Carbondale: Southern Illinois University Press, 1968), 119; quoted in Bieder, 21.

46. Alexis de Tocqueville, *Democracy in America,* 2 vols. (New York: Random House, 1990), 1:345–46 n. 17.

47. Quoted in Robinson, 15.

48. Quoted in Jordan, 480.

49. Quoted in Jordan, 547.

Chapter 3

1. On the discovery and dating of *Virginian Luxuries* see Barbara Luck, "AARFAC Acquires Unusual Painting," *Colonial Williamsburg News* (October 8, 1993): 3.

2. Abolitionist organizing in the 1820s was comprised primarily of the American Colonization Society, which had been founded in 1816 on a platform of gradual aboli-

tionism with black deportation. The society took great pains not to anger or alienate Southern slaveholders. See P. J. Staudenraus, *The African Colonization Movement, 1816–1865* (New York: Columbia University Press, 1961).

3. For this definition of amalgamation, see the *Liberator*, July 19, 1834.

4. This number is according to the count of the three leading anti-slavery newspapers. See Leonard L. Richards, *"Gentlemen of Property and Standing": Anti-Abolition Mobs in Jacksonian America* (Oxford: Oxford University Press, 1970), 157.

5. Richards, 43. Like Richards and Ronald G. Walters, I take the amalgamation rhetoric used by both sides seriously. Ronald G. Walters, "The Erotic South: Civilization and Sexuality in American Abolitionism," *American Quarterly* 25 (1973): 177–201. Walters finds that "If abolitionists worried about licentiousness and the decline of order, then so did men who opposed them in anti-slavery mobs, fearful that emancipation would upset conventional social relations and promote miscegenation" (192). For the view that these riots were a culmination of economic anxieties instead, see Linda Kerber, "Abolitionists and Amalgamators: The New York City Race Riots of 1834," *New York History* 48 (January 1967): 28–39. She writes of the 1834 New York City riot in that "1834 was a recession year. What New Yorkers may have sensed hidden behind abolitionist egalitarianism was an economic challenge quite as much as a social one; though they claimed the riot was caused by outraged sensibilities, the outrage may well have been to pocketbooks" (34). But as Richards notes, "Kerber . . . rests her argument on one quote from . . . a Washington, D. C., newspaper. On the basis of this quote, she implies that the rhetoric of amalgamation was only a cover for the tension between white and black labor. I disagree: the behavior of the rioters indicates that the rhetoric of amalgamation reflected their deepest fears" (115).

6. See David Brion Davis, "The Emergence of Immediatism in British and American Antislavery Thought," in *From Homicide to Slavery: Studies in American Culture* (Oxford: Oxford University Press, 1986): 238–57.

7. The *Liberator*, January 1, 1831.

8. The law had been subsequently reenacted in 1786. Garrison first stated his opposition to the Massachusetts law in the *Liberator* on January 8, 1831. In the early months of 1831, he also reprints and/or comments on the law on January 22, 1831, January 29, 1831, February 19, 1831, February 26, 1831, March 4, 1831, and March 19, 1831.

9. The shift to companionate marriage has been documented by Lawrence Joseph Stone in *The Family, Sex and Marriage in England, 1500–1800* (London: Weidenfeld & Nicolson, 1977). On the shift to companionate marriage in the United States, see Ellen K. Rothman, *Hands and Hearts: A History of Courtship in America* (New York: Basic Books, 1984), 17–87.

10. See Michael Grossberg, "Guarding the Altar: Physiological Restrictions and the Rise of State Intervention in Matrimony," *The American Journal of Legal History* 26 (July 1982): 197–226, 201.

11. On James Kent's influence, see Norma Basch, *In the Eyes of the Law: Women, Marriage, and Property in Nineteenth-Century New York* (Ithaca, N.Y.: Cornell University Press, 1982), 60.

12. Quoted in Michael Grossberg, *Governing the Hearth: Law and Family in Nineteenth-Century America* (Chapel Hill: University of North Carolina Press, 1985), 70–71.

13. Daniel Scott Smith, "Parental Power and Marriage Patterns: An Analysis of Historical Trends in Hingham, Massachusetts," in *The American Family in Social-Historical Perspective*, ed. Michael Gordon, 2nd ed. (New York: St. Martin's Press, 1983), 87–100.

14. The restrictive nature of nuptial law has been made most clear recently by feminist scholars and queer theorists who oppose the right to same-sex marriages. See, for example, Paula Ettelbrick, "Since When Is Marriage a Path to Liberation," in *Lesbians, Gay Men and the Law*, ed. William Rubenstein (New York: Columbia University Press, 1993), 401–5.

15. See Daniel Scott Smith, "The Long Cycle in American Illegitimacy and Premarital Pregnancy," in *Bastardy and its Comparative History: Studies in the History of Illegitimacy and Marital Nonconformism in Britain, France, Germany, Sweden, North America, Jamaica, and Japan*, ed. Peter Laslett (London, Arnold, 1980).

16. Quoted in Grossberg, *Governing the Hearth*, 18.

17. See 149 n.3.

18. See Werner Sollors, *Neither Black Nor White Yet Both: Thematic Explorations of Interracial Literature* (New York: Oxford University Press, 1997), 396–97, for this and other laws against inter-racial sex and marriage listed in chronological order.

19. On the various effects of the ban, see Eva Saks, "Representing Miscegenation Law," *Raritan* 8:2 (fall 1988): 39–69.

20. The *Liberator*, March 4, 1831.

21. The *Liberator*, January 29, 1831. See also January 8, 1831, 2nd issue. Of course, the pursuit of happiness is not protected by the Constitution per se, although the latter is spelled out in the Declaration of Independence and is commonly believed to be protected by the so-called Bill of Rights, or first ten amendments to the Constitution.

22. In *Loving v. Virginia* (1967), Virginia argued that the law banning inter-racial marriage there was constitutional because it discriminated equally against blacks and whites. The Supreme Court found this argument specious. The Supreme Court's decision is reprinted in Rubenstein, *Lesbians, Gay Men and the Law*.

23. David Fowler notes that "even though the laws have usually applied the same penalties to both races and have occasionally penalized whites more severely than non-white . . . [these] statutes have discriminated against non-whites because their actual effect has been to add legal support to the common characterization of non-whites as socially inferior to whites" (7 n. 2). David Fowler, *Northern Attitudes Towards Interracial Marriage: Legislation and Public Opinion in the Middle Atlantic and the States of the Old Northwest, 1780–1930* (New York: Garland Publishing, 1987).

24. Lydia Maria Child, *An Appeal in Favor of That Class of Americans Called Africans* (Amherst: University of Massachusetts Press, 1996), 187.

25. On the first notice taken by the colonizationists of Garrison, see Staudenraus, 194–206. For one of the early accusations that the abolitionists were in favor of amalgamation, see the *Methodist Magazine and Quarterly Review of New York* 15 (January 1833), 111–16. The *Courier and Enquirer* began to make similar charges in October 1833. On the rumor that Garrison was seeking a black wife, see Wendell Phillips Garrison and Francis Jackson Garrison, *William Lloyd Garrison, 1805–1879: The Story of His Life Told by His Children*, 4 vols. (Boston: Houghton, Mifflin, 1889), 1: 331 n.

26. Richards devotes an entire section of his book to the "New York Phase" of anti-abolitionist violence, noting that "It was Arthur Tappan and his New York associates, rather than Garrison and his Boston radicals, whom . . . Americans saw as frightening Americans 'out of their senses.' . . . What frightened . . . Americans was the apparent power and efficiency of Arthur Tappan and his New York associates—their ability to establish numerous societies and presses rapidly and to flood the country with their literature" (48).

27. *Courier and Enquirer*, July 4, 1834. Chatham Street Chapel was a theater leased by Lewis Tappan for reformist activities.

28. See Henry Fowler, *The American Pulpit* (New York, 1856), 374–75.

29. See E. S. Abdy, *Journal of a Residence and Tour in the United States of North America from April, 1833, to October, 1834*, 3 vols. (London, 1835), 3: 123.

30. Ludlow denied the charge in a letter to the editors of the *Journal of Commerce*, July 24, 1834.

31. On the rumor regarding the Reverend Peter Williams, Gustave de Beaumont sites the *Mercantile Advertiser* and the *New York Advocate*, July 12, 1834. See his *Marie; Or, Slavery in the United States*, 248 n. 4.

32. The *Morning Courier and New-York Enquirer*, July 7, 1834. The rumor about his children was reprinted in the *Liberator*, July 26, 1834, from the *Boston Courier*.

33. That Arthur Tappan was rumored to want his daughter to marry a black man is reported in Abdy, 3: 123.

34. Quoted in Richards, 116.

35. See, for example, the *Philadelphia Saturday Courier*, May 19, 1838.

36. Sarah and Angelina Grimké were two of the first women to take to the platform and were ridiculed for it. See Keith E. Melder, "Forerunners of Freedom: The Grimké Sisters in Massachusetts, 1837–38," *Essex Institute Historical Collections* 103 (July 1967): 223–49; Larry Ceplair, introduction to *The Public Years of Sarah and Angelina Grimké: Selected Writings, 1835–1839* (New York: Columbia University Press, 1989).

37. The *Morning Courier and New-York Enquirer*, July 7, 1834.

38. Ibid., July 7, 1834.

39 On the nineteenth-century and early-twentieth-century belief that the tinge of the fingernails revealed one's race, see Sollors, 142–61.

40. The *Morning Courier and New-York Enquirer*, 7 July 1834.

41. On Clay's life and work, see Nancy Reynolds Davidson, "E. W. Clay: American Political Caricaturist of the Jacksonian Era" (Ph.D. diss., University of Michigan, 1980). Unlike Clay's *Life in Philadelphia* lithographs (1828–30), which consisted of fourteen numbered plates, the amalgamation prints were introduced as single-sheet caricatures, nor were they numbered. But their common theme of flirtation and romance across race lines indicates that they comprised a series and must be considered as such. Of the seven prints related to inter-racial romance, six published in 1839 and one in 1845, six have the term "amalgamation" in the title, three of which are further linked by the title "practical amalgamation." *Johnny Q* is related to the series, if not perhaps a part of it, by its direct reference to inter-racial sex in the dedication to "Miss. Caroline Augusta Chase, & the 500 ladies of Lynn, who wish to marry Black husbands." Further evidence that Clay came to consider all of these prints, including

Johnny Q," a series or at least a themed group is a line below the title of *Practical Amal-gamation* (*The Wedding*)." There Clay notes, "Also. Just Published—The Amalgama-tion Waltz—The Courtship—The Fruits—Johnny Q—& Black Cut—." (I have not been able to identify the last print he lists here.)

42. On Clay's move to New York, see the entry on Clay in Harry Twyford Peters, *America on Stone* (Garden City, N.Y.: Doubleday, 1931).

43. Clay misspells Aroline Chase's first name to avoid charges of libel.

44. For a photo of Garrison at age 30 in 1835, see John L. Thomas, *The Liberator William Lloyd Garrison: A Biography* (Boston: Little, Brown, 1963), following p. 246.

45 On the abolitionist fight against racism in the 1830s, see Herbert Aptheker, *Anti-Racism in U.S. History: The First Two Hundred Years* (New York: Greenwood Press, 1992), 129–46.

46. Quoted in Aptheker, 129.

47. For examples of testimony and practice rhetoric in anti-abolitionist rhetoric, see the *New York Times*, July 9, 1834; The *Evening Post* (quoting the *Courier*), July 16, 1834; and the *New-York Commercial Advertiser*, July 11, 1834.

48. On marriage as a sign of equality, see Kingsley Davis, "Intermarriage in Caste Societies," *American Anthropologist*, n.s., 43.3 (July–September 1941): 376–95.

49. The rumor that Arthur Tappan had married a black woman was reported and denied in the *Emancipator*, August 19, 1834.

50. Fabricated ads ran or were discussed in the following: the *New York Times*, July 8, 1834; The *New-York Commercial Advertiser*, July 7, 1834; and the *Morning Couri-er and New-York Enquirer*, July 8, 1834.

51. The *New-York Commercial Advertiser*, July 11, 1834.

52. Ibid., July 7, 1834.

53. It thus seems strange that Gustave de Beaumont read the ad in the *New-York Commercial Advertiser* as sincere. Perhaps because he believed inter-marriage was a sound political solution—he argues in *Marie* that "Intermarriages are . . . the most obvious index of equality"—he didn't want to believe the ad was only so much hyper-bole intended to turn the public against the abolitionists (245).

54. The *New York Times*, July 9, 1834.

55. Ibid., July 8, 1834.

56. The *New-York Commercial Advertiser*, July 7, 1834.

57. *Memorial History of Utica, New York*, ed. M. M. Bagg (Syracuse, N.Y., 1892), 224.

58. Minute Book of the Utica Literary Club, Sept. 7, 1833, the Oneida Historical Society, Utica, New York. On Jerome's attendance at the Utica debates, see William C. Holgate diary, December 29, 1833–February 5, 1834; October 22, 1834–March 5, 1835, The Defiance College, Defiance, Ohio.

59. For such a resolution on January 13, 1834, see *Memorial History of Utica, New York*, 223.

60. Beaumont cites as his source for this rumor the *National Intelligencer*, Febru-ary 1834. And he links it directly to the riot: "Early in the year 1834 a minister of the Anti-Slavery Society, the Reverend Doctor Beriah Green, performed in Utica the mar-riage of a Negro to a young white girl, and there was a sort of popular uprising in the

city, following which the reverend doctor was hanged in effigy on the public street" (245). Beaumont again has trouble, however, distinguishing fact from rumor.

61. [Jerome B. Holgate], *A Sojourn in the City of Amalgamation in the Year of Our Lord 19– by Oliver Bolokitten–Esq.* (New York, 1835), 70–72. Page numbers will hereafter be cited parenthetically in the text. It was pointed out to me by David L. Greene that the name "Bolokitten" was probably derived by Jerome from his own middle initial, "B.," together with the first part of his last name, "hol," and the second part of his last name translated into English from the Spanish for cat, "gato." For the only critical reading to date of this novel, see James Kinney, *Amalgamation! Race, Sex, and Rhetoric in the Nineteenth-Century American Novel* (Westport, Conn.: Greenwood Press, 1985). Kinney recognizes that Bolokitten is a pseudonym, which, indeed, is indicated in the *National Union Catalog.* But he assumes that the author is Southern and thus is unable to fit him comfortably into any antebellum tradition (38–39).

62. The *New York Times,* July 7, 1834.

63. A reproduction of E. B. and E. C. Kellogg's "The Dance" can be found in Helen Comstock, *American Lithographs of the Nineteenth Century* (New York: Barrows, 1950), 88. For examples of minstrel sheet music, see Eric Lott, *Love and Theft: Blackface Minstrelsy and the American Working Class* (Oxford: Oxford University Press, 1993), 118, 121, and 128.

64. See Alain Corbin, *The Foul and the Fragrant: Odor and the French Social Imagination* (Cambridge, Mass.: Harvard University Press, 1986).

65. Catharine E. Beecher, *A Treatise on Domestic Economy, for the use of Young Ladies at Home, and at School* (Boston, 1841), 294.

66. Corbin, 143.

67. I use Frank Weitenkampf's dating here. He notes of *Professor Pompey* that "'ca. 1862'" has been suggested but costumes do not seem to fit that period." See his *Political Caricature in the United States* (New York: New York Public Library, 1953), 85.

68. Gillian Brown explains that mesmerism was called "variously mental alchemy, electrical psychology, animal or vital magnetism, supernal theology, somnolism, somnambulism, psycheism, the science of the soul, spiritual physiology, or simply psychology" (88). See her *Domestic Individualism: Imagining Self in Nineteenth-Century America* (Berkeley: University of California Press, 1990), 88.

69. Dr. Joseph Haddock, "Mesmeric phenomena" (1849), quoted in Brown, 89.

70. Nathaniel Hawthorne, *Centenary Edition,* ed. William Charvat, Roy Harvey Pearce, and Claude M. Simpson, 23 vols. (Columbus: Ohio State University Press, 1962–), *The Letters, 1813–1843,* 15: 588.

71. T. W. Strong, *Boy's Own Book of Fun* (New York, n.d.), 148.

72. The *New York Times,* July 7, 1834.

73. The *Morning Courier and New-York Enquirer,* July 7, 1834.

74. The *Mercantile Advertiser and New York Advocate,* July 7, 1834.

75. The *New York Times,* July 8, 1834.

76. The *New-York Commercial Advertiser,* July 10, 1834.

77. Ibid., July 7, 1834.

78. Pierre Bourdieu, *Distinction: A Social Critique of the Judgement of Taste.* trans. Richard Nice (Cambridge, Mass.: Harvard University Press, 1984), 1–2.

79. A List of the Members of the Literary Club, Minute Book, Utica Literary Club, the Oneida Historical Society, Utica, New York. See Richards for a list of mob participants, 171–73.

80. Samuel J. Webb, *Some Recollections of our Antislavery Conflict* (Boston: Fields, Osgood, 1869), 166.

81. Historians have disagreed on the extent to which the abolitionists supported inter-marriage. In *The Struggle for Equality: Abolitionists and the Negro in the Civil War and Reconstruction* (Princeton, N.J.: Princeton University Press, 1964), James M. McPherson asserts, "It is not recorded whether any daughter of a white abolitionist did marry a Negro, but it is known that the abolitionists did not shrink from discussing the issue. In the face of popular odium and violence, abolitionists struggled to remove laws marring intermarriage from the statute books of Massachusetts and other states" (147). However, George M. Fredrickson argues of McPherson in *The Black Image in the White Mind: The Debate on Afro-American Character and Destiny, 1817–1914* (New York: Harper & Row, 1971) that "he somewhat exaggerates the egalitarianism of the abolitionists. His discussion, for example, of abolitionist advocacy of intermarriage . . . gives a misleading impression because it consists mainly of statements from the relatively few abolitionists who took a strong and unequivocal stand on this issue." (Fredrickson, 127 n. 60). My own findings are in keeping with Fredrickson's.

82. On one occasion Garrison did insist that "intermarriage is neither unnatural nor repugnant to nature, but designed to unite people of different tribes and nations." But he was careful to add that inter-marriage would only happen in the future. "As civilization, and knowledge, and republican feelings, and Christianity prevail in the world, the wider will matrimonial connexions extend; and finally people of every tribe and kindred and tongue will freely intermarry. By the blissful operation of this divine institution, the earth is evidently to become one neighborhood or family" (The *Liberator*, May 7, 1831).

83. The *Liberator*, February 5, 1831.

84. On such assumptions about white womanhood, see Barber Welter, "The Cult of True Womanhood," in her *Dimity Convictions: The American Woman in the Nineteenth Century* (Athens: Ohio University Press, 1976), 21–41. On white ideas about black male sexuality, see Jordan, 32–34, 150–54.

85. The *Liberator*, February 5, 1831.

86. Ibid., January 29, 1831.

87. The *Liberator*, April 30, 1831.

88. Ibid., February 15, 1839.

89. The *New-York Commercial Advertiser*, July 14, 1834; The *New York Times*, July 14, 1834; and elsewhere.

90. The *New York Times*, July 14, 1834.

91. The *Emancipator*, 5 August 1834. On July 29, 1834, the *Emancipator* printed the first of three lists of the rumors and accusations they wished to refute. Of the fourteen rumors in the first list, three were about amalgamation: "'IT IS NOT TRUE,' That . . . Rev. Mr. Ludlow married a white to a colored person—Or—that black dandies have been parading Broadway in search of white wives —. . . . Or—that a certain leading abolitionist wished his daughter to marry a negro" (The *Emancipator*, July 29, 1834). On

August 19, 1834, a third list was published in the *Emancipator* of "False Accusations" against the abolitionists. The first, and therefore most important to the abolitionists, is that they are accused of championing amalgamation.

1. Of trying to persuade the Blacks and whites to intermarry together.
2. Of exciting resistance to the laws.
3. Of violating the U. S. Constitution.
4. Of seeking to dissolve the Union.
5. Of exciting the slaves to rise against their masters.
6. Of being unfriendly to the people of the south.
7. Of "bitter malignity and cruel hatred' to the members of the Colonization Society. (The *Emancipator*, August 19, 1834)

Abolitionist societies across the Northeast followed suit in issuing denials and passing resolutions, many of which the *Emancipator* reprinted. The following from the Pawtucket Anti-Slavery Society is one example—note that once again, inter-racial marriage is the first issue addressed: "1. Resolved, That the charges against abolitionists, that they design and encourage an amalgamation of the white and colored races by intermarriage, intend to excite the slaves to rebellion and dissolve the Union, are entirely unfounded and slanderous" (quoted in the *Emancipator*, Aug. 19, 1834). William Jay of New York, a staunch anti-slavery leader, also sought to dispel misapprehensions about abolitionists in his 1835 *An Inquiry into the character and tendency of the American Colonization and American Anti-Slavery Societies*:

Men of all ranks have united in charging upon . . . [the abolitionists] designs which they indignantly disclaim, and in support of which, not a particle of evidence has been, or can be adduced. One of the designs falsely imputed to them, is that of bringing about an amalgamation of colors by intermarriages. In vain have they again and again denied any such design; in vain have their writings been searched for any recommendation of such amalgamation. No Abolitionist is known to have married a negro, or to have given his child to a negro; yet has the charge of amalgamation been repeated, and repeated, till many have, no doubt, honestly believed it. . . . No one, in the possession of his reasoning faculties, can believe it to be the duty of white men to select black wives; and Abolitionists have given every proof the nature of the case will admit, that they countenance no such absurdity. (Quoted in Fowler, 149)

92. *The Emancipator*, August 5, 1834.
93. The data compiled by Richards on mob violence in the 1830s shows it peaking between 1834 and 1837 and declining thereafter.
94. A bill to revise the Commonwealth of Massachusetts marriage code had been introduced to the House by Whig member John P. Bigelow within a few months of Garrison's initial complaint in 1831. Another attempt was made to repeal the law in 1832 but, like Bigelow's, failed. For a history of the attempts to repeal the Massachusetts law, see Louis Ruchames, "Race, Marriage, and Abolition in Massachusetts," *Journal of Negro History* 40.3 (July 1955): 250–73.
95. See the following in the *Liberator*: "The Marriage Law," February 15, 1839, 27;

"Doings in the Legislature, Satirical Petition on the fair Ladies who admire 'Gentlemen of Color," "Scurrilous Petition from Lynn," and "Equal Laws—The Lynn Petition," February 22, 1839, 30; "Report Respecting Distinctions of Color,' " March 15, 1839, 41; and "The Law of Caste," March 22, 1839, 47.

96. See Lorman Ratner, *Powder Keg: Northern Opposition to the Antislavery Movement, 1831–1840* (New York: Basic Books, 1968), 139–41.

Chapter 4

1. *History of Pennsylvania Hall Which Was Destroyed by a Mob on the 7th of May, 1838*, ed. Samuel Webb (Philadelphia, 1838), 4.

2. Pennsylvania Hall cost forty thousand dollars and could seat two thousand. See Wendell Phillips Garrison and Francis Jackson Garrison, *William Lloyd Garrison, 1805–1879: The Story of His Life Told by His Children* (Boston: Houghton, Mifflin, 1889), 2: 211.

3. Quoted in Webb, 154.

4. The *Pennsylvanian*, May 18, 1838.

5. Quoted in Webb, 169.

6. Quoted in Webb, 136.

7. *Proceedings of the Anti-Slavery Convention of American Women, held in Philadelphia, May 15th, 16th, 17th and 18th, 1838* (Philadelphia, 1838), 10.

8. Quoted in Webb, 169.

9. Webb, 167–68.

10. Quoted in Webb, 167–68.

11. Sarah M. Grimké to Elizabeth Pease, Manlius, N.Y., May 20?, 1838, in *The Public Years of Sarah and Angelina Grimké: Selected Writings, 1835–1839*, ed. Larry Ceplair (New York: Columbia University Press, 1989), 317–18, 318.

12. See Webb, 117, 127.

13. The *Pennsylvanian*, May 18, 1838.

14. Quoted in Webb, 140. One might argue that Samuel Webb's account of the Philadelphia riot was strongly biased in favor of the abolitionists, of which he was a member. And, indeed, one historian who claims to provide an "objective" account bases it almost solely on published accounts in the *Public Ledger*, "the city's largest penny daily and . . . non-partisan," a paper, he argues, whose "steady tone lends credibility to its accounts." See Sam Bass Warner, Jr., *The Private City: Philadelphia in Three Periods of Its Growth* (Philadelphia: University of Pennsylvania Press, 1968), 132–3, n. 12. But in overlooking Webb's account and the numerous sources quoted in Webb, Warner fails to see the prevalence of amalgamation rhetoric that instigated and shaped accounts of the riot on both sides.

15. See David Grimsted, "Rioting in Its Jacksonian Setting," *American Historical Review* 77.2 (April 1972): 361–97; 373; and Warner, 137.

16. The *Pennsylvanian* reported after Pennsylvania Hall burned that "no impediment would be offered by those in authority" (May 19, 1838). The *Ledger* also suggested

on May 18 that the fire company allowed the hall to burn. The Police Committee reported, however, that the firemen were afraid to anger the mob further.

17. The delegates frequently linked the franchise to amalgamation. See the *Proceedings and Debates of the Convention of the Commonwealth of Pennsylvania. To Propose Amendments to the Constitution, Commenced at Harrisburg, May 2, 1837*, 5:414, 418, 443; 7:3, 272, 295, 357, 384; 8:40, 91, 92, 113, 117, 161, 241, 267; 9:83, 293, 321–28, 339, 349; 10:22, 23, 94, 106. Quote from 9:322.

18. Leonard L. Richards, *"Gentlemen of Property and Standing": Anti-Abolition Mobs in Jacksonian America* (Oxford: Oxford University Press, 1970), 132.

19. Webb, 154.

20. The *Pennsylvanian*, May 19, 1838.

21. Quoted in Warner, 136–37.

22. Emma Jones Lapsansky, "'Since They Got Those Separate Churches': Afro-Americans and Racism in Jacksonian Philadelphia," *American Quarterly* 32.1 (spring 1980): 54–78, 57.

23. Quoted in Jones Lapsansky, 70.

24. Quoted in Jones Lapsansky, 66–67.

25. On *Life in Philadelphia* and its popularity, see Nancy Reynolds Davidson, "E. W. Clay: American Political Caricaturist of the Jacksonian Era" (Ph.D. diss., University of Michigan, 1980), 85–100.

26. A commission which investigated the causes of the 1834 riots concluded that

An opinion prevails, especially among white laborers, that certain portions of our community, prefer to employ colored persons . . . to the employing of white people; and that, in consequence of this preference, many whites, who are able and willing to work, are left without employment. . . . Whoever mixed in the crowds and groups, at the late riots, must so often have heard these complaints, as to convince them, that . . . they . . . stimulated many of the most active among the rioters. (Quoted in Jones Lapsansky, 61)

See also John Runci, " 'Hunting the Nigs' in Philadelphia: The Race Riot of August, 1834," *Pennsylvania History* 29 (April 1972): 187–218.

27. On the location of the shelter, see Warner, 136.

28. Jones Lapsansky, 63.

29. John Fanning Watson, *Annals of Philadelphia* (Philadelphia, 1830), 479, quoted in Jones Lapsansky, 62.

30. Jones Lapsansky notes, correctly I think, that "it is worth speculating that it was, perhaps, intermarriage for the purpose of upward mobility that was abhorred by the riotous whites, and not necessarily amalgamation per se" (62).

31. Clay never titled the amalgamation series as a whole, but three of the seven prints that seem to compose it, if we include *An Amalgamation Polka* (1845), have the phrase "practical amalgamation" in the title. See Chapter 3.

32. See Stewart Button, *The Guitar in England, 1800–1924* (New York: Garland Publishing, 1989).

33. In his book, *Love and Theft: Blackface Minstrelsy and the American Working Class* (Oxford: Oxford University Press, 1993), Eric Lott notes of banjos in the minstrel

tradition that they were "deployed in ways that anticipated the phallic suggestions of rock'n'roll" (117). The illustrations in his book reveal as much and may have served as Clay's inspiration (118).

34. The *Philadelphia Saturday Courier*, May 19, 1838. A similar resolution was made at the Philadelphia Convention in 1838 but whether or not this was popularly known is unclear: "Resolved, . . . That it is . . . the duty of abolitionists to identify themselves with these oppressed Americans, by sitting with them in places of worship, by appearing with them in our streets, by giving them our countenance in steam-boats and stages, by visiting them at their homes and encouraging them to visit us, receiving them as we do our white fellow citizens." *Proceedings of the Anti-Slavery Convention of American Women, held in Philadelphia, May 15th, 16th, 17th and 18th, 1838*, 8. Webb declined to reprint this portion of their minutes in his book on the riot, undoubtedly thinking it would cause further furor.

35. In 1845, Clay produced *An Amalgamation Polka*. But the separation of six years from the rest of *Practical Amalgamation* makes it an afterthought in the series.

36. John Quincy Adams, "Misconceptions of Shakspeare [*sic*] upon the Stage," *New England Magazine* 9.54 (December 1, 1835): 435–40. Adams concludes that "The great moral lesson of 'Othello' is, that black and white blood cannot intermingle in marriage without a gross outrage upon the law of Nature" (438). See William Jerry MacLean, "Othello Scorned: The Racial Thought of John Quincy Adams," *Journal of the Early Republic* 4 (summer 1984): 143–60. And on the ways in which American productions of *Othello* "dramatized some of this country's racial reality and its racial fantasies," see Tilden G. Edelstein, "*Othello* in America: The Drama of Interracial Marriage," in *Region, Race and Reconstruction: Essays in Honor of C. Vann Woodward*, ed. J. Morgan Kousser and James M. McPherson, 179–97 (New York: Oxford University Press, 1982).

37. Kathryn Kish Sklar, *Catharine Beecher: A Study in American Domesticity* (New Haven, Conn.: Yale University Press, 1973), 137.

38. Karen Halttunen, *Confidence Men and Painted Women: A Study of Middle-Class Culture in America, 1830–1870* (New Haven, Conn.: Yale University Press, 1982), 60.

39. Quoted in Charles White, *An Account of the Regular Gradation of Man* (London, 1799), 51.

40. See Londa Schiebinger, *Nature's Body: Gender in the Making of Modern Science* (Boston, Mass.: Beacon Press, 1993), 253.

41. Stephen Jay Gould, "American Polygeny and Craniometry Before Darwin: Blacks and Indians as Separate, Inferior Species," in *The "Racial" Economy of Science: Toward A Democratic Future*, ed. Sandra Harding, 84–115 (Bloomington: Indiana University Press, 1993), 102.

42. Schiebinger, 149–50. William Dandridge Peck, professor of natural history at Harvard, recorded similar measurements in the United States. See William Martin Smallwood, *Natural History and the American Mind* (New York: Columbia University Press, 1941), 302–4.

43. Georges-Louis Leclerc Comte de Buffon, *Histoire naturelle, générale et particulière*, 44 vols. (Paris, 1749–1804), 14:50–51.

44. On the popularity of natural history in the nineteenth century, see Lynn Barber, *The Heyday of Natural History, 1820–1870* (Garden City, N.Y.: Doubleday & Co., Inc., 1980).

45. *Philadelphia Gazette,* August 20, 1839. Similar announcements were also made in the *Public Ledger,* July 1, 1839, the *Pennsylvania Inquirer,* July 1, 1839, and the *Saturday Courier,* July 6, 1839.

46. *A Natural History of the Globe, of Man, and of Quadrupeds* (1833), 2:253.

47. Quoted in Anthony Ambrogio, "Fay Wray: Horror Films' First Sex Symbol," in *Eros in the Minds' Eye: Sexuality and the Fantastic in Art and Film,* ed. Donald Palumbo (New York: Greenwood Press, 1986), 135.

48. The exact date of Poe's arrival in Philadelphia is not known. In "Poe in Philadelphia, 1838–1844: A Documentary Record" (Ph.D. diss., University of Pennsylvania, 1978), which provides more detail on this than his later published *The Poe Log: A Documentary Life of Edgar Allan Poe* (Boston: G. K. Hall, 1987), Dwight Rembert Thomas notes:

> Traditionally, Edgar Allan Poe is said to have moved from New York City to Philadelphia during "the summer of 1838," but there are apparently no documents to support this dating. Poe had arrived in New York by February 28, 1837, and he was still in this city on May 27 of that year. On July 19, 1838, he was in Philadelphia, writing James Kirke Paulding, then Secretary of the Navy, to request a clerkship. Between June, 1837, and July, 1838, there is no precise evidence of his location. No items of his correspondence are known to survive, and no mention of him in the contemporary newspapers or in the correspondence of his acquaintances has been discovered. In all probability, Poe remained in New York until late 1837 or early 1838. (1)

Of course, Poe may have arrived slightly after the riot in 1838. But discussions and debates about it would still have been echoing throughout the local press.

49. Several critics have noted that the simian on display at Masonic Hall may have served as Poe's inspiration. Dwight Rembert Thomas muses in "Poe in Philadelphia," for example, that "When Poe selected an ourang outang as a protagonist for 'The Murders in the Rue Morgue,' he was almost certainly mindful of the popular sensation caused by the exhibition of this chimpanzee in August and September, 1839" (51). More recently, Jeffrey Meyers argues in *Edgar Allan Poe: His Life and Legacy* (New York: Charles Scribner's Sons, 1992) that "The murderer was undoubtedly inspired by the huge, hairy, red ourang-outang that was exhibited before astonished crowds at the Masonic Hall in Philadelphia in July 1839" (123). Neither Thomas nor Meyers, however, ponders the precise nature of the public's fascination and thus, by extension, what might have prompted Poe to use this animal. Terence Whalen, one of the few who sees the story's connection to antebellum race ideologies, also notes the exhibition of the "orangutan" at Masonic Hall in "Edgar Allan Poe and the Horrid Laws of Political Economy," *American Quarterly* 44.3 (1992): 381–417, 415 n. 53.

50. Edgar Allan Poe, "The Murders in the Rue Morgue," in *Collected Works of Edgar Allan Poe,* vol. 2: *Tales and Sketches, 1831–1842,* ed. Thomas Ollive Mabbott, 521–74 (Cambridge. Mass.: Harvard University Press, 1978), 559. Hereafter, page numbers will be cited parenthetically in the text.

51. Quoted in Thomas, "Poe in Philadelphia," 950.

52. Poe's full remarks about *The Conchologist's First Book* (1839) read as follows:

I wrote it, in conjunction with Professor Thomas Wyatt, and Professor McMurtrie of Pha — my name being put to the work, as best known and most likely to aid its circulation. I wrote the Preface and Introduction, and translated from Cuvier, the accounts of the animals etc. *All* schoolbooks are necessarily made in a similar way. The very title-page acknowledges that the animals are given "according to Cuvier." (Quoted in Thomas, "Poe in Philadelphia," 950, Poe's emphasis)

Poe must have also read Cuvier's *Animal Kingdom* in English, particularly insofar as he claimed to have written *The Conchologist's First Book* with the translator, H. McMurtrie. Charles F. Heartman and James R. Canny include Wyatt's *Synopsis* in their *Biography of First Printings of the Writings of Edgar Allan Poe* (New York: Kraus Reprint, 1972), 45–46.

53. Quoted in Schiebinger, 80.

54. *Dr. Ree's New Cyclopaedia*, vol. 1, part 2.

55. Lincoln was called the "Illinois Ape" in the *Richmond Examiner* on April 23, 1861. On this and other such nicknames used, see J. G. Randall, *Lincoln: The Liberal Statesman* (New York: Dodd, Mead, 1947), 65–66.

56. On this and other exhibits of monkeys at Peale's Museum, see Charles Coleman Sellers, *Mr. Peale's Museum: Charles Willson Peale and the First Popular Museum of Natural History & Art* (New York: W. W. Norton, 1980), 207, 216.

57. Charles Godfrey Leland, *Memoirs* (New York, 1893), 38–39.

58. Cyprian Clamorgan, *The Colored Aristocracy of St. Louis*. 1858. Rpt. in *The Bulletin of the Missouri Historical Society* 31.1 (October 1974): 9–31, 18.

59. Herman Melville, "Benito Cereno," in *Billy Budd, Sailor and Other Stories*, 144–223 (New York: Bantam Books, 1986), 185, 186.

60. Clamorgan, 18.

61. Roger Lane, *William Dorsey's Philadelphia and Ours: On the Past and Future of the Black City in America* (New York: Oxford University Press, 1991), 115.

62. W. E. B. Du Bois, *The Philadelphia Negro: A Social Study* (Philadelphia, 1899), 142–43.

63. Clamorgan, 17.

64. Melville, 186–88.

65. For years, "The Murders in the Rue Morgue" has elicited what critic Shawn Rosenheim calls "bad Freudian readings" in "Detective Fiction, Psychoanalysis, and the Analytic Sublime," in *The American Face of Edgar Allan Poe*, ed. Shawn Rosenheim and Stephen Rachman, 153–78 (Baltimore: The Johns Hopkins University Press, 1995), 167. For scholars who have attempted to grapple with the story's racial context, see Whalen; Joan Dayan, "Romance and Race," in *The Columbia History of the American Novel*, ed. Emory Elliott et al., 89–109 (New York: Columbia University Press, 1991); Frankie Y. Bailey, *Out of the Woodpile: Black Characters in Crime and Detective Fiction* (New York: Greenwood Press, 1991); and, in addition to my own reading of the tale in *Romancing the Shadow: Poe and Race*, a somewhat different version of this chapter, see Lindon Barrett, "Presence of Mind: Detection and Racialization in 'The Murders in

the Rue Morgue,' " in *Romancing the Shadow: Poe and Race*, ed. J. Gerald Kennedy and Liliane Weissberg, 157–76 (Oxford: Oxford University Press, 2001).

66. Judith Fetterley, "Reading about Reading: 'A Jury of Her Peers,' 'The Murders in the Rue Morgue,' and 'The Yellow Wallpaper,'" in *Gender and Reading: Essays on Readers, Texts, and Contexts*, ed. Elizabeth A. Flynn and Patrocinio P. Schweickart, 147–64 (Baltimore: The Johns Hopkins University Press, 1986), 156.

67. For an extended argument on Poe's racism and its relationship to his work, see John Carlos Rowe, "Poe, Antebellum Slavery, and Modern Criticism," in *Poe's Pym: Critical Explorations*, ed. Richard Kopley, 117–38 (Durham, N.C.: Duke University Press, 1992). Rowe asserts that "Poe's sympathy with the Southern aristocracy, plantation life, and the institution of slavery have been treated as personal prejudices which are not consistently displayed in his literary writings. . . . My own argument is that Poe's proslavery sentiments are fundamental to his literary production and thus demand a searching reconsideration of his aesthetic canon" (117). Dayan remarks similarly, in "Romance and Race," that "Critics, myself included, have ignored the way the romance of the South and the realities of race were fundamental to . . . [Poe's] literary production" (93). In *Playing in the Dark: Whiteness and the Literary Imagination* (Cambridge, Mass.: Harvard University Press, 1992), "an investigation into the ways in which a nonwhite Africanlike (or Africanist) presence or persona was constructed in the United States, and the imaginative uses this fabricated presence served," Toni Morrison asserts that "no early American writer is more important to the concept of American Africanism than Poe" (6 and 32). Perhaps the best treatment to date of race and Poe's oeuvre is Joan Dayan's "Amorous Bondage: Poe, Ladies, and Slaves," *American Literature* 66.2 (June 1994): 239–73. In it, she recounts her own institutional experience with the academia's "coercive monumentalization of certain writers" whereby, in Poe's case, there has been a determined attempt to excise considerations of Poe's proslavery sentiments from his literary production. See also the recent compilation of essays *Romancing the Shadow: Poe and Race*, ed. Kennedy and Weissberg.

68. Bared white breasts were considered shocking at the time. In the 1840s, Hiram Powers's statue *The Greek Slave* raised a ruckus in part because the general public was not ready to see a bare-breasted white woman. See Jean Fagan Yellin, *Women and Sisters: The Antislavery Feminists in American Culture* (New Haven, Conn.: Yale University Press, 1989), 99–124.

69. On the detective's role "in annihilating the libidinal possibility, the 'inner' truth that each in the group might have been the murderer" (59), see Slavoj Zizek, *Looking Awry: An Introduction to Jacques Lacan through Popular Culture* (Cambridge, Mass.: Harvard University Press, 1992).

70. For a similar conclusion, see Gould, 98.

71. See Stanton, 69.

72. Stanton, 77.

73. J. C. Nott, "The Mulatto a Hybrid—probable extermination of the two races if the Whites and Blacks are allowed to intermarry," *American Journal of the Medical Sciences* 6 (1843): 252–56, 253.

74. Ibid., 254.

75. Stanton, 75, 112; Gould, 95.

76. Quoted in Morton, "Hybridity in Animals considered in reference to the Unity of the Human Species," *American Journal of Science,* 2nd ser., 3 (1847): 39–50, 203–12, 210.

77. Ibid., 211.

78. Ibid., 212.

79. In *The Black Image in the White Mind: The Debate on Afro-American Character and Destiny, 1817–1914* (New York: Harper & Row, 1971), George Fredrickson devotes an entire chapter to refuting "the belief of historians that the theory [of polygenesis] was rejected out of hand" (85). Fredrickson explains that

The exact importance for the slavery controversy of the new scientific attitudes towards race— that is, the extent to which the theory was promulgated to serve conscious proslavery purposes or was, in any case, appropriated and used by the defenders of slavery—needs to be reexamined. William Stanton . . . has argued that its doctrines . . . were peripheral to the defense of slavery . . . because it conflicted with orthodox religious beliefs about human origins. . . . But there is evidence, some of it presented by Stanton himself, to support a somewhat different view. (76)

Fredrickson notes that "Argued on a scientific basis, the theory [of polygenesis] was abstruse and difficult for those without some knowledge of biology. But the basic idea was disseminated by popularizers, who not only simplified the concepts but labored to remove the single objection that carried real weight—the impression that pluralism conflicted with scripture" (86–87). The result was what Fredrickson calls a "Biblical theory of polygenesis" (89). Fredrickson takes as one example the career of Josiah C. Nott. "Adherents of the common descent of mankind accused him and his supporters of infidelity for denying the accepted Biblical view of the origin of all races in the progeny of Adam" (82). But, as Fredrickson notes, despite initial resistance from clergymen, Nott "eventually gained widespread and influential support for his most fundamental conceptions" (81). "What is most striking is not that polygenesis encountered opposition from the spokesmen of conservative Christianity but that, even in its aggressively secular form as put forth by Nott, it won as much acceptance as it did" (84–85). Fredrickson concludes that, polygenesis "raised prejudice to the level of science; thereby giving it respectability" in the mid-nineteenth century (89).

80. See review by John Bachman published in the *Charleston Medical Journal* in four installments in 1854. Quoted in Stanton, 172. Bachman noted that those who supported the doctrine of unity were "stigmatized as abolitionists" unfairly. As a Southerner, he explained, he found the process of "amalgamation" "revolting" (quoted in Stanton, 172). A reviewer of Nott and Gliddon's next book, *Indigenous Races of the Earth* (1857), also expressed the fear of being branded a "northern abolitionist" (Stanton, 177).

81. The *Pennsylvanian,* May 21, 1838.

82. The *Philadelphia Saturday Courier,* May 26, 1838.

Chapter 5

1. So stated the constitution of the New England Anti-Slavery Society and those

of most abolitionist societies. Quoted in Louis Ruchames, "Race, Marriage, and Abolition in Massachusetts," *Journal of Negro History* 40.3 (July 1955): 250–73, 254.

2. See, for example, the argument in the Lowell *Journal* that "Matrimony is an affair that may safely be left to the tastes of the contracting parties." Reprinted in the *Liberator*, May 10, 1839, and quoted in Ruchames, 266.

3. Quoted in the *Commonwealth*, July 17, 1863, and quoted in James M. McPherson, *The Struggle for Equality: Abolitionists and the Negro in the Civil War and Reconstruction* (Princeton, N.J.: Princeton University Press, 1964), 148.

4. Quoted in George M. Fredrickson, *The Black Image in the White Mind: The Debate on Afro-American Character and Destiny, 1817–1914* (New York: Harper & Row, 1971), 121.

5. McPherson finds statements in support of inter-racial marriage evidence of the abolitionists' great egalitarianism. "The remarkable fact about the abolitionists was not that as champions of the Negro *some* of them believed in racial differences, but that in a nation where popular belief *and* scientific learning overwhelmingly proclaimed the Negro's absolute inferiority, there were men and women who dared to affirm their faith in the innate equality of all men, regardless of race" (147). As for inter-marriage, he adds, "It is not recorded whether any daughter of a white abolitionist did marry a Negro, but it is known that the abolitionists did not shrink from discussing the issue. In the face of popular odium and violence, abolitionists struggled to remove laws marring intermarriage from the statute books of Massachusetts and other states" (147). Like me, Fredrickson finds of McPherson's book that "he somewhat exaggerates the egalitarianism of the abolitionists. His discussion, for example, of abolitionist advocacy of intermarriage . . . gives a misleading impression because it consists mainly of statements from the relatively few abolitionists who took a strong and unequivocal stand on this issue." (127 n. 60). Fredrickson explains that

Views on amalgamation as bold and forthright as those of Moncure Daniel Conway and [Gilbert] Haven represented an extreme position, even among abolitionists. Antislavery radicals who addressed themselves to this question during the war were usually more tentative in their evaluation of race mixing. Their characteristic response to the charge that emancipation would lead to wholesale amalgamation was that they did not advocate intermarriage as a deliberate policy and felt that short-run miscegenation would actually decrease once the slavemaster lost control of his black concubines. But they were opposed to legal prohibitions on intermarriage, believing that such alliances should be a matter of personal choice, and they held out the possibility that in the course of centuries, the Negro blood would be absorbed by the white. Some antislavery spokesmen, however, actually shared the strong aversion of intermarriage characteristic of Northern opinion in general and were receptive to the views of the American school of ethnology on the dire consequences of racial mixture. (122–23)

6. The *New-York Commercial Advertiser*, July 7, 1834.

7. Quoted in Samuel G. Morton, "Hybridity in Animals, considered in reference to the question of the Unity of the Human Species," *American Journal of Science*, 2nd ser., 3 (1847): 39–50, 203–12.

8. David Goodman Croly and George Wakeman], *Miscegenation: The Theory of the Blending of the Races, Applied to the American White Man and Negro* (New York,

1863–64), 1. Hereafter, page numbers will be cited in the text. Because the pamphlet title was entered for copyright on December 29, 1863, it is often listed in bibliographies with either a publishing date of 1863 or 1864. See J. M. Bloch, *Miscegenation, Melaleukation, and Mr. Lincoln's Dog* (New York: Schaum Publishin, 1958), 62 n. 82. For a history of the pamphlet and its reception, see Bloch; Fredrickson, 171–86; Sidney Kaplan, "The Miscegenation Issue in the Election of 1864," *Journal of Negro History* 34 (July 1949): 274–343; and Forrest G. Wood, *Black Scare: The Racist Response to Emancipation and Reconstruction* (Berkeley: University of California Press, 1968), 53–79.

9. Articles about and references to the *Miscegenation* pamphlet appeared in both Republican and Democrat newspapers and as far away as Virginia City, Nevada, where Mark Twain remarked on it in the *Territorial Enterprise* on May 24, 1864, and London, where the status of the pamphlet as a hoax was revealed in the *Morning Herald* . See Bloch, 24–28, 34–36.

10. *The Lincoln-Douglas Debates*, ed. Harold Holzer (New York: HarperCollins, 1993), 67.

11. *Abraham Lincoln: Speeches and Writings, 1832–1858*, ed. Don E. Fehrenbacher (New York: The Library of America, 1989), 636–37.

12. See [John Van Evrie], *Subgenation: The Theory of the Normal Relation of the Races; An Answer to "Miscegenation"* (New York, 1864) and the West Chester *Jeffersonian*, quoted in Kaplan, 312.

13. On the revelation that the pamphlet was a hoax, see Bloch, 34–36, and Kaplan, 326–33.

14. Quoted in Kaplan, 296–97.

15. The New York *Tribune*, March 16, 1864.

16. The *Independent*, February 25, 1864; quoted in Kaplan, 300.

17. See David R. Roediger, *The Wages of Whiteness: Race and the Making of the American Working Class* (London: Verso, 1991), 154.

18. The London *Times*, 8 February 1864, quoted in Kaplan, 295.

19. Quoted in Kaplan, 306.

20. This would seem to indicate that the specter of inter-mixing at mid-century was raised, not as a means of policing white women in particular, as some scholars argue, but as a means of controlling both white women and men. For the argument that gender was the pivotal axis along which race was policed in the nineteenth century, see, for example, Martha Hodes, *White Women, Black Men: Illicit Sex in the Nineteenth-Century South* (New Haven, Conn.: Yale University Press, 1997).

21. Quoted in Kaplan, 317 n. 59.

22. George W. Stocking, Jr., characterizes Prichard's career as one devoted to defending the common humanity of blacks (lvii). He views Prichard's inability to accept the popular theory of polygenesis as stemming from his Quaker humanitarianism (xlix). George W. Stocking, Jr., introduction to *Researches into the Physical History of Man*, by James Cowels Prichard (Chicago: University of Chicago Press, 1973).

23. Van Evrie, 5–6.

24. The *National Anti-Slavery Standard*, November 9, 1861.

25. Charles Sumner, "The Question of Caste" (October 21, 1869), in *The Works of Charles Sumner* (Boston: Lee and Shepard, 1870–83), 13:176. Fredrickson argues that the

abolitionists "were on the defensive on this question [of human origins] and preferred to avoid the whole subject" (127 n.60). It is certainly true that the abolitionists did not look to science very frequently, but that they largely believed in the theory of monogenesis is not questioned.

26. Sumner, 176.

27. See William Stanton, *The Leopard's Spots: Scientific Attitudes Toward Race in America, 1815–59* (Chicago: University of Chicago Press, 1960).

28. Quoted in Bloch, 35.

29. Reprinted in the *World*, Nov. 18, 1864, quoted in Bloch, 34.

30. Nott, "The Mulatto a Hybrid—probable extermination of the two races if the Whites and Blacks Are allowed to intermarry," *American Journal of the Medical Sciences* 6 (1843): 252–56, 255.

31. New York *Leader*, March 26, 1864.

32. Van Evrie, 68.

33. Quoted in Wood, 64–65.

34. Quoted in Fredrickson, 107.

35. Quoted in Fredrickson, 120.

36. *Commonwealth*, October 18, 1862; quoted in McPherson, 144. Even as they meant to promote the humanity of the slaves, Lowell, Parker, and Conway all imagine in racist fashion that "the African race" is somehow less "strong" than "Caucasians," Conway going so far as to term the "African element" "child-like."

37. Harriet Beecher Stowe, *Uncle Tom's Cabin* (New York: Bantam, 1981), 350.

38. Quoted in the *Liberator*, April 8, 1864.

39. Quoted in the New York *World*, April 4, 1864.

40. The *New York Times*, March 21, 1864.

41. Ibid., March 21, 1864.

42. Van Evrie, iii.

43. The *New York Times*, March 21, 1864.

44. The *New York Times*, April 3, 1864.

45. Louisa May Alcott, "M. L." (1863), in *Louisa May Alcott on Race, Sex, and Slavery*, ed. Sarah Elbert, 2–28 (Boston: Northeastern University Press, 1997), 7, 5, 7. Hereafter, page numbers will be cited parenthetically in the text.

46. On the motto "Am I Not a Man and a Brother?" and its history, see Jean Fagan Yellin, *Women and Sisters: The Antislavery Feminists in American Culture* (New Haven, Conn.: Yale University Press, 1989), 5–8.

47. Alcott also transforms the stereotype that blacks are talented singers. Of course, ultimately Paul is revealed to have black ancestry that may, in hindsight, explain his singing talents for some readers. But for most of the story, his singing is experienced as completely distinct from his blackness.

48. Quoted in Wood, 72.

49. Quoted in Kaplan, 276.

50. Quoted in Wood, 62–63.

51. Quoted in Kaplan, 334.

52. Quoted in *Miscegenation Indorsed*, [sic] *by the Republican Party, Campaign Document, No. 11.*, 6.

53. Quoted in Kaplan, 287.

54. Quoted in Kaplan, 289.

55. Quoted in Kaplan, 293.

56. Quoted in Kaplan, 288.

57. Quoted in Kaplan, 286–87.

58. See Kaplan, 291 n. 16.

59. June 26, 1857, in *Abraham Lincoln: Speeches and Writings, 1832–1858*, ed. Don E. Fehrenbacher (New York, 1989), 397.

60. Ibid., 397–98.

61. *Abraham Lincoln: Speeches and Writings, 1832–1858*, 636–37.

62. Quoted in Byron Curti Martyn, "Racism in the United States: A History of the Anti-Miscegenation Legislation and Litigation" (Ph.D. diss., University of Southern California, 1979), 436.

63. Quoted in Kaplan, 294.

64. The New York *Tribune*, March 16, 1864.

65. The New York *Tribune*, March 16, 1864.

66. The New York *Tribune*, March 16, 1864.

67. The London *Morning Herald*, November 1, 1864, quoted in Kaplan, 278.

68. Croly and Wakeman, 18. After Croly and Wakeman's pamphlet was published, the Civil War was also termed a "war of miscegenation." See, for example, the *New York Freeman's Journal and Catholic Register*, April 30, 1864; quoted in Kaplan, 319. Karl Marx, *Grundrisse: Foundations of the Critique of Political Economy*, trans. Martin Nicolaus (New York: Random House, 1973), 105–6. For a concise explanation of Marx's "simple abstraction," see Michael McKeon, *The Origins of the English Novel, 1600–1740* (Baltimore: The Johns Hopkins University Press, 1987), 15–20.

69. Quoted in Wood, 71, 62.

70. L. Seaman, *What Miscegenation Is! And What We Are to Expect Now that Mr. Lincoln is Re-elected* (New York, n.d.), 3.

71. See 173 n. 5

72. *National Sermons*, 548–49; quoted in Fredrickson, 122.

73. Dana Nelson, introduction to *A Romance of the Republic*, by Lydia Maria Child (Lexington: University Press of Kentucky, 1997), xix.

74. "Final Report of the American Freedman's Inquiry Commission to the Secretary of War, May 15, 1864," in *War of the Rebellion: A Compilation of the Official Records of the Union and Confederate Armies*, series 3, (Washington, D.C. 1990), 4:289–382, 377.

75. I have only found one book prior to the recent *Africana* that complained about the usage of the term "miscegenation." In *Racism and Psychiatry* (New York: Brunner/Mazel, 1972), Alexander Thomas and Samuel Sillen note that "The acceptance of this term ["miscegenation"] is a graphic example of how racist ideas achieve uncritical circulation. . . . The word was picked up by the racists as a term of opprobrium and its unthinking use today represents a victory for the Copperheads who concocted it" (111).

Epilogue

1. The assertion that race is a social fiction is now made repeatedly. George Lipsitz begins *The Possessive Investment in Whiteness: How White People Profit from Identity Politics* (Philadelphia: Temple University Press, 1998), for example, with what he assumes is now a commonplace:

> whiteness is, *of course*, a delusion, a scientific and cultural fiction that like all racial identities has no valid foundation in biology or anthropology. Whiteness is, however, a social fact, an identity created and continued with all-too-real consequences for the distribution of wealth, prestige, and opportunity. (vii, emphasis added)

Most recently, in another example, Dr. Eric S. Lander of the Whitehead Institute for Biomedical Research at Massasschusetts Institute of Technology was quoted in the *New York Times* for declaring of the human genome sequence that "these data have tremendous potential to deconstruct simplistic notions of race and ethnicity." Nicholas Wade, "Genome Mappers Navigate the Tricky Terrain of Race," The *New York Times* (July 20, 2001), A17.

2. Jared Diamond, "Race without Color," *Discover* (November 1994): 83–89, 83.

3. Diamond, 89.

4. As this book goes to press, the marriage figures for the 2000 federal census are still unavailable. The 97 percent rate is from the 1990 census. U.S. Bureau of the Census.

5. Carmela Ciuraru, "In Stark Black and White, a Mixed Family Unravels," review of *Resurrecting Mingus*, by Jenoyne Adams, *USA Today* (March 22, 2001): 5D.

Bibliography

PRIMARY SOURCES

MANUSCRIPTS

Minute Book of the Utica Literary Club, the Oneida Historical Society, Utica, New York.
William C. Holgate Diary, The Defiance College, Defiance, Ohio.

NEWSPAPERS

Courier and Enquirer (N.Y.)
Emancipator
Evening Post (N.Y.)
Ledger (Pa.)
Liberator
Mercantile Advertiser and New York Advocate
Methodist Magazine and Quarterly Review of New York
Morning Courier and New-York Enquirer
National Anti-Slavery Leader
New-York Commercial Advertiser
New York *Leader*
New York Times
New York *Tribune*
New York *World*
Pennsylvanian
Philadelphia Gazette
Philadelphia Inquirer
Philadelphia *Port Folio*
Philadelphia Saturday Courier
Public Ledger (Pa.)
Richmond *Recorder*
Saturday Courier (Pa.)

OTHER PUBLISHED SOURCES

Abdy, E. S. *Journal of a Residence and Tour in the United States of North America from April, 1833, to October, 1834.* 3 vols. London, 1835.

Adams, John Quincy. "Misconceptions of Shakspeare [*sic*] upon the Stage." *New England Magazine* 9.54 (December 1, 1835): 435–40.

Africana: The Encyclopedia of the African and African American Experience. Ed. Kwame Anthony Appiah and Henry Louis Gates, Jr. New York: Basic Books, 1999.

Alcott, Louisa May. "M. L." In *Louisa May Alcott: On Race, Sex, and Slavery*, ed. Sarah Elbert, 3–28. Boston: Northeastern University Press, 1997.

Beaumont, Gustave de. *Marie; Or, Slavery in the United States.* Trans. Barbara Chapman. Stanford, Calif.: Stanford University Press, 1958.

Beecher, Catharine E. *A Treatise on Domestic Economy, for the use of Young Ladies at Home, and at School.* Boston, 1841.

Best, George. In *The English Literatures of America, 1500–1800*, ed. Myra Jehlen and Michael Warner, 54–58. New York: Routledge, 1997.

Blackstone, Sir William. *Commentaries on the Laws of England.* 4 vols. London, 1768.

Bryant, William Cullen. *The Embargo, or Sketches of the Times: A Satire.* Gainesville, Fla.: Scholars' Facsimiles and Reprints, 1955.

Buffon, Georges-Louis Leclerc Comte de. *Histoire naturelle, générale et particulière.* 44 vols. Paris, 1749–1804.

Byrd, William. *William Byrd's Histories of the Dividing Line betwixt Virginia and Carolina.* Ed. William K. Boyd. Raleigh: The North Carolina Historical Commission, 1929.

Child, Lydia Maria. *An Appeal in Favor of That Class of Americans Called Africans.* Amherst: University of Massachusetts Press, 1996.

Ciuraru, Carmela. "In Stark Black and White, a Mixed Family Unravels." Review of *Resurrecting Mingus*, by Jenoyne Adams. *USA Today*, March 22, 2001, 5D.

Clamorgan, Cyprian. *The Colored Aristocracy of St. Louis.* 1858. Reprint, *The Bulletin of the Missouri Historical Society* 30.1 (October 1974): 9–31.

Cobbett, William. *The American Gardener.* 1819.

Cooper, James Fenimore. *The Last of the Mohicans.* New York: Penguin Books, 1986.

[Croly, David Goodman and George Wakeman]. *Miscegenation: The Theory of the Blending of the Races, Applied to the American White Man and Negro.* New York, 1863–64.

Cuvier, Baron Georges. *The Animal Kingdom arranged according to its organization.* Ed. and trans. H. McMurtrie. London: Orr and Smith, 1834.

Dante, Alighieri. *The Divine Comedy: Purgatory.* Trans. Dorothy L. Sayers. Harmondsworth: Penguin, 1995.

Diamond, Jared. "Race Without Color." *Discover* (November 1994): 83–89.

Dr. Ree's New Cyclopaedia. Philadelphia, 1806–21.

Fessenden, Thomas Green [Christopher Caustic, L.L.D., pseud.]. *Democracy Unveiled or, Tyranny Stripped of the Garb of Patriotism.* 3rd ed. New York, 1806.

"Final Report of the American Freedmen's Inquiry Commission to the Secretary of War, May 15, 1864." In *The War of the Rebellion: A Compilation of the Official*

Records of the Union and Confederate Armies, ser. 3, vol. 4. Washington, D.C., 1900.

Fowler, Henry. *The American Pulpit.* New York, 1856.

Grimké, Sarah M. Letter to Elizabeth Pease. Manlius, N.Y., May 20?, 1838. In *The Public Years of Sarah and Angelina Grimké: Selected Writings, 1835–1839,* ed. Larry Ceplair, 317–18. New York: Columbia University Press, 1989.

Grimké, Sarah and Angelina Grimké. *The Public Years of Sarah and Angelina Grimké; Selected Writings, 1835–39.* Ed. Larry Ceplair. New York: Columbia University Press, 1989.

Hawthorne, Nathaniel. *Centenary Edition.* Ed. William Charvat, Roy Harvey Pearce, and Claude M. Simpson. 23 vols. Columbia: Ohio State University Press, 1962–.

History of Pennsylvania Hall Which Was Destroyed by a Mob on the 7th of May, 1838. [Ed. Samuel Webb]. Philadelphia, 1838.

[Holgate, Jerome B.]. *A Sojourn in the City of Amalgamation in the Year of Our Lord 19– by Oliver Bolokitten–Esq.* New York, 1835.

Horace (Quintus Horatius Flaccus), *The Complete Works of Horace.* Trans. Charles E. Passage. New York: Frederick Ungar Publishing Company, 1983.

Jefferson, Thomas. *Thomas Jefferson: Writings.* Ed. Merrill D. Peterson. New York: The Library of America, 1984.

———. *Thomas Jefferson and James Thomson Callender, 1798–1802.* Ed. Worthington Chauncy Ford. Brooklyn: Historical Printing Club, 1897.

Leland, Charles Godfrey. *Memoirs.* New York, 1839.

Lincoln, Abraham. *Abraham Lincoln: Speeches and Writings, 1832–1858.* Ed. Don E. Fehrenbacher. New York: The Library of America, 1989.

———. *The Lincoln-Douglas Debates.* Ed. Harold Holzer. New York: Harper Collins, 1993.

Melville, Herman. "Benito Cereno." In *Billy Budd, Sailor and Other Stories.* 144–223. New York: Bantam Books, 1986.

Memorial History of Utica, New York. Ed. M. M. Bagg. Syracuse, N.Y., 1892.

Miscegenation Indorsed [*sic*] *by the Republican Party. Campaign Document, No. 11.* New York, 1864.

Morton, Samuel George. *Crania Americana; or, A Comparative View of the Skulls of Various Aboriginal Nations of North and South America: To Which is Prefixed an Essay on the Varieties of the Human Species.* Philadelphia, 1839.

———. "Hybridity in Animals considered in reference to the Unity of the Human Species." *American Journal of Science,* 2nd ser., 3 (1847): 39–50, 203–12.

A Natural History of the Globe, of Man, and of Quadrupeds; From the Writings of Buffon, Cuvier . . . and Other Eminent Naturalists. 2 vols. New York, 1833.

Nott, J. C. "The Mulatto a Hybrid—probable extermination of the two races if the Whites and Blacks are allowed to intermarry." *American Journal of the Medical Sciences* 6 (1843): 252–56.

Poe, Edgar Allan. "The Murders in the Rue Morgue." In *Collected Works of Edgar Allan Poe,* ed. Thomas Ollive Mabbott, vol. 2, 521–74. Cambridge, Mass.: Harvard University Press, 1978.

Prichard, James Cowles. *Researches into the Physical History of Man.* Ed. George W. Stocking, Jr. Chicago: University of Chicago Press, 1973.

Proceedings and Debates of the Convention of the Commonwealth of Pennsylvania. To Propose Amendments to the Constitution, Commenced at Harrisburg, May 2, 1837. 14 vols. Harrisburg: Packer, Barrett, and Parke, 1837–39.

Proceedings of the Anti-Slavery Convention of American Women, held in Philadelphia, May 15th, 16th, 17th and 18th. Philadelphia, 1838.

Quincy, Josiah. "Journal of Josiah Quincy Junior, 1773." *Massachusetts Historical Society, Proceedings* 49 (June 1916): 424–81.

Rolfe, John. "Letter of John Rolfe, 1614." In *Narratives of Early Virginia: 1606–1628*, ed. Lyon Gardiner Tyler. New York: C. Scribner's Sons, 1907.

Seaman, L. *What Miscegenation Is! And What We Are to Expect Now that Mr. Lincoln is Re-elected.* New York, n.d.

Strong, T. W. *Boy's Own Book of Fun.* New York, n.d.

Sumner, Charles. *The Works of Charles Sumner.* 15 vols. Boston: Lee and Shepard, 1870–83.

Tocqueville, Alexis de. *Democracy in America.* 2 vols. New York: Random House, 1990.

[Van Evrie, John H.]. *Subgenation: The Theory of the Normal Relation of the Races; An Answer to "Miscegenation."* New York, 1864.

Wade, Nicholas. "Genome Mappers Navigate Tricky Terrain of Race." *New York Times* (July 20, 2001), A17.

Webb, Samuel J. *Some Recollections of our Antislavery Conflict.* Boston: Fields, Osgood, 1869.

White, Charles. *An Account of the Regular Gradation of Man.* London, 1799.

Wyatt, Thomas. *A Synopsis of Natural History: Embracing the Natural History of Animals, with Human and General Animal Physiology, Botany, Vegetable Physiology and Geology. Translated from the Latest French Edition of C. Lemmonnier.... With Additions from the Works of Cuvier, Dumaril, Lacepede, Etc.; And Arranged as a Textbook for Schools.* Philadelphia, 1839.

SECONDARY SOURCES

Ambrogio, Anthony. "Fay Wray: Horror Films' First Sex Symbol." In *Eros in the Mind's Eye: Sexuality and the Fantastic in Art and Film*, ed. Donald Palumbo. New York: Greenwood Press, 1986.

Aptheker, Herbert. *Anti-Racism in U.S. History: The First Two Hundred Years.* New York: Greenwood Press, 1992.

Bailey, Frankie Y. *Out of the Woodpile: Black Characters in Crime and Detective Fiction.* New York: Greenwood Press, 1991.

Bailey, Thomas. *Voices of America: The Nation's Story in Slogans, Sayings, and Songs.* New York: The Free Press, 1976.

Barber, Lynn. *The Heyday of Natural History, 1820–1870.* Garden City, N.Y.: Doubleday, Inc., 1980.

Bardaglio, Peter W. *Reconstructing the Household: Families, Sex, and the Law in the Nineteenth-Century South.* Chapel Hill: University of North Carolina Press, 1995.

Barker, Martin and Roger Sabin. *The Lasting of the Mohicans: History of an American Myth.* Jackson: University Press of Mississippi, 1995.

Barrett, Lindon. "Presence of Mind: Detection and Racialization in 'The Murders in the Rue Morgue.'" In *Romancing the Shadow: Poe and Race*, ed. J. Gerald Kennedy and Liliane Weissberg, 157–76. Oxford: Oxford University Press, 2001.

Basch, Norma. *In the Eyes of the Law: Women, Marriage, and Property in Nineteenth-Century New York*. Ithaca, N.Y.: Cornell University Press, 1982.

Baym, Nina. "Putting Women in Their Place: *The Last of the Mohicans* and Other Indian Stories." In *Feminism and American Literary History: Essays by Nina Baym*, 19-35. New Brunswick, N.J.: Rutgers University Press, 1992.

Bieder, Robert E. "Scientific Attitudes Toward Indian Mixed-Bloods in Early Nineteenth Century America." *The Journal of Ethnic Studies* 8.2 (summer, 1980): 17–30.

Bloch, J. M. *Miscegenation, Melaleukation, and Mr. Lincoln's Dog*. New York: Schaum Publishing Company, 1958.

Bloch, R. Howard. *Etymologies and Genealogies: A Literary Anthropology of the French Middle Ages*. Chicago: University of Chicago Press, 1983.

Boulton, Alexander O. "The American Paradox: Jeffersonian Equality and Racial Science." *American Quarterly* 47.3 (September 1995): 467–92.

Bourdieu, Pierre. *Distinction: A Social Critique of the Judgement of Taste*. Trans. Richard Nice. Cambridge, Mass.: Harvard University Press, 1984.

———. *Outline of a Theory of Practice*. Cambridge: Cambridge University Press, 1997.

Brodie, Fawn. *Thomas Jefferson: An Intimate History*. New York: W. W. Norton, 1974.

Brown, Gillian. *Domestic Individualism: Imagining Self in Nineteenth-Century America*. Berkeley: University of California Press, 1990.

Burg, B. R. "The Rhetoric of Miscegenation: Thomas Jefferson, Sally Hemings, and Their Historians." *Phylon* 47.2 (1986): 128–38.

Button, Stewart. *The Guitar in England, 1800–1924*. New York: Garland Publishing, 1989.

Camporesi, Piero. *Juice of Life: The Symbolic and Magic Significance of Blood*. Trans. Robert R. Barr. New York: Continuum, 1995.

Chappell, William. *The Ballad Literature and Popular Music of the Olden Time: A History of the Ancient Songs, Ballads, and of the Dance Tunes of England, with Numerous Anecdotes and Entire Ballads; also, A Short Account of the Minstrels*. 2 vols. New York: Dover Publications, 1965.

Comstock, Helen. *American Lithographers of the Nineteenth Century*, New York: Barrows, 1950.

Corbin, Alain. *The Foul and the Fragrant: Odor and the French Social Imagination*. Cambridge, Mass.: Harvard University Press, 1986.

Davidson, Nancy Reynolds. "E. W. Clay: American Political Caricaturist of the Jacksonian Era." Ph.D. diss., University of Michigan, 1980.

Davis, David Brion. "The Emergence of Immediatism in British and American Anti-slavery Thought." In *From Homicide to Slavery: Studies in American Culture*, ed. David Brion Davis, 238–57. Oxford: Oxford University Press, 1986.

Davis, Kingsley. "Intermarriage in Caste Societies." *American Anthropologist*, n.s., 43.3 (July–Sept. 1941): 376–95.

Dayan, Joan. "Amorous Bondage: Poe, Ladies, and Slaves." *American Literature* 66.2 (June 1994): 239–73.

———. "Romance and Race." In *The Columbia History of the American Novel*, ed. Emory Elliott et al., 89–109. New York: Columbia University Press, 1991.

Dowling, William C. *Literary Federalism in the Age of Jefferson: Joseph Dennie and* The Port Folio, *1801–1811.* Columbia: University of South Carolina Press, 1999.

———. *Poetry and Ideology in Revolutionary Connecticut.* Athens: University of Georgia Press, 1990.

Drinnon, Richard. *Facing West: The Metaphysics of Indian-Hating and Empire Building.* Minneapolis: University of Minnesota Press, 1980.

Durey, Michael. *"With the Hammer of Truth": James Thomsom Callender and America's Early National Heroes.* Charlottesville: University Press of Virginia, 1990.

Edelstein, Tilden G. *"Othello* in America: The Drama of Interracial Marriage." In *Region, Race and Reconstruction: Essays in Honor of E. Vann Woodward,* ed. J. Morgan Kousser and James M. McPherson, 179–97. New York: Oxford University Press, 1982.

Egerton, Douglas R. "Thomas Jefferson and the Hemings Family: A Matter of Blood." *The Historian* 59.2 (Winter 1997): 327–45.

Ettelbrick, Paula. "Since When Is Marriage a Path to Liberation." In *Lesbians, Gay Men and the Law,* ed. William Rubenstein, 401–5. New York: Columbia University Press, 1993.

Fetterley, Judith. "Reading About Reading: 'A Jury of Her Peers,' 'The Murders in the Rue Morgue,' and 'The Yellow Wallpaper.'" In *Gender and Reading: Essays on Readers, Texts, and Contexts,* ed. Elizabeth A. Flynn and Patrocinio P. Schweickart, 147–64. Baltimore: The Johns Hopkins University Press, 1986.

Fisher, Philip. *Hard Facts: Setting and Form in the American Novel.* New York: Oxford University Press, 1987.

Foster, Eugene A. et al. "Jefferson Fathered Slave's Last Child." *Nature* 196 (November 5, 1998): 27–8.

Foucault, Michel. *The History of Sexuality, Volume I: An Introduction.* Trans. Robert Hurley. New York: Random House, 1980.

Fowler, David. *Northern Attitudes Towards Interracial Marriage: Legislation and Public Opinion in the Middle Atlantic States of the Old Northwest, 1780–1930.* New York: Garland Publishing, 1987.

Fredrickson, George M. *The Black Image in the White Mind: The Debate on Afro-American Character and Destiny, 1817–1914.* New York: Harper & Row, 1971.

———. *White Supremacy: A Comparative Study of American and South African History.* Oxford: Oxford University Press, 1981.

French, Scot A. and Edward L. Ayers. "The Strange Career of Thomas Jefferson: Race and Slavery in American Memory, 1943–1993." In *Jeffersonian Legacies,* ed. Peter S. Onuf, 418–56. Charlottesville: University Press of Virginia, 1993.

Garrison, Wendell Phillips and Francis Jackson Garrison. *William Lloyd Garrison, 1805–1879: The Story of His Life Told by His Children.* 4 vols. Boston: Houghton, Mifflin, 1889.

Gordon-Reed, Annette. *Thomas Jefferson and Sally Hemings: An American Controversy.* Charlottesville: University Press of Virginia, 1997.

Gould, Stephen Jay. "American Polygeny and Craniometry Before Darwin: Blacks and Indians as Separate, Inferior Species." In *The "Racial" Economy of Science: Toward a Democratic Future*, ed. Sandra Harding, 84–115. Bloomington: Indiana University Press, 1993.

———. "The Geometer of Race." *Discover* (November 1994): 65–69.

Grossberg, Michael. *Governing the Hearth: Law and Family in Nineteenth-Century America*. Chapel Hill: University of North Carolina Press, 1985.

———. "Guarding the Altar: Physiological Restrictions and the Rise of State Intervention in Matrimony." *The American Journal of Legal History* 26 (July 1982): 197–226.

Halttunen, Karen. *Confidence Men and Painted Women: A Study of Middle-Class Culture in America, 1830–1870*. New Haven, Conn.: Yale University Press, 1982.

Heartman, Charles F. and James R. Canny. *Biography of First Printings of the Writings of Edgar Allan Poe*. New York: Kraus Reprint Co., 1972.

Hendrickson, Robert. *QPB Encyclopedia of Word and Phrase Origins*. New York: Facts on File, 1997.

Herbert, T. Walter. *Dearest Beloved: The Hawthornes and the Making of the Middle-Class Family*. Berkeley: University of California Press, 1993.

Hodes, Martha. *White Women, Black Men: Illicit Sex in the Nineteenth-Century South*. New Haven, Conn.: Yale University Press, 1997.

Horseman, Reginald. *Race and Manifest Destiny: The Origins of Racial Anglo-Saxonism*. Cambridge, Mass.: Harvard University Press, 1981.

Jack, Ian. *Augustan Satire: Intention and Idiom in English Poetry, 1660–1750*. Oxford: Clarendon Press, 1966.

Jordan, Winthrop D. *White over Black: American Attitudes Toward the Negro, 1550–1812*. New York: W. W. Norton, 1968.

Kaplan, Sidney. "The Miscegenation Issue in the Election of 1864." *Journal of Negro History* 34 (July 1949): 274–343.

Kelly, James C. and B. S. Lovell. "Thomas Jefferson: His Friends and Foes." *The Virginia Magazine of History and Biography* 101.1 (January 1993): 133–57.

Kerber, Linda. "Abolitionists and Amalgamators: The New York City Race Riots of 1834." *New York History* 48 (January 1967): 28–39.

———. *Federalists in Dissent: Imagery and Ideology in Jeffersonian America*. Ithaca, N.Y.: Cornell University Press, 1970.

Kerber, Linda K. and Walter John Morris. "Politics and Literature: The Adams Family and the *Port Folio*." *William and Mary Quarterly*, ser. 3, vol. 1, 23 (1966): 450–76.

Kinney, James. *Amalgamation! Race, Sex, and Rhetoric in the Nineteenth-Century American Novel*. Westport, Conn.: Greenwood Press, 1985.

Lane, Roger. *William Dorsey's Philadelphia and Ours: On the Past and Future of the Black City in America*. New York: Oxford University Press, 1991.

Lapsansky, Emma Jones. "'Since They Got Those Separate Churches': Afro-Americans and Racism in Jacksonian Philadelphia." *American Quarterly* 32.1 (spring 1980): 54–78.

Laqueur, Thomas. *Making Sex: Body and Gender from the Greeks to Freud*. Cambridge, Mass.: Harvard University Press, 1990.

Lawrence, Vera Brodsky. *Music for Patriots, Politicians, and Presidents: Harmonies and Discords of the First Hundred Years*. New York: Macmillan, 1975.

Lesbians, Gay Men and the Law. Ed. William Rubenstein. New York: Columbia University Press, 1993.

Lipsitz, George. *The Possessive Investment in Whiteness: How White People Profit from Identity Politics.* Philadelphia: Temple University Press, 1998.

Lott, Eric. *Love and Theft: Blackface Minstrelsy and the American Working Class.* Oxford: Oxford University Press, 1993.

Lovejoy, Arthur O. *The Great Chain of Being: A Study of the History of an Idea.* Cambridge, Mass.: Harvard University Press, 1966.

Luck, Barbara. "AARFAC Acquires Unusual Painting." *Colonial Williamsburg News* (October 8, 1993): 3.

MacLean, William Jerry. "Othello Scorned: The Racial Thought of John Quincy Adams." *Journal of the Early Republic* 4 (summer 1984): 143–60.

Martyn, Byron Curti. "Racism in the United States: A History of the Anti-Miscegenation Legislation and Litigation." Ph.D. diss., University of Southern California, 1979.

Marx, Karl. *Grundrisse: Foundations of the Critique of Political Economy.* Trans. Martin Nicolaus. New York: Random House, 1973.

McKeon, Michael. *The Origins of the English Novel, 1600–1740.* Baltimore: The Johns Hopkins University Press, 1987.

McPherson, James M. *The Struggle for Equality: Abolitionists and the Negro in the Civil War and Reconstruction.* Princeton, N.J.: Princeton University Press, 1964.

Melder, Keith E. "Forerunners of Freedom: The Grimké Sisters in Massachusetts, 1837–38." *Essex Institute Historical Collections* (July 1967): 223–49.

Meyers, Jeffrey. *Edgar Allan Poe: His Life and Legacy.* New York: Charles Scribner's Sons, 1992.

Morgan, Edmund S. *American Slavery, American Freedom: The Ordeal of Colonial Virginia.* New York: W. W. Norton, 1975.

Morrison, Toni. *Playing in the Dark: Whiteness and the Literary Imagination.* Cambridge, Mass.: Harvard University Press, 1992.

Moss, Sidney P. and Carolyn Moss. "The Jefferson Legend in British Travel Books." *Journal of the Early Republic* 7 (fall 1987): 253–74.

Nelson, Dana. Introduction. In *A Romance of the Republic,* by Lydia Maria Child. Lexington: University Press of Kentucky, 1997.

Oberholtzer, Ellis Paxson. *The Literary History of Philadelphia.* Philadelphia, 1906.

Peters, Harry Twyford. *America on Stone.* Garden City, N.Y.: Doubleday, 1931.

Peterson, Merrill D. *The Jefferson Image in the American Mind.* New York: Oxford University Press, 1960.

———. *Thomas Jefferson and the New Nation: A Biography.* New York: Oxford University Press, 1970.

Quimby, Maureen O'Brien. "The Political Art of James Akin." In *Winterthur Portfolio* 7, ed. Ian M. B. Quimby, 59–112. Charlottesville: University Press of Virginia, 1972.

Randall, J. G. *Lincoln: The Liberal Statesman.* New York: Dodd, Mead, 1947.

Randall, Randolphe C. "Authors of the *Port Folio* Revealed by the Hall Files." *American Literature* 11 (1940): 379–416.

Ratner, Lorman. *Powder Keg: Northern Opposition to the Antislavery Movement, 1831–1840.* New York: Basic Books, 1968.

Richards, Leonard L. *"Gentlemen of Property and Standing": Anti-Abolition Mobs in Jacksonian America.* Oxford: Oxford University Press, 1970.

Robinson, Forrest G. "Uncertain Borders: Race, Sex, Civilization in *The Last of the Mohicans." Arizona Quarterly* 47.1 (spring 1991): 1–28.

Roe, John Carlos. "Poe, Antebellum Slavery, and Modern Criticism." In *Poe's Pym: Critical Explorations,* ed. Richard Kopley, 117–38. Durham, N.C.: Duke University Press, 1992.

Roediger, David R. *The Wages of Whiteness: Race and the Making of the American Working Class.* London: Verso, 1991.

Romancing the Shadow: Poe and Race, ed. J. Gerald Kennedy and Liliane Weissberg. Oxford: Oxford University Press, 2001.

Rosenheim, Shawn. "Detective Fiction, Psychoanalysis, and the Analytic Sublime." In *The American Face of Edgar Allan Poe,* ed. Shawn Rosenheim and Stephen Rachman, 153–178. Baltimore: The Johns Hopkins University Press, 1995.

Rothman, Ellen K. *Hands and Hearts: A History of Courtship in America.* New York: Basic Books, 1984.

Rothman, Joshua D. "James Callender and Social Knowledge of Interracial Sex in Antebellum Virginia." In *Sally Hemings and Thomas Jefferson: History, Memory, and Civic Culture,* ed. Jan Ellen Lewis and Peter S. Onuf, 87–261. Charlottesville: University Press of Virginia, 1999.

Rubin, Gayle. "The Traffic in Women: Notes Toward a Political Economy of Sex." In *Toward an Anthropology of Women,* ed. Rayna Reiter, 157–210. New York: Monthly Review Press, 1975.

Ruchames, Louis. "Race, Marriage, and Abolition in Massachusetts." *Journal of Negro History* 40.3 (July 1955): 250–73.

Runcie, John. "'Hunting the Nigs' in Philadelphia: The Race Riots of August, 1834." *Pennsylvania History* 29 (April 1972): 187–218.

Saks, Eva. "Representing Miscegenation Law." *Raritan* 8.2 (Fall 1988): 39–69.

Scheckel, Susan. *The Insistence of the Indian: Race and Nationalism in Nineteenth-Century American Culture.* Princeton, N.J.: Princeton University Press, 1988.

Schiebinger, Londa. *Nature's Body: Gender in the Making of Modern Science.* Boston: Beacon Press, 1993.

Schneider, David. *American Kinship: A Cultural Account.* Englewood Cliffs, N.J.: Prentice-Hall, Inc., 1968.

———. *A Critique of the Study of Kinship.* Ann Arbor: University of Michigan Press, 1984.

Sellers, Charles Coleman. *Mr. Peale's Museum: Charles Willson Peale and the First Popular Museum of Natural History and Art.* New York: W. W. Norton, 1980.

Sheehan, Bernard W. *Seeds of Extinction: Jeffersonian Philanthropy and the American Indian.* Chapel Hill: University of North Carolina Press, 1973.

Sklar, Kathryn Kish. *Catharine Beecher: A Study in American Domesticity.* New Haven, Conn.: Yale University Press, 1973.

Slotkin, Richard. *Regeneration Through Violence: The Mythology of the American Frontier, 1600–1860.* Middletown, Conn.: Wesleyan University Press, 1973.

Smallwood, William Martin. *Natural History and the American Mind.* New York: Columbia University Press, 1941.

Smith, Daniel Scott. "The Long Cycle in American Illegitimacy and Premarital Pregnancy." In *Bastardy and its Comparative History: Studies in the History of Illegitimacy and Marital Nonconformism in Britain, France, Germany, Sweden, North America, Jamaica, and Japan*, ed. Peter Laslett et al. London: Arnold, 1980.

————. "Parental Power and Marriage Patterns: An Analysis of Historical Trends in Hingham, Massachusetts." In *The American Family in Social-Historical Perspective*, 2d ed., ed. Michael Gordon, 87–100. New York: St. Martin's Press, 1983.

Smits, David D. "'We Are Not to Grow Wild': Seventeenth-Century New England's Repudiation of Anglo-Indian Intermarriage." *American Indian Culture and Research Journal* 11.4 (1987): 1–32.

Sollors, Werner. *Neither Black nor White yet Both: Thematic Explorations of Interracial Literature.* Oxford: Oxford University Press, 1997.

Stanton, William. *The Leopard's Spots: Scientific Attitudes Toward Race in America, 1815–59.* Chicago: University of Chicago Press, 1960.

Staudenraus, P. J. *The African Colonization Movement, 1816–1865.* New York: Columbia University Press, 1961.

Stocking, George W. Jr. Introduction. In *Researches into the Physical History of Man*, by James Cowles Prichard, ix-cxviii. Chicago: University of Chicago Press, 1973.

Stoler, Ann Laura. *Race and the Education of Desire: Foucault's History of Sexuality and the Colonial Order of Things.* Durham, N.C.: Duke University Press, 1995.

Stone, Lawrence Joseph. *The Family, Sex and Marriage in England, 1500–1800.* London: Weidenfeld & Nicolson, 1977.

Thomas, Alexander and Samuel Sillen. *Racism and Psychiatry.* New York: Brunner/Mazel, 1972.

Thomas, Dwight Rembert. "Poe in Philadelphia, 1838–1844: A Documentary Record." Ph.D. diss., University of Pennsylvania, 1978.

————. *The Poe Log: A Documentary Life of Edgar Allan Poe.* Boston: G. K. Hall, 1987.
Thomas, John L. *The Liberator William Lloyd Garrison: A Biography.* Boston: Little, Brown, 1963.

Vaughan, Alden T. "From White Man to Redskin: Changing Anglo-American Perceptions of the American Indian." *The American Historical Review* 87 (October 1982): 917–53.

Walters, Ronald G. "The Erotic South: Civilization and Sexuality in American Abolitionism." *American Quarterly* 25 (1973): 177–201.

Warner, Sam Bass, Jr. *The Private City: Philadelphia in Three Periods of Its Growth.* Philadelphia: University of Pennsylvania Press, 1968.

Weitenkampf, Frank. *Political Caricature in the United States.* New York: New York Public Library, 1953.

Welter, Barbara. "The Cult of True Womanhood." In *Dimity Convictions: The American Woman in the Nineteenth Century*, 21–41. Athens: Ohio University Press, 1976.

Weston, Kath. *Families We Choose: Lesbians, Gays, Kinship.* New York: Columbia University Press, 1991.

Whalen, Terence. "Edgar Allan Poe and the Horrid Laws of Political Economy." *American Quarterly* 44.3 (1992): 381–417.

Wood, Forrest G. *Black Scare: The Racist Response to Emancipation and Reconstruction.* Berkeley: The University of California Press, 1968.

Yellin, Jean Fagan. *Women and Sisters: The Antislavery Feminists in American Culture.* New Haven, Conn.: Yale University Press, 1989.

Young, Mary. "Racism in Red and Black: Indians and Other Free People of Color in Georgia Law, Politics, and Removal Policy." *The Georgia Historical Quarterly* 73.3 (fall 1989): 492–518.

Zirkle, Conway. "The Early History of the Idea of an Inheritance of Acquired Characters and of Pangenesis." *American Philosophical Society Transactions* n.s. 35, pt. 2 (1945): 91–151.

Zizek, Slavoj. *Looking Awry: An Introduction to Jacques Lacan through Popular Culture.* Cambridge, Mass.: Harvard University Press, 1992.

References to illustrations are printed in
italics.

Acknowledgments

I am indebted to several agencies for supporting the writing of this book. A recent fellowship from the National Endowment for the Humanities gave me a year of release time from my teaching duties at Purchase College, the State University of New York, to finish the manuscript. In its earlier incarnation, the project was supported by a Charlotte W. Newcombe Doctoral Dissertation Fellowship from the Woodrow Wilson National Fellowship Foundation and a Kate B. and Hall J. Peterson Fellowship from the American Antiquarian Society.

At the Antiquarian Society, I was fortunate to be warmly and expertly assisted by Georgia Barnhill, Nancy Burkett, Joanne Chaison, Marie Lamoureux, and Laura Wasowicz. I also thank the wonderful librarians at the Library Company of Philadelphia, the Historical Society of Pennsylvania, the New York Public Library, the Oneida County (New York) Historical Society, the Defiance (Ohio) Public Library, the Defiance College Library, the Library of Congress, the John Hay Library at Brown University, the Alexander Library at Rutgers University, and the Purchase College Library.

This project was shaped by comments and suggestions in response to presentations I made at the annual conferences of the Modern Language Association and the American Studies Association, as well as at Donald Pease's Institute in American Studies at Dartmouth College. I am grateful, too, for the comments of my two anonymous readers at the University of Pennsylvania Press, as well as for those of the editorial board of the press. The book is much stronger for these generous efforts as well as for those of my editor, Jerry Singerman. All remaining errors and shortcomings are solely my own.

An earlier version of Chapter 4 appeared in *Romancing the Shadow: Poe and Race*, edited by J. Gerald Kennedy and Liliane Weissberg (Oxford: Oxford University Press, 2001).

I have received much in the way of guidance, support, and inspiration from my teachers, mentors, and colleagues. At Rutgers, Myra Jehlen and Michael Warner taught me to think historically about the contemporary issues that I thought were just distracting me from the work of being a scholar but that were, of course, the consuming passions that make scholarship imperative and sustaining. At Purchase, my mentor and friend Louise Yelin has taught me how to be a professor. That she has also taken the time to read and comment on my work is more appreciated than she knows. Gari LaGuardia, head of the Purchase Humanities Division, has been wonderfully supportive of my professional and personal goals. I have been able to write this book while working at a student-centered college in no small part because of his creative solutions to scheduling and other dilemmas. Charles Ponce de Leon and Lynn Mahoney have kindly answered every question about American history (and everything else) that I have ever asked them. I am lucky to have them as my colleagues.

I am also indebted to Karen Riggs Skean for standing still for this and other projects; to Joan and James Taylor, Sr. for always pointing out the places whiteness is at work in America; and to my parents, Robert and Virginia Lemire, for being with me on the journey of this book as well as the journeys that led to it.

Finally, this book has had two very able and caring midwives. It simply would not have happened without my writing partner and friend Audrey Fisch. She and my partner in life, Jim Taylor, asked the hardest questions about the project and made answering them when I could a pleasure. In recent months, Jim's willingness to do all of the domestic chores and more than half of the child care has allowed me to complete this book. It is dedicated to him with gratitude and love. It is also, of course, for my real baby, our son Eli, whose arrival during the last months of writing was sweet inspiration to finish.